W9-DFV-157

MORE THAN LOVE

MORE THAN LOVE

Adopting and Surviving Attachment Disorder Children

Sherril M. Stone, Ph.D.

Writers Club Press
New York Lincoln Shanghai

GRAND ISLAND PUBLIC LIBRARY

MORE THAN LOVE
Adopting and Surviving Attachment Disorder Children

All Rights Reserved © 2001 by Sherril M. Stone

No part of this book may be reproduced or transmitted in any form or by any means, graphic, electronic, or mechanical, including photocopying, recording, taping, or by any information storage retrieval system, without the written permission of the publisher.

Writers Club Press
an imprint of iUniverse, Inc.

For information address:
iUniverse, Inc.
2021 Pine Lake Road, Suite 100
Lincoln, NE 68512
www.iuniverse.com

ISBN: 0-595-19294-7

Printed in the United States of America

GRAND ISLAND PUBLIC LIBRARY

To: Marty, our families, and friends

Contents

Preface

The story that follows is one of joy, sadness, hope, and despair. Although some of the material may be difficult to read, this story is one that must be told. We are only one of the many families who have experienced the pain of a disrupted adoption. All too often, the family wants to forget the pain and proceed with their lives. However, the story begs to be told. If for no other reason, this story must be told to inform other parents of the possible problems that may arise when they adopt older, emotionally damaged children. This book is meant to provide comfort and hope to the hopeless, strength to the weary, and encouragement to the discouraged. It is my intention to provide the reader with as many accounts, good and bad, as possible. It is not my intention to dissuade any adopting parent from pursuing their dream of a family. Yet, parents and other family members must be fully aware of the possible heartache, financial ruin, and emotional toil that these children may bring into the adoption. Children with attachment problems can splinter even the strongest family ties. It is, therefore, very important to be prepared for the chaos that may occur within the family; immediate and extended family members.

This book began as a daily journal of our quest to bond as a family. I soon began to receive hundreds of requests for copies of the journal from others besides the adoptive community. Many people were interested in our daily struggles, our triumphs, and our defeats. Therefore, what began as a journal of our first year as an adoptive family, eventually became a testament of endurance covering nine years of parenting attachment disorder children.

Attachment disorder children do not, unfortunately, encourage or enhance strong family relationships. In contrast, many attachment disorder children can, and will, go to great lengths to keep family members away or in a constant state of turmoil. The closer the family members try to get to the attachment disorder child, the further away the child pushes in an attempt to dissolve the relationship and bond. The behaviors themselves are designed to specifically keep the family members, especially the mother figure, at a controllable distance. The family becomes confused over the child's distancing behaviors. In return, the family responds by trying harder to develop a closeness with the child or removing themselves from the child's environment. Unfortunately, these methods are often misunderstood by society and the family may be labeled as the problem. Yet, when these children attend counseling, they are seen as very charming and likeable individuals. Ironically, this type of behavior is an enormous insight into the controlling aspect of the Attachment Disorder child.

It is my hope that this book not only provides truthful and accurate accounts of our struggles to parent attachment disorder children, but also to prevent other parents from enduring similar hardships. I have included many suggestions and examples for working with these children. I hope that they may serve as a guideline and inspiration to parents who are looking for alternative behavioral measures.

The appendix to this book provides helpful information about Attachment Disorder. Additional information is presented for therapists, parents, and family members involved with children experiencing attachment difficulties. Please refer to the reference list for other valuable resources including current research, behavioral studies, and treatment procedures.

Chapter 1

Life Decisions

It is 9:30 p.m., they are in bed asleep and the house is calm and quiet. If all goes well, it will remain this way until morning. A tremendous amount of hard work was exerted to make it through the day and to insure everyone was still in one piece at the day's end. Without a doubt, it required "More than Love".

Little did I realize when I met my husband that our lives were being prepared for the most demanding situation anyone could imagine. We met in Germany while serving in the Air Force. We spent many long hours talking and getting to know each other. I knew what I expected in a mate and was determined to stick to my preferences. Luckily, my husband felt the same. The more acquainted we became, the more apparent it was that we shared the same values. In fact, it seemed as if I was talking to myself when we discussed various issues. Soon, we realized we had more in common, and shared more views on life, than most married couples we had met. This companionship and shared ideas laid a solid foundation for our relationship; a foundation that, to this day, has held us together through the most trying times.

One requirement I adhered to very strongly was to retain my last name if I married. To my surprise, my husband informed me that he had told his family of his intention to take his wife's last name when he married. When I heard this I was flabbergasted and felt it must have been a sign of things to come. My stand on keeping my last name was not out of the realm of possibility after all. There existed a man who would accept my stance of retaining my last name, and, who even wanted to change his last name to mine! I knew immediately that I better pay close attention to our growing relationship. Many other commonalties also arose between us, however one in particular eventually sealed our fate. It was the desire we both had to adopt some non-infant, sibling brothers. This would be our most important commonality; one that led to a decision which changed our lives forever.

We were married a year later. We spent our first year as a married couple establishing ourselves as civilians. We had both served our time in the military and decided that, due to the frequent separations and moves, military life was not the atmosphere to raise our children. The next year we began the tedious process required of adopting parents. We asked for a set of brothers between the ages of four and eight years old. Because most of the siblings in this particular age group had experienced abuse and/or neglect, we were required to successfully complete parent training for special needs children. In addition, we also were asked to compile a photo album of ourselves, our family, our pets, our interests, and our hobbies. After approval for placement of children the case manager would use the album as a 'show and tell' instrument to ease the children's transition into our family. Of all the paperwork required for the adoption, the photo album served as our symbol of hope. We included as many pictures depicting our lifestyle as possible. We also contacted our families and asked for their pictures. After all, we wanted the album to be perfect. Not only did preparing the album give us great joy then, it still resides in our bookshelf and serves as a reminder of a much happier time, the birth of our family.

We attended a series of workshops, training seminars, and classes on parenting special needs' children and learned valuable information from the specialized training. One discussion in particular struck us both and to this day we follow the philosophy behind it. We were told "All the training in the world will never fully prepare you for what lies ahead in parenting special needs' children. You must follow your gut instincts when raising these children and never forget that you did not cause their problems and behaviors." We were also enlightened about the ridiculing we would encounter from those who do not understand the behaviors these children are capable of displaying or the discipline approaches we would need to use. We were advised not to doubt ourselves based on the accusations of others. To do this would result in our children's insecurity as well as our own self-defeat. Being naive, first time adopting parents, we did not fully appreciate the usefulness of this advice until we were faced with the daily problems that accompany parenting of behavioral problem children.

Not only did we learn parenting skills for special needs' children, we were also informed of the many offensive questions and comments we would hear from society. Many could be overcome with a simple smile, but the remark most offensive to adoptive parents, we were told, was the one regarding our parental status. For instance, remarks such as "where are their *real* parents", "who are their *natural* parents", and "why did you not have *your own* kids" were the ones considered by other adoptive parents as being the most insensitive. At that time, however, we convinced ourselves these would not be a significant problem. It did not take long to learn that these questions are more common, more poignant, and more hurtful than we had first anticipated. They infer negative connotations of adoption which are easily picked up by the adopted children and causes them to feel they are *not real* or that they are only *second choice* children. Adoptive parents, likewise, begin to sense that society views them as merely baby-sitters not as loving, caring, and devoted parents. Quite the contrary, adoptive parents could not love their adoptive children any more then if they had given birth to them. These remarks also tend to undermine the parents' feelings of validity and worth. Unfortunately, the majority of people in society are not aware of the hurt feelings resulting from these statements. However, we have witnessed that once they are informed of the feelings conjured by these remarks, most people tend to become proactive in the sanctity of the adoptive family. By educating society on the preferred adoptive status terms, the adoptive family's validity is further solidified. *Adoptive parent*, or simply *Parent*, are the terms preferred by these families while the adoptive family prefers the term *birthparents* for the biological parents of the children. Not only do these titles distinguish the families involved, they also ease the insecurity felt by so many adoptees. This allows the adopted children the chance to feel wanted and, hopefully, they will be capable of accepting the fact that they are part of a family with a Mom and Dad who love them unconditionally.

During our last training session we were provided an opportunity to role-play with other prospective parents. We were split into groups; the spouses were placed in separate groups. Each group was given a behavioral situation and told to act out the child and parental roles of the scenario. Those playing the parent role were allowed to consult with each other on ways of handling the child's behavior. The person acting as the child was told to make it "hard" on the parents. By sharing ideas with each other, we learned which consequences worked and which ones did not. We then met as an entire group and discussed the small group scenarios. By splitting the spouses, each couple came away with several different ways of responding to problem behaviors. Before we received our certification for parenting special needs' children, we were free to ask questions of an experienced foster mother who helped with our training. She had opened her house as a receiving home. These are the homes where the children who are removed from the birthparents are first placed until a long-term foster home can be located. She related several examples of behaviors she had witnessed and passed along some techniques she had picked up. We have used some of the techniques she related to us. One statement that clearly stands out in our minds was her reply to the question "Why do you put yourself through this?" She simply said, "when I think about quitting it never fails that one of my kids will return to thank me for being firm with them. My thoughts of quitting immediately disappear because I am reminded that I have made a difference in a child's life." We left that night with the same hope for ourselves, that somehow we could make the difference in an abused child's life.

With the classes and training behind us we began the long wait. Another year passed and our hopes were beginning to fade. When our optimism was at its lowest point, we received an invitation to a "Kids Fest" sponsored by the state's Family and Child Services Department. It was a gathering of children waiting to be adopted and parents wanting to adopt. By bringing prospective parents and waiting children together in a party atmosphere, tensions of the parents disseminated and anxieties of the children were eased. Each child's case manager was on hand to answer any questions from the prospective parents. They could also provide further information if the parents felt drawn to a specific child. By handling information in this manner, the children were not put on display or subjected to any type of rejection. They were simply allowed to enjoy the party.

Ironically, my husband and I almost turned down our invitation to this event. We had waited so long for children and were afraid it would only result in another disappointment. After much thought, however, we decided to attend. At least if we attended, we told ourselves, we could confirm our belief that there were indeed available children who needed a family. As it turned out, our decision to attend the Fest changed the course of our lives and has affected us dramatically. It was on this day that we were led to the path of parenthood.

Kids will be kids! However, kids who have endured abuse or neglect come to their adoptive parents with unhealed sores and emotional scars. The children deal with their pain the only way they know how—through their behaviors. Their behaviors can range from mildly irritating to dangerous and severe. Parenting these children is not an easy task; it is the hardest work a person could ever endure. However, the rewards, no matter how small, are better than anything imaginable.

The remainder of this book is devoted to our experiences as parents of special needs' children. It was not a walk in the park, but rather a road with many twists and turns. Not only did we experience extreme behavioral problems from the boys, we were the target of many allegations from others. Those who were not familiar with our family accused us of child abuse and reported us to the child welfare agency. They based their accusations on the behaviors of the boys and justified their reporting with "these boys must be being abused or they would not behave this badly." The first few times we were investigated we were terrified and, although we did not enjoy the pain the false allegations caused, we remained secure knowing we were innocent of any wrongdoing. We simply accepted each time as "here we go again." Every time the authorities investigated us, it resulted in the same outcome. We received an apology for the interruption, were praised for the work we had done with the boys, and offered suggestions for dealing with the boys' deviant behaviors. The praise reassured us while the suggestions provided additional avenues to try. We then returned to our daily life.

The heartaches we experienced were made tolerable by times of great joy. Our sons' positive accomplishments not only supplied us with tremendous pride, but also the motivation we needed to continue parenting during the worst times. It was during those moments of pride that we were once again reassured that we had done, and continued to do, the best parenting job humanly possible under such difficult circumstances. The painful, rough times seemed worth all our efforts when one of the boys experienced a sense of self-pride and could not wait to tell 'MOM and

DAD!' of his accomplishment. Although my husband and I no longer have daily contact with any of our sons, we are thankful for the good times we experienced as a family. Yet we fully appreciate the solitude of being just the two of us

By sharing our experiences, both good and bad, it is my hope that I can convey encouragement to other families feeling defeated and hopeless. Knowing that we have experienced and survived horrible situations can bring great comfort to other struggling parents. Even during the times when we felt totally abandoned by the outside world, a hug accompanied by a simple "I love you Mom and Dad" melted away all doubt and heartache! We will live the rest of our lives satisfied with the job we did even though the outcome was not one that we anticipated when we began our journey into parenthood.

Chapter 2

Getting Together

We arrived at the Kids Fest nervous, yet hopeful, that we would not leave disappointed. We were met at the door by a social worker from the state. She told us to mingle and have a good time. She showed us where we could ask for information on any of the children. The kids were having a wonderful time playing games, having their faces painted, coloring, dancing, and drinking Kool-Aid. We chatted with several adults as well as children and very quickly felt comfortable and at ease. Several small children asked if they could sit on our laps or color pictures with them. Most of the older children either kept to themselves or stayed with their case manager. However, if an older child had something to say they were more assertive and blunt than the younger children. For instance, one of the 12-year-old boys asked me "Do you want to adopt me." I quickly replied "Hum, do you want me to?" He turned around and left. My training had saved me this time. We had been instructed not to give the children any false hopes. The older children, we had been informed, would try to reject us before we had a chance to reject them.

While strolling to the area where some street dancers were performing with the kids, my husband and I noticed a boy around seven years of age. He passed in front of us and I said, "Are you going to dance with them?" He looked at me strangely as if he were thinking, "Are you crazy lady or what?" I immediately turned to my husband and noticed he was smiling. I told my husband that the boy's look reminded me of something I would do. He replied "that is why I am smiling." A few minutes later we decided to ask for his information. We soon learned that his younger brother was also there. We had already noticed the younger boy but did not realize they were brothers. We decided to find their case manager and discuss the boys further.

When we located their case manager, she was talking to the younger brother, Charlie. He was talking very openly with her until he noticed us. He then whispered in her ear. I remember thinking, "Well you've blown it now, he is afraid of you." After he left she told us that he needed to find the bathroom but he was too embarrassed to tell her when he saw us. We visited with her for quite awhile and learned more about the boys. We informed her we were waiting for a set of brothers and were interested in the two boys. She began by relating to us some of their background history.

She informed us that they had been abused and neglected by the birth-parents, had lived in six different foster homes, and had been kidnapped twice while in foster care. She told us the boys were in extensive counseling and were now living in a specialized foster home for very needy children. She then described their personalities. Wayne, which we had already witnessed, was a loner and tended to be superficial with his emotions. Charlie was more outgoing and friendly. This accounts for the reason we had noticed him earlier; he tended to be the life of the party. She then told us that many parents had inquired about Charlie but none had asked about Wayne. She said the state had considered separating them so they would have a better chance of being adopted. When she learned that we were interested in both of them she appeared hesitant, but hopeful. It was then that she sprang some additional news on us—The boys had a younger brother in another foster home! Well, my husband and I almost fainted. It was as if they were the boys we had been waiting on. We both smiled and said, "that's fine, we will consider all three of them." I could see the skepticism in her face when she told us of the third boy. I think she was afraid a third boy would be enough to scare us off entirely. When she saw that it did not, she seemed relieved. As a matter of fact, she admitted to us, much later, that our reaction to the third boy was what she had hoped for and a catalyst to her support.

When she saw that we did not hesitate when she revealed the existence of the third boy, she was convinced that we were very serious in our adoption pursuits. We exchanged names and phone numbers and then she introduced us to the boys. We spent some time with them and talked about their hobbies, school, and friends. Before we realized it, the time had passed and everyone was packing to leave. We said good-bye to the boys and again mentioned our interest to their case manager. After reaffirming our intention to call her the next week to initiate the process, we left for home with a renewed feeling of hope.

On the drive home we talked incessantly. We discussed the two boys we had seen and tried to picture Chris. All we knew about him was his name and age so we could only speculate about what he looked like. Our minds were spinning faster than our mouths could communicate our thoughts. Trying not to get ahead of ourselves with possibilities of the future was difficult. We found ourselves asking "what if this and what if that..." In my mind I was already arranging bedrooms, shopping for clothes and toys, and putting in for maternity leave at work. First time parent syndrome had hit!

The next week was a flurry of phone calls between us, our adoption worker, and the boys' case manager. Since the boys were in the state foster care system and we had registered with a private agency, there was a tremendous amount of paperwork to be exchanged. Our worker sent our paperwork, including our physical, emotional, and financial statements and an autobiography from both my husband and I to the boys' case manager. We then waited for approval from the professionals working with the boys. During the wait, I called the boys' case manager daily to check on the progress and to find out if a decision had been made. She informed me that it would take approximately a week for the circulation of the paperwork and that she would call us when the decision was final. We waited a day but heard nothing so I called her again. I knew she was probably sick of hearing from me, but as I told her, we were sincere and did not give up easily. This fact, she has since admitted to me, was one of the deciding factors in approving us for the trial visits. The therapists involved with this case were aware of the extreme behaviors the two older boys could exhibit, so they were more hesitant than the boys' case manager. It was her persuasion that convinced those involved to give us a chance. Without her supporting us, the boys would more than likely have been split apart and adopted separately.

Nine days after meeting the boys, their case manager called our worker to announce the news—we were approved for a trial placement of all three boys. She next called my husband to inform him of the decision. He immediately called and told me. I was so ecstatic that I wanted to verify the news myself so I got in touch with her. When I reached her she was not surprised to hear from me. She told me, "I knew I'd be hearing from you within a matter of minutes of my call." She reassured me that the news was correct and we could now initiate the visits. She said we would start slowly and progress from there. The first visit would consist of a few hours. From this we would increase to overnight visits then a full weekend. If all went well during the next couple of months, she said the state would place the boys with us before the new school year. Then after a period of six months following their placement, if we were still interested, the final adoption could take place.

Our first visit was scheduled for two weeks later. The state representatives, Charlie's therapist, and both foster mothers wanted to meet with us prior to our first visit. Since the boys were located 5 hours away in another city, plans were made for us to have the meeting and a brief hello with the boys the first day. A longer visit was planned for the second day.

My husband and I attended the first meeting with the state representatives, the therapist, and foster mothers in a room divided by a one-way mirror. The boys were on the other side in a playroom. This allowed us to observe them while we attended the meeting. This was our first time to see Chris and he was just as cute as their case manager had told us. He had not seen his brothers in quite awhile so we observed their reunion. Wayne, the oldest brother, crowded out Charlie, the middle brother, when Chris, the youngest brother, entered the room. At the time we did not think much of it, but during the meeting we soon heard information that explained Wayne's behavior. After the boys were settled in the playroom the meeting began. To our disadvantage the boys' case manager was not able to attend this meeting. My husband and I had prepared a list of questions we wanted to ask. When we began asking them, the supervisor stopped us and began to relate some of the boys' behaviors. It was not that we were uninterested in this information, but as naive as we were, we did not fully appreciate the importance of the behavioral information we were receiving. We wanted to know things such as their birthdays, school grades, church affiliations, and physical well being. We did receive answers to our questions but they seemed to be matter of fact issues with the therapists and supervisor. At this point we decided it was best to listen to the information they were presenting and deal with our personal interests at a later time. For the rest of the meeting we felt as if we were on trial. In truth, that is exactly what was happening. They were presenting us with information and watching our reactions to each bit. I was actively writing down everything and this seemed to ease their skepticism. It also was a visual display of our interest in the boys' extreme and problematic behaviors.

The therapist for the two older boys related some additional background information to us. She informed us that the boys had been found during a drug raid after the second kidnapping. The children, including an older half sister, had previously been removed from the birthparents after allegations of child abuse. During their removal the police confiscated pornographic photographs of two infant boys with both birthparents. There were also loaded weapons and sexual devices found in the house. After the children were removed they were placed in the foster care system pending an investigation of the abuse charges. Prior to their removal, there was quite a bit of time that remained unaccounted for. We were informed that it might never be fully known what took place during the children's early life. At this point, the therapist, foster mothers, and supervisor began explaining the concerns and issues of each boy. As first time adopting parents, we did not comprehend the information they were relating to us. As we look back on that first meeting, we realize we were being forewarned of the trouble ahead. Thinking no child could possibly behave as badly as they were describing, we listened with cynicism. Once again our naive presumption displayed itself! However, we have not forgotten one question raised by the therapist at the conclusion of that meeting. She bluntly asked, "Are you prepared for any kind of *Hell* these boys will put you through?"

At the time she asked that question I thought to myself, "How much hell can three young boys cause?" My husband and I convinced ourselves that "love would be enough to see us through any difficult and hard times. After all they can't be that bad!" We brushed off her question as a scare tactic. We presumed it was an attempt to check our stamina and frighten us away. However, we held onto our steadfast nature and remained poised during the bombardment of negative information. At one point I thought to myself that if all adopting parents are put through this routine, it is amazing any children are adopted. The foster mother for the older boys was the first to speak.

Wayne displayed insecurity behaviors. His self-esteem was very low and he craved love and acceptance. He wanted to know that was okay and part of a group. He tried almost too hard to be liked and did inappropriate kinds of bonding. This came across with a false ring such as "This soup is the best soup I've ever eaten. You're the best cook in the world!" His foster mother stated that he did not know how to relate in appropriate ways. In addition, he internalized his feelings and was quiet, reserved, angry, and very moody. He denied his birthfamily's problems, but would gladly tell how they beat him. He had much knowledge of drugs and alcohol, and was afraid of the police. Along with boundary issues in touching other children, he and Charlie masturbated each other.

Charlie displayed intense anger outbursts, but was also quite volatile. He could become angry easily, but just as easily, could recover and return to good relations with others. He was much more physically active than his older brother was. He was animated and friendly, although he also did little things to annoy and provoke others such as making noises, staring, and mocking. He liked chaos and fighting and was constantly causing problems. He urinated on the walls of the foster home. Unlike his older brother, he sought affection but he was affectionate in appropriate ways. He did not appear to be as emotionally needy as his older brother. However, he too, had much knowledge of drugs and alcohol, and was also afraid of the police. Whereas Wayne was bright, Charlie had a learning disorder and poor memory.

Chris' foster mother then described his situation. He was thought to be the least damaged of the boys and appeared to learn inappropriate behaviors from them. However, he had recently been placed with another adoptive family. After eight weeks they chose to return him to the foster family. His foster mother said she was told that the man could not accept a child that was not his by birth. The woman told her that Chris had crawled in her lap and fondled her breasts. The foster mother informed us she was unsure of the true reasoning behind his return. She further added that the situation had left him confused and he tended to blame himself. Several times she overheard him saying, "I am a bad person, that's why nobody wants me." It seems ironic now, but after the foster mothers told us about the boys we were more determined than before to proceed with the adoption. My emotions crowded out the reality of the hardships we would endure in the future. My husband, an emotional person himself, and I decided we were all the boys needed to overcome their problems. It was pretentious on our part, but we thought we could be their heroes by loving their hurts away!

The following day we met all of the boys and Chris' foster mother at a park for a supervised visit. At first we did not welcome the supervision restriction, but afterwards we were glad. It allowed us a chance to talk freely with the foster mother. She related additional background information to us. Even though she only had Chris now, she told us that she had all three of them at one time. After a few weeks, she requested that the two older boys be placed in another foster home. They were exhibiting extreme behaviors and she suggested they receive intense therapy for those behaviors. When she informed the state authorities that the older boys were teaching Chris to masturbate, they were soon moved to a therapeutic foster home. In addition, their therapy sessions were increased from once a week to three times a week.

After our picnic lunch, we played ball with the boys, took them on some carnival rides, and let them ride ponies. We had brought our camera to take pictures for our families. The boys seemed to love having their picture taken. After we left the park we drove all the boys to Chris' foster home. His foster mother told us there was a neighborhood park at the end of their street and she felt it was fine for us to spend a little "unsupervised" time with the boys. This allowed us a chance to interact with them. They climbed on the jungle gym while we watched and played with them. An hour later we took the boys to the foster home and said our good-byes. We told the boys we hoped to see them again very soon and asked if that was okay with them. They were quick to tell us that their foster parents had told them about our interest in adopting them and they wanted to see us again also. On the drive home, my husband and I were quiet. In our own way we were thinking through the last two days. That night we had no doubts about pursuing the adoption. We were already becoming emotionally involved with them and felt a parental bond that can not be explained.

The two weeks until our next visit seemed like an eternity. To busy ourselves we prepared the boys' rooms. The members of my softball team threw us a "kid shower". They gave us various toys, games, and books for the boys. I told my husband that it was so exciting to participate in all of the same first time parent events just as birthparents. He reassured me that we were "giving birth" to them, in fact our family as a whole was being "reborn."

Before our next visit with the boys, we met with their case manager and the director of the community mental health center where the two older boys received therapy. This meeting was more informal than the first. The director suggested we find a therapist in our area and have all resources in place when the boys moved in with us. We agreed this was an excellent idea. He then asked if we had any questions and we were grateful for the opportunity to ask them. We learned that the boys would be in the first and third grades. Charlie had been held back due to some learning difficulties so he and the youngest would be in the same grade. We all agreed it would be best to talk to the school principal and request separate classes for them. Charlie also needed special education classes for emotionally disturbed children. The next question we asked was concerning their birthdates and birthplaces. Their case manager said that the records listed a separate town in Oklahoma for each of the boys. I could have been knocked over with a feather when she told us this. Oklahoma was my home and I was only out-of-state due to the military. In fact, my husband and I planned to move back to Oklahoma once the adoption was final. The look on her face was as stunned as the look on mine when I told her they were all born within 30 minutes to an hour away from my hometown. This was one more assurance to us that this adoption was meant to be and we belonged together as a family.

After our meeting, their case manager took all of us, boys included, to McDonald's and then we headed for the beach. While my husband played with the boys, I talked with her. We had a pleasant conversation and I felt very comfortable. She learned more about us as individuals, and as a couple. The more she learned, the more confident she became of our abilities to parent the boys and more sure of her decision to recommend us. She told us we could take the boys on an unsupervised visit the next day. We arranged to pick the boys up at their foster homes and take them to a lake for a picnic and swimming. By doing this we could visit more with the foster parents.

We arrived to pick up the boys and visited with each of the foster parents. We soon began to feel more at ease with each set of foster parents. We learned that Chris' foster father was in the Air Force. Since my husband and I had just been discharged from the Air Force, we knew this was another coincidence, which reassured us we were the right adoptive parents. At the end of our visit, we told the boys we would pick them up the next week and they could stay at our house for a couple of nights. They were very eager to see our house and anxious about spending the night in "their rooms." After dropping them off at their foster parents, we drove back home with a feeling of emptiness that I now know only parents can feel.

The next visit was a true experience in parenthood. The boys stayed at our home from Thursday morning to Sunday afternoon. We received a full dose of preparing meals, taking baths, going to bed, and refereeing arguments. However, it also gave us the chance to become more acquainted with each of them. It was then that we personally witnessed the personality traits we had been told about. We had already planned for the weekend to be full of activities so there would not be a moment of boredom. This also gave us the opportunity to learn the kinds of activities each boy enjoyed. (I would recommend this tactic to all adopting parents for the first few visits. Remembering you were not with the older children during their early years leaves much to be learned. The more that is learned about the children during the visits, the more prepared you are for the placement.) By the end of this visit my husband and I had mixed emotions about returning them to their foster homes. Sad because they had to leave, but also worn out and ready for some rest and time to reflect on the last few days. By the end of the next week however, we were rested, ready, and very excited about the next visit.

The rest of that summer was a combination of home visits and overnighters. A couple of weeks before the start of school we felt we were ready for the boys to move in. Their case manager, knowing their placement would put a financial strain on us, arranged for their placement as foster children until the adoption. This allowed us to receive financial assistance, therapy services, and medical and dental care for the boys. Then after the adoption was final, we would still receive assistance through the Medicaid system and a monthly subsidy from the state. Also, the Adoption Support Program would upon approval, pay any expenses not paid by Medicaid. My husband and I experienced conflicting feelings about the assistance. We felt that if we were not able to provide for the boys then we should not be adopting them. Their case manager convinced us that we would be grateful for the assistance. She explained that, although we may not think so at the time, there would be many expenses involved in their mental and physical recovery. The abuse they had suffered in the past had resulted not only in their emotional instability, but their physical and dental health as well. Reluctantly we accepted the state's assistance. Looking back on this now, I wonder why we had doubts in the first place. Of course, at that time, we were still in the "love can conquer all" mode of thinking.

Once all the paperwork and legal processes of their placement were complete, their case manager arranged for the move in date. We readied their rooms, stocked up on groceries, and waited for them to arrive. I wrote the "stoplight rules" and hung them on the board in front of the breakfast counter so the boys could read them every morning. They were dubbed the stoplight rules because they were written on corresponding colors of construction paper, depending on their purpose. The green rules, for instance, were those that were okay to do any time. They included family hugs or brushing teeth. The yellow rules consisted of rules that were conditional upon other circumstances. For example, if all school-work was completed and rooms picked up then, with permission, the boys could ride their bikes or play in the backyard. Finally, the red rules were those that were absolutely forbidden. These were intended more for safety than anything else. As we got to know the boys better we began to add to the red rules. For instance, when Charlie climbed on the roof or started fires these behaviors were added to the red rules. When Chris picked at scabs or told false stories they were also added. Finally, stealing food or hurting self became part of the red rules because of Wayne. The stoplight rules were posted in every house we lived in from that moment forward.

We were expecting to spend the first day unpacking and arranging the boys' belongings. To our surprise this was not the case. They had very little. They came with only a few clothes and some toys the foster parents had given them as going away gifts, most of which was packed in paper sacks. I suddenly realized—they truly had not lived a normal childhood up to that point!

I had requested and received maternity leave from work and it was the best thing I could have done. My husband received a week's paternity leave and I was very grateful to have his assistance during that first week. We had already promised ourselves that each night before the boys went to sleep we would tuck them in, hug them, and tell them that we loved them. It was not until a few months later, when we missed a night, that we realized how important this routine had become to the boys. They let us know about it the next day when Wayne said, "No one ever did that for us before you and we really like it." We made sure that we never missed a night again. Even if we were not home when they went to bed, we went out of our way to call them on the phone to tell them we loved them. We told them that we would hug and kiss them when we came home. When Charlie replied, "we won't know if we are asleep," we assured him that they would know "because they would feel an angel's wings during the night."

Although we had a schedule worked out for the boys, we strayed from it during the first week. My husband's parents took vacation time to meet the boys and arrived the morning after they moved in. This was an excellent time for the boys to become acquainted with their new family. It also was a tremendous help to my husband and I to have some experienced parents available for help and advice. They stayed a week and I was sorry to see them leave because now I knew I was "home alone" during the day and wondered if I would do everything correctly.

For the next couple of weeks, the boys ran me ragged. By the time my head hit the pillow each night, I was exhausted and began wondering if I could keep up. I could only imagine that what I was experiencing was comparable to the postpartum "baby blues" experienced by birthmothers. Not only was I exhausted from my motherly duties, but also from the constant watch I had to keep over the boys. If one of them was quiet my maternal instincts immediately kicked in. It was usually at this time that one of the other boys would be getting into something that also needed my attention.

Everything imaginable happened during this time period. Charlie constantly climbed on the roof of our house when he became angry, an event which occurred at least once a day, sometimes more. While outside trying to coax him down, it never failed that one of the other boys would involve himself in a situation just as pressing as the one on the roof. For instance, Chris was constantly crying "I want my mother" or "you're going to send me back because you don't love me." I would try to comfort Chris while keeping watch over Charlie on the roof. If I was lucky I could calm him down before Wayne instigated mischief of his own. Unfortunately this did not happen very often. One time in particular will always be implanted in the depths of my brain—the day the police came to our house to "protect the boys." They informed me that Wayne had called 911 and reported child abuse. I could not believe my ears. I informed the police that Charlie continually climbed up on the roof and explained our adoptive situation. The only thought running through my mind at this time was "What have

I gotten myself into?" Fortunately the police officers' attitudes changed from rescuing the boys to rescuing me. They apologized for interrupting my attempt to corral the boys and lectured Wayne for causing so much trouble. The only thing I could do at this point was *pray for school to start*!

After the police incident, I kept a tighter rein on all three of the boys. I immediately implemented the schedule that I had become so lax about. I told them they had to be where I could always see them. They had a specific time for everything. Meals were served at the same time every day, they lined up to brush their teeth, they read the family rules at every meal, and many other monitored routines. If they wanted to go outside, they were not allowed anywhere but in our fenced backyard. I also placed a chair at the sliding door so I could watch their every move. Oh speaking of the sliding door, my husband quickly invented the "door lesson." The boys would come in and out hundreds of times a day and it never failed that they would leave the door open letting **out** the air conditioning and letting **in** the bugs. After warning them to close the door for the 1,999th time, on the 2,000 and each subsequent time they left it open they were "invited" to perform the door lesson. It consisted of going out the door, closing it, opening it, coming back in, and closing it again. Soon they became so accustomed to this lesson that they began to do it without being told. I knew they had learned it well when the neighbor kids would come over, leave the doors open, and the boys immediately giggled and shouted "DOOR LESSON." Situation conquered!

We invented many similar lessons just for them! For instance, we had the shoe lesson, the light lesson, the bed lesson, and even the "hit the toilet hole" lesson. The light lesson was not one of turning on and off the lights, but rather for every light they left on they had to pay a penny for the use of the electricity. This amount would then increase each time the same light was involved in the light lesson. Usually by the time they had worked their way up to a nickel for each light, they were able to "remember" to turn it off. After all, it cut into their spending money and they just could not stand for that!

The "hit the toilet hole" lesson helped me, the only female in the house, the most. Not only did they read "We will aim and hit the toilet" rule at least three times a day, I also told them numerous times to keep the seat dry and the lid down. The final straw came one early morning when I got up to use the restroom. Not wanting to wake up my husband, I left the light off. Boy did I get a surprise when I sat down! The next day I told my husband it would be the last time I sat down in *a puddle of piddle!* So he marched all three of them into the bathroom, visually showed them how to lift the lid, unzip their zippers, do their boy thing, zip up their zippers, flush the stool, and finally put the lid down. When they wanted to practice this we wondered if they had ever had been taught such a mundane task. I never experienced this problem again.

Chapter 3

The Honeymoon Period

I convinced myself that the boys' mischief would decrease after they had time to adjust to their new surroundings and us. By justifying their antics this way, each new day brought hope of a normal family life. But this way of thinking was simply a rewording of the ideal society holds. The phrase "all they need is to be loved more and they will be fine" does not magically cure the abused child. As each chaotic day passed, we began encouraging ourselves by changing our phrase to "things will be better after the adoption is final and the boys know they are secure." It is easy to get caught up in this way of thinking but it does not help anyone involved. It is merely a myth that prolongs the denial of the depth of the child's problems. It is easy to look back on this time period and realize we ignored all the signs of what was to come. The desire we had to have a family clouded our otherwise normal brain functioning. The boys' misbehaviors and deteriorating mental health were feeding off each other. It was not until sometime later that we *woke up* and realized, "*Love is not enough to make everything all right.*"

We had been told in our training classes that the first few weeks, or even months, after the kids arrived was known as the Honeymoon Period. This, we were informed, was the time when the kids were on their best behavior in hopes that the parents would not be scared away or be tempted to send them back to foster care. I remember thinking "honeymoon, how bad can it really be." Well, this was my first mistake, never question if things can get worse because *they can and probably will!!*

We started the boys in therapy the week after their arrival. Our first session was spent getting to know the therapist. She had read the boys' files and asked us what we wanted her to work on with each boy. We related some of the misbehaviors we had already witnessed and those with which we needed assistance.

Wayne had self-esteem problems and wanted to be in control of everything. We told her that we had found him hiding in his closet several times. When we told him to come out he would purposely inflict injury upon himself in some way. For instance, he would bang his head against the wall or bend his arms around his back. His other misbehaviors consisted of not obeying the rules, cramming his meals into his mouth, and isolating himself behind books. The books were a constant problem. He would sit and read books and do nothing else, even when asked. His personal hygiene was also a concern for us. He did not care to be clean. When we did manage to get him in the bath or shower, he would empty all the shampoo bottles and blame it on one of his brothers.

Charlie had very explosive anger outbursts. Not only would he crawl up on the roof, he would also hit and kick others when he was angry. He felt as if everyone was coming to hurt him and he had to defend himself when, in all actuality, he instigated the outbursts. I told the therapist that I had made a "deal" with him that seemed to be working. He and I had sat down and came up with an alternative way to handle his anger. When he felt himself becoming angry he would come to me and I would hold him while we counted to ten. Then, when he felt he was in control, he could go back to his activities. I admitted to the therapist that I was quite confused the first time he actually followed through with this. After a few seconds I remembered our "deal" and praised him for following through. In addition to his anger, there were other dangerous behaviors such as fire setting and stealing. He was very sly about his behaviors and if my husband or I did not catch him in the act, we would begin to doubt ourselves and believe his extremely charming and convincing stories. He had an amazing way of lying and it was very difficult to know when he was telling the truth and when he wasn't. Fortunately I began to learn the signs he displayed while lying.

Chris displayed many insecure behaviors. He was very negative about the placement and was sure to remind us daily that, "This is not going to work anyway so just send me back." We knew this was a result of his prior disrupted placement but we felt these feelings would fade with time. He was also very immature for his age. He constantly whined if things did not go his way or if he was not the center of attention. We related several instances when he would throw tantrums and begin his "send me back demands." These incidents always lead to several hours of crying. In addition to this, he was a very accident-prone child. Just in the week since he had moved in with us, he had fallen off his bike and cut his knees, cut his foot on a rock, and left his bike behind the mail truck which resulted in the bike being run over and destroyed. Of course all of these events led to hours of "send me back" episodes and whining. It took, on the average, 2-3 hours of comforting to calm him.

After we finished telling her the problem areas, we decided she should meet with the boys once a week. She also agreed to meet with us as a family, as well as, my husband and I together. Our naïve manner once again showed itself when we asked her how long she expected it would take to change the boys' misbehaviors. In a kind, yet professional manner, she informed us "the causes of these behaviors did not happen overnight and they will not disappear overnight. Each child is different and it is not possible to estimate an amount of time."

The next couple of weeks were a mixture of good and bad days. The good days persuaded us that we had done the right thing by getting the boys. However, we quickly learned the good days should be enjoyed to the fullest because they served as a signal that something big was about to happen. We began to think, subconsciously, that the boys had a good day just to mess with our minds and give us a false sense of hope.

I began writing a journal of the boys' activities and milestones on the day of their arrival. I did this for several reasons; first, to give them something to look back on when they were grown, secondly, to make up for the childhood years they had already missed, and thirdly, for my own mental health. Writing every night seemed to help me unwind from the day and put the day's events in perspective. Even though I did not realize it at the time, the journal provided me with an extra benefit. I soon found myself reading it as a progress report. I received my greatest inspiration when it refreshed my memory of the fun times. For instance, there was the time the boys took their sack lunches and a shovel to the woods to dig up worms. As they headed off to the woods they slung their shovels over their shoulder and disappeared into the trees singing "Hi Ho Hi Ho it's off to work we go." Or another time when they colored pictures for us simply because they "loved us." In addition, my husband and I were reminded that we really were parents when the boys began losing their baby teeth and the tooth fairy <u>had</u> to come the same night. With the three of them losing their teeth at the same time, the tooth fairy nearly went broke, but truly did not mind at all. It was a pleasure to have the opportunity to enjoy this normal childhood event!

A week after my husband's parents left, my parents arrived for their vacation. It was a 3-day drive for them so they called the boys every night to tell them where they were. To help the boys visualize their trip I bought a map and hung it on the dining room wall. We drew a yellow line from their city to ours. Then, each night after my parents called we would trace the yellow line with a red line and put a star on the city from where they had called. By the time my parents were only hours away, the boys could barely contain their excitement. When they finally pulled into the driveway I was very relieved. Not only would the boys settle down but also I would get a much needed and welcome BREAK.

During the next week the boys enjoyed many activities with my parents. But this is not to say it was smooth sailing, there were daily problems that had to be dealt with. The first incident had to do with the gifts my parents brought from home. Chris threw a tantrum when he opened the box containing new jeans and a shirt. After throwing down the clothes, he ran to his room and hid behind the dresser. My husband and I persuaded him to come back and open the rest of his gifts. We never found out why this incident occurred so we dropped it after he decided to rejoin the rest of us.

Another tantrum he threw during that week revolved around his birthparents. We had dealt with this issue several times since meeting him and decided this time he needed to know the truth. He did not understand why he was "taken" away from his birthparents. I asked him "do you remember our green rule about always getting a true answer to our questions?" He said he did so I explained that his birthmother had signed some papers that allowed him to be adopted. He quickly replied, "It was my birthfather not her." I told him "I'm sorry but it was both." At this point he began crying so I told him that I knew it was sad and hurtful and it was good for him to cry. I reassured him several times that Dad and I loved him and the only way he would leave us would be by his own behaviors and actions. I then asked him if he wanted to be with us. He calmed down and said, "YES! I love you Mom and Dad." He then put on his *happy face* and was fine for the rest of the night. We could only assume that no one had ever told him the truth of his birthparents and why he had been placed in foster care. He seemed to feel better after having it explained. Not only did he have to deal with his birthparents' rejection but also the failed adoption prior to coming to us. He had only lived with the other adoptive family for eight weeks so he had in his mind that we would send him back to his foster parents' house after eight weeks. No amount of denying it on our part convinced him that would not happen. So, my husband and I made plans to take him on a camping trip on the 8-week anniversary of his placement with us. His insecurity is something that has never left him. In addition, he was always the boy who would do *anything* to get some attention. When we notice it, we immediately say something to him and increase his counseling sessions in an attempt to curtail his behaviors before they are out of control.

Each day that passed exposed more insight into each boy's behavior problems. I wanted everything to go smoothly while all the grandparents visited but soon accepted the fact that it would not. At least, I told myself, the grandparents would see what we were dealing with and would have a better understanding of the boys. Looking back, I realize they held the same thought as everyone else. That is, "things will be better after the boys become adjusted to us and the adoption is finalized." For instance, Wayne would stop stuffing meals into his mouth, taking money from his bank to secretly buy food from vending machines, and cease setting up his brothers for punishment so he could defend them when they were disciplined. Charlie, we told ourselves, would also stop his lying, stealing, and dangerous anger outbursts. Even though not absolute, the optimism of this thinking provided us with a source of hopefulness that helped us survive each tumultuous day.

I do not believe there has been any mother alive happier to see the first day of school than I was. I rose with the sun that morning making breakfast, singing like a lark, and getting the boys dressed in their school clothes. This was very unusual because I had never been a morning person, especially before a cup of coffee. But this day was an answer to my prayers and I was not going to waste a second of it. The boys, although nervous and excited about school, were more dumbfounded by my cheerfulness than their feelings of anxiety.

Off to school we went. My husband escorted Chris, I escorted Charlie, and my mother escorted Wayne. We dropped them off in their classrooms, informed their teachers of their foster/adoption status and met back at the office with a collective sigh of relief. My only hope was that they made it through the entire day without me receiving a phone call from the school. My husband went back to work and my mother and I went home. I sat on the sofa and just knew something was wrong—it was too quiet. It was then that my mother reminded me *"it is okay, they are at school."*

Chapter 4

The Wave of Trials and Tribulations

After the Honeymoon period ended, which I am not sure when, or if, it ever started, we began to witness more bizarre behaviors. We attributed the behaviors to the growing anxiety of going to court and finalizing the adoption. In all actuality, the boys were testing us in an attempt to have us reject them before the finalization. By doing this, they could confirm their belief that they were bad; which was the reason they believed their birth-parents did not want them. However, we had assured them many times that we DID want them and they were not bad, rather their birthparents had done some bad things. Since the first visit, we had informed them that we did not want to split them up so it was all three of them or none of them. Our purpose for telling them this was to take the burden off their shoulders concerning their adoption. They did not have to compete with each other for the chance of being adopted, but rather they were part of a family package.

The anticipation of the next few months was bittersweet. Sweet because we were eager to finalize the adoption and move on with our life, bitter due to the boys' continued antics. We continued to cling to the ever-deceiving idea that things would be okay after the finalization. Their behaviors, however, made the wait difficult. Each boy had his own problem behaviors and staying ahead of them was a challenge. Just when I felt I was one step ahead of them, and felt confident in heading off trouble, they, individually or as a whole, caught me off guard.

To discourage them from repeating an unwanted misbehavior I had to invent creative consequences. For instance, our youngest persisted in telling everyone he came in contact with to f(*uck*) off. We had tried all of the customary consequences with no success. We explained that it was a bad word, lectured, took away TV time, and had him brush his teeth. The last consequence threw us a curve ball though. Instead of using toothpaste, we chose mouthwash. We figured, even though he was unaware of it, the mouthwash was beneficial to his oral hygiene. Unfortunately this resulted in a scare when he formed blisters in and around his mouth. It took a trip to the Emergency Room to relieve our worry. The doctor informed us that it was a common reaction so we should not beat ourselves up about it. He also assured us that there was no way of knowing he would have this allergic reaction. He suggested we wait a few years and then allow our son to use mouthwash again since he would probably outgrow the allergic reaction.

This alleviated our guilt but we were once again faced with the dilemma when he, once again, began using the f... off phrase. I had to come up with a consequence that would once and for all curtail this problem. Looking around our living room, the answer suddenly came to me! We had a corner table that was used to display our family Bible and a statue of Jesus. After telling myself that God would understand my situation, I had my son put his hands on the statue and say the f... off phrase 20 times. I did not hear this phrase again for six more years. Two points for Mom, another situation conquered.

Conquering this behavior instilled in me a renewed sense of determination. Of course, the boys did not wait long to offer me the chance to test it. Less than a week later, I received a call from Charlie. He was in the school principle's office and crying hysterically when I answered. I was finally able to calm him down enough to decipher what had caused his devastation. His older brother had gone to school that morning and told several kids that his dad had sexually abused the middle brother. He revealed explicit details of the abuse. The kids wasted no time in ridiculing Charlie. They asked Charlie to demonstrate the abuse, taunted him, and further assumed it was my husband, since they were unaware of his adoptive status.

When he told me the story I was bombarded with feelings. I felt empathy and protectiveness for Charlie, anger at Wayne for hurting his brother in an attempt to gain friends, and a deep protectiveness of my husband's reputation. I composed myself for Charlie's sake and was able to calm him. I told him I loved him and I would take care of the situation. He reluctantly decided to return to his class after I suggested he stay inside at recess and help his teacher. She agreed to let him be her "special helper" until he felt comfortable enough to go outside.

Meanwhile, I told the principle that I would be at the school in a few minutes and pick up Wayne. Being ex-military, I immediately called the nearest military recruiting office. It happened to be the Marines. When I explained the incident to the recruiter and told him that this was a continuing problem with Wayne, that is, trying to sabotage his middle brother, the recruiter agreed to put on his military persona and "have a talk with the young man." He told me he would attempt to leave a lasting impression on our son. After picking up our son, I drove directly to the Marine office. My son did not know where we were headed so when I pulled up to the office and he saw the Marines in their crisp uniforms it was all I could do to maintain my stern composure. His eyes became as large as saucers and he snapped to when the Marine said "Son step into my office. Ma'am, I will handle this so please have a seat." I do not know what all was said in that office, but I could tell by looking through the window that my son was getting a lesson in humanity. I saw him stand at attention, quieted when he tried to interrupt and finally cry when the Marine stared intently at him. At the conclusion of their "meeting" the Marine opened the door and Wayne saluted him. The Marine told me if I had any more problems with "the young man" to call him immediately. He then gave my son his business card and said he would be checking in on his behavior. The ride home was quiet and any lecture by me at this point would have been fruitless. After all, even though I was becoming an accomplished lecturer, I could not beat the one he had just received from "one of the few good men—A Marine Sergeant!"

In addition to all of the unusual behaviors we dealt with, there were also the normal growing boy behaviors. We knew we were just like all parents when we had to tell the boys to do something time after time. I felt like a broken record each time I had to remind them to pick up their clothes and toys, tie their shoe laces, wash their hands, brush their teeth, and stop jumping on their beds. To counteract these everyday annoyances we invented more "lessons" similar to the door lesson. For the scattered clothes we, after telling them numerous times, emptied their dressers and supervised as they neatly folded them and put them back where they belonged. The shoe lace lesson was invented especially for our youngest. It consisted of putting on his socks and shoes, tying the laces, taking off the shoes and socks, and putting them all back on. I only had to implement this lesson once. It happened to be after school one day. I warned him until I was blue in the face and finally said, "OK shoe lesson until Dad gets home from work." Those few minutes must have been some of the longest of his life but until he outgrew those shoes, he never failed to keep them tied. The next pair of shoes, until he wore them out, fixed the problem. Thank goodness Velcro was available in kid's sizes!

By the fourth month we felt we had things under control. That is until we learned that Charlie was stealing from neighbors, friends, and schoolmates. We had noticed unaccounted for loose change, but were so busy surviving each day that we accepted his "Oh I found it on the ground today" excuses. Not only was he stealing, but also he had the uncanny ability to lie and make even the most alert person believe him. However, the day I was notified by the principle that his classmates' lunch money was disappearing, was the day I realized I had been duped.

I looked in all the hiding places throughout the house and found coins and bills stashed everywhere. When we confronted our son he, of course, denied it "with his life." If we had not been absolutely positive of our sanity, we could have fallen for his convincing act. Thankfully our brains fired the correct signals this time. My husband told him he might as well spill the beans because "continuing to deny it is putting yourself deeper and deeper in the hole you are digging." Finally, he realized no amount of denial would get him out of this episode and admitted to more than we were even aware of. His downfall was when he told us he had stolen a dollar from our neighbor's son and used it to pay the football wager he had made with his Dad. We had thought it came from his piggy bank money. We immediately dispensed his consequences—writing apology letters and loss of his bike for a week. The next thing I knew he was in the car with his Dad heading for the police station. Since the Marine had assisted in Wayne's prank, my husband hoped the police officer could enlighten Charlie about the life of a thief. He indeed received a scare when the police officer took him on a tour of the jail while explaining the consequences of stealing. When the officer realized he had gotten our son's full attention he asked him "Do you know what is worse than jail? It is the feeling you have to carry around in your heart." My husband told me he knew the message had sunk in when on the drive home he asked our son how he felt and he answered, "I'll tell you after my heart stops beating so fast."

Along with being on a constant watch for the boys' misbehaviors, we also tried to ease the transition by having family meetings. We would begin by talking about the problems of the day and ask the boys to tell us what they had learned. This provided us with an insight into the boys' emotional and cognitive processes. My husband and I soon discovered that with abused kids, honesty is the best policy. We were always very open with the boys and did not hide the truth from them. Since they had endured so much already, lying to them would only collapse the trust that had been established between us. Besides that, the boys could instinctively detect half-truths. If they felt you were lying to them, problems arose immediately.

Chris, despite all of his whimpering and whining, was never at a loss for words. He would jabber on for hours unless directed to pinpoint a specific subject. At least with him, we never have had to guess at what he was feeling or thinking. Charlie, on the other hand, was the silent type. Trying to get a simple yes or no answer from him is like pulling nails. If we asked for explanations to accompany his answers we might as well have been talking to a brick wall. He would not say anything for hours. Our frustration would build until finally my husband or I would say "Okay fine" and continue with our family discussion. This would normally persuade him to start mumbling. When we did not respond to him, he would loudly blurt out in frustration. Furthermore, if we ignored him long enough, he would become extremely upset at not receiving attention and would attempt to give an honest answer or opinion.

We also learned very quickly to view everything Wayne said with a bit of skepticism. He tended to say whatever he thought would put him in good graces with us. At times his conversation was so outlandish or syrupy sweet that we would have to say something to bring him back to reality. Although he could communicate well, it was very superficial and never truly his inner thoughts. The only thing I knew to do was listen and attempt to get him to open up with his honest feelings. Still, the times I thought his conversation was sincere, I was never quite sure if it was a ploy to manipulate me for his own gain. I felt there had to be some way for me to get through to him so I tried every tactic imaginable. I tried to identify with him as the oldest sibling (since I myself am the oldest sibling). When this failed, I spoke to him as a friend, mother, therapist, and even a spiritual leader. I wanted so much to develop a bond with him, similar to the one I had with the younger boys, but it never fully emerged. I hoped the few occasions he told me "I love you and it was meant for me to be here" would be the breakthrough I was searching for. Unfortunately, I was wishing for something that was completely out of my control and that, frankly, would never happen. All the same, I cherish the few, rare moments of mother-son tenderness that we were able to share. The moment I hold most precious was the night he crawled up on my lap and asked "Mom can I talk to you?"

We spent the next couple of hours talking about trust, friendship, and love. He told me about his worries for his brothers and wanted to know why he was *no good*. I explained that he was a *good boy* and how his brothers looked up to him as their hero. Being their hero, they would follow almost everything he did. He said, "Yea, I should be a good example." He then went on to tell me about a friend in their past and a pile of tires they used to live by. He was shocked when I said "Yes that man was a friend and he hid you in those tires." I assured him that it was good to remember the nice friends and be thankful for them. I told him that he would have many friends in his life and his true friends would always do good things. My explanation that a good friend is like "God kissing you on your cheek and you will be kissed lots during your lifetime" brought a smile to his somber face.

At this point he told me that his birthparents never cared if he was alive or not. He said the only time they may have cared was when he was in school. I tried to explain, in a loving way, that it might have been because they did not want to be responsible adults. He cringed when he said, "They never came in my room or told me goodnight." However, he seemed to melt in my arms when he told me "I am glad you and Dad do and I like it." When I asked if he knew why we did this, he cried and said, "Yea because you love me." I replied "that's right" and I hugged him tight. The final sentiment we shared that night was one that will always be special. It was the last time that our hearts emotionally meshed as one. He said, "I love you and I'll meet you in my bedroom so you can kiss me and tell me goodnight."

Chapter 5

Court Date—Another Beginning

The time to go to court and finalize the adoption was drawing near. My husband had left a few weeks earlier to find a job closer to home and establish residency so we would be ready to move after our court appearance. On his last Friday night at home, we arranged for a baby-sitter so we could go out to dinner. The boys had already eaten their dinner and dessert so we had them take their baths and get their pajamas on before we left. When the baby-sitter arrived we told her the boys could watch a movie then go to bed at 9:30. We also told her we would call and check in while we were gone. We kissed the boys goodnight, said we would see them the next morning, and told them to be good and enjoy the movie.

When we called after their bedtime, our sitter told us she had problems with the boys all night. Among other things, our oldest made popcorn without permission and smoke filled the house. She also had to stop several fights between them and they refused to go to bed after the movie. She said she had just gotten them to their rooms but they were not asleep. My husband told her we would be home sooner than we had planned and he apologized for all the trouble.

Before we went home we discussed what we should do about the situation. We knew we were getting close to the court date but justifying their behavior as anxiety this time did not ease our aggravation. After much thought we chose to use a consequence that we had been told about by the foster mother during our last parent training session. She told us that when she had children who refused to go to bed on time, she would tell them they could watch TV. She would fix them popcorn and drinks then turn on the TV. After they appeared to be quite comfortable and pleased with themselves for getting their way, she sprang the "condition" on them. They could stay up as late as they wanted and enjoy all the snacks she had prepared but they "had to stand up the entire time." She said a few minutes of standing and they decided bed "sounded very good." She told us that she had never had the same child pull this stunt twice. Well, we thought, if it worked for her it should work for us also.

We arrived home and thanked the sitter for her patience. After she left, my husband went into action. He banged on their bedroom doors and, in his military voice, shouted, "Get up and out here NOW!" The boys came flying out of their rooms and immediately stood at attention. If we had not been so upset with them, we both would have laughed hysterically. He proceeded from this point with a series of questions. We had already learned not to phrase our questions as "*Did* you do it?" but rather, "*Why* did you do it?" Asking them if they did something would only result in denials that could convince anyone. When we asked why they did such and such, by naming the specific behavior, they were trapped. They at least had to come up with some kind of excuse. The answer we received that night was "because I wanted to and you can't tell me what to do" from our oldest, "I didn't do anything" from Charlie, and, mixed with crying and whining, "they made me do it" from our youngest. We then told the boys that this time their excuses were not going to work and if they did not want to be in our family they better tell us now. I explained that they were running out of time before we went to court to finalize the adoption. If they did not want to be adopted, I told them, then I needed to make arrangements with their case manager to place them with foster parents. But, on the other hand, if they wanted to stay they would have to work at making us a family just as hard as we were. At this point, my husband took over.

He spelled out their activities for the rest of the night. First they would get their laundry and start washing their clothes. Next, they would do their exercises. Lastly they would stand in the hall and wait on the dryer so he could watch them while he did some work on the computer. All the while, he continued with a lecture that would put even the most wide-awake person to sleep. I went to bed so I could be alert enough to handle the next day. At 4:00 a.m. my husband crawled into bed and said that, although it was a battle of wills, the boys finally gave out and pleaded to go to bed. Needless to say, the boys behaved perfectly the rest of the weekend.

The following Monday morning my husband left to hunt for a job and I was home alone with the boys. It was a daily challenge keeping the boys and house together. My leave from work was over and I also had to concentrate on my job. After a couple of weeks of this, I told my husband I wanted a vacation once we were moved and settled in. I did not realize at the time that I made the comment that my desire would grow immensely.

The boy's case manager called and told us when we found an attorney and completed the paperwork the court date could be set. I immediately contacted the attorney referred to us by our agency. He compiled the legal paperwork while I gathered the adoption agency paperwork. Once everything was in order, I called my husband to tell him we would go to court in two or three weeks. He made plans to come back the week of the court date. I had handled the boy's mischief fairly well by myself and was feeling fairly confident, however, that was before all *hell* broke loose. Two days after my husband made his plans to return for our court date, I had to call him back and move his return date ahead of schedule.

I had dropped the boys off at the sitters and told them that I had a class to attend and would not be at my desk that morning. I told them I would see them after school. After my class I went back to the office. Within a matter of a few minutes, I received a phone call from the school counselor about all three boys. He told me they were having a terrible day and it had gotten continually worse. He told me he was taking care of the boys at school but wanted me to know what had happened before they got home. At the end of our conversation he apologized for not becoming involved with the boys sooner. He told me he now realized the seriousness of what I had been trying to tell him and he now planned to visit with them daily.

Wayne was caught reading a comic book that he had hidden in his math book. When his teacher told him to put it away and finish his work, he folded his arms and said NO! She told me his voice and statuesque posture was very eerie and she was frightened by what he might do next. She said the look on his face was so terrifying that it sent chills through her. Knowing that she had taught for many years, I realized it was very serious if she admitted being leery of him.

At the bus stop that morning, Charlie was swinging a tent stake at the other kids. The bus driver told him to stop but he would not. She also asked him to give it to her but he refused to do that also. He received a bus warning ticket even though the counselor told the driver it would not help. His teacher had to take the tent stake away from him when he got to school. He then got into a boy's face and called him "stupid faggot." When he was told to apologize he said he wouldn't. He was immediately sent to the counselor. Then later that day he had run out of his room twice. The first time the secretary found him behind a tree and talked him into going back into his room. The second time he was gone longer. All the staff looked for him. Finally the janitor found him hiding under the bleachers in the gym. The counselor then informed me that the recess monitors did not want to handle him anymore. He had received several complaints from other kids and no one wanted to be around him because of his aggressive behavior. When he complained to his teacher that the kids were chasing him, she replied "they can't chase someone who isn't moving." I had never thought about it in that way and began to immediately use this phrase every time he justified his misbehaviors because of being chased. Soon this excuse began to subside and only resurfaced when he ran out of other excuses.

Chris had his own share of mischief that morning. While at the bus stop another boy told him that his pants were unzipped. Our son then kicked the boy in his "privates." The bus driver wanted to give him a bus warning ticket also, but the counselor convinced the driver that he would take care of it. The counselor talked to him and explained it was wrong and inappropriate to hit or kick anyone. Our son was embarrassed to talk about it and the counselor suggested I discipline him for the behavior since he had talked to our son.

I went back home to recover from the morning. I prepared for the boys' return from school. I did not call my husband because I knew he was busy interviewing for jobs. The counselor had left a message on our answering machine just in case he missed me at work. By now I was very upset and felt almost hopeless. It was the first time I honestly wanted to be rid of all of the problems. I felt very resentful. The problem was I did not know whom my resentment was directed towards. Was it the boys for their continual misbehavior and lack of trust; the birthparents for abusing the boys; the caseworkers and counselors for their "Band-Aid therapy"; my husband for being away; friends for their "you asked for the boys" attitude; other parents for having well-adjusted kids and lack of appreciation for my 110% effort; the school for not listening in the beginning; or God for not helping the boys. I took a couple of deep breaths and picked up the boys at school.

While waiting in the school parking lot to pick up the boys, Chris' teacher waved me down. She told me that she was going to call because she was having trouble with our son tearing up his desk. He was using his scissors to drill holes in the desk table. I could not believe it. I was ready to pack them up and deliver them to their case manager that instant. The school counselor told me he had called all three boys into his office and talked to them. I think he finally accepted the fact that they were a handful and I was pretty much a basket case at this point. He told me he was able to calm them down and they agreed to be good the rest of the night. He attributed all their behaviors to anxiety of going to court. When I told him that was the same excuse I used in justifying their actions, he assured me that after the adoption was final and court was over, "Things would be much better." Once again, I fell for the theory and convinced myself that "it will get better." After all, I reasoned, how much worse can it get? Big mistake to ask that question!

I chose to make the best out of the rest of the day and let the boys watch cartoons, color, play checkers, and help with dinner. I decided not to mention the day unless they brought it up. After they got home, they had their snacks and seemed to be on their best behavior. While watching cartoons, Wayne and Chris decided to go to their rooms and color in their activity books. Charlie stayed with me in the living room and watched Flipper and Lassie on the television. During one of the commercials, he went to the bathroom. I did not think anything of it and we continued to watch the shows when he returned. A few minutes later I decided to check on the other boys. As I began walking down the hall to their rooms, I smelled something in the bathroom. When I reached the door, I immediately recognized the odor. It was Smoke! I ran into the bathroom and found smoldering cups in the sink and one in the trash can. I looked in the toilet and one had been thrown in there. I must have gone on autopilot at this point. I immediately began putting out the fire and yelled for the boys to "get your little butts in here now." All the love in the world, I admitted to myself, was insufficient to conquer this incident. To cope with this, I needed much, much more.

After I put out the fire, I began looking around the house. I had noticed Charlie in the kitchen on his way back from the bathroom. I had seen him standing by the microwave so I began searching there. When he saw me looking at him he said while pointing to his oldest brother's room "I saw him put something in his pocket." Although I knew he was such an accomplished liar, I believed him and immediately confronted Wayne. He was sitting on his bed reading a book. When I told him to tell me what he was hiding, he said he did not know what I was talking about. With all the problems he had caused for Charlie lately, I did not know whom to accuse. So, I told Wayne to empty his pockets. When I did not find anything I then told him to strip down to his underwear. I was determined to find out what was used to start the fire.

In the meantime, I continued searching the kitchen with no success. I knew Charlie had been in there but found myself doubting my own eyes. After I was satisfied that Wayne did not have a fire-producing object, I went back to the kitchen. During this entire time, Charlie followed my every step and told me his "suspicions of where his brother had hidden something." I began to believe that Charlie was correct and he was trying to help me get to the bottom of the fire. I was so naive and ignorant; he was playing me the whole time. It was not until I moved the microwave and found a lighter that I knew Charlie was responsible for the fire. I became so angry that I paced the floor and knew I could not even talk to him right then. My mind was going in about a million different directions. The realization that Charlie could have burnt down the house, combined with the misbehaviors of the day was more than I could comprehend. I knew I was about to lose my composure so I called my husband and told him "get in your car now and come home." Even with the 36 hours drive time, just knowing that help was on the way brought some relief.

I proceeded to the two younger boys' room and pulled the sheets off Charlie's bed. As I pulled them, they became caught against the wall and the mattress flipped over. After I finally got the sheets free, I took them to the backyard and put the grill lid upside down on the patio. I then placed the sheets along with my son's favorite stuffed animal in the lid. I told him to stand where he could watch what fire could do and I lit the articles. He stood glaring at his sheets and toys while they burned. While he watched the fire destroy his belongings I explained that fire is very dangerous. Not only does it destroy our things, I told him, but it can also hurt people if they are unable to get out of their burning house. I was also able to use the fire example to explain how a lie can be like a fire and destroy people's trust in a liar. "Anger too," I said, "can build up inside someone and if it is not dealt with properly can destroy the angry person and others around the angry person." I stressed to him the importance of talking to someone and dealing with problems. Misbehaving, I told him, could lead to some-one getting "hurt real bad." "When you play with fire you always get burned" I told him.

After dinner, I sent the boys to bed. All three of them gave me a hug and told me they were sorry for all the "bad things" they had done that day. I told them I was still upset but that I also loved them and hoped they learned some good lessons. Our youngest told me he now knew that, "You mean business and you will always find out what I do." I smiled and told him to remember that and it would save him a lot of trouble. Our oldest said goodnight in his superficial way and went to bed. Charlie stayed around for a bit longer. He did not say much but with his head hung low he whispered "I'm sorry Mom. I just can't control my anger. Do you still love me?" I held him close and assured him that I still loved him and always would no matter what happened. He then went to bed. I checked on them 10 minutes later and found that they were all sound asleep. It was not until then that I collapsed on the sofa thankful that the day from hell was finally over. I just prayed that tomorrow would not be as bad as the day I just lived through. After all, my husband would be back in 34 more hours *and* he was also bringing my mother to help.

The next morning the boys got off to school without any problems. I called work and asked for two days of vacation. I then went next door and spent the morning with two of my neighbors. Both had boys of their own and they offered to give me some relief that night. One of them would take the boys to the Art and Science Fair at school and buy them a Popsicle. The other neighbor took them to rent a movie.

While they were gone, two other friends stopped by. When I related the events of the previous day they stayed and helped me clean the house. Then one of my friends took me to see a movie. I was very grateful for the break. That night the boys stayed with one of our neighbors. They offered to keep them overnight so when my husband arrived the next morning we would have time to discuss our plans. It was so peaceful that night that I was asleep as soon as my head hit the pillow.

By driving day and night, my husband and mother arrived early the next morning. We discussed everything that I had been through. I told them all the counselors were convinced the boys would calm down after we finalized the adoption and felt they were secure. After discussing the pros and cons of continuing the adoption, we decided to go ahead with it. We already were emotionally tied to the boys and felt that it was meant for us to have them. We could not imagine life without them at this point. Now that I had help with them and had been given a break by friends, I was in a much better position to think it through clearly. I continued to cling to the dream that it would get better after the adoption and the boys knew they were our sons. The problem with that dream was that, although I was thinking in rational and logical terms, the boys would never be able to think in that manner. Whether this was due to cognitive inability or purposively determined by each one I will never know.

We spent the next week taking care of all the legalities of the adoption. We had to drive to the state Capital to get the necessary forms filed before our attorney could get his paperwork ready. In addition, we began packing so we would be ready to leave when court was over. Chris came home from school while we were busy packing and said, "Boy the house got bald." He was so sincere that we had to bust out laughing. It felt wonderful to be able to laugh; it helped ease the anxiety of going to court, packing, and waiting.

Two days before court, my mother and I went shopping to buy each of the boys a new blue suit. Each received a new shirt and an individualized special tie for their suit. When we brought them home the boys' eyes lit up like candles. They were very eager to try them on but I told them they would have to wait until after their showers. It did not take them long to finish the dishes and showers that night. When I saw all three boys in their suits, reality hit me—they were going to be part of our family! The next morning my husband took the boys to the barbershop. "They have to have a new haircut for the big event," my husband told me. It was 'men's morning out' as he put it. When they got back they all looked so cute. I remember thinking, how could such innocent looking, cute boys be so mischievous?

Well, the day was finally here. I got up and got ready so I could then get the boys ready. My mother and I were in charge of getting the boys dressed. My husband was in charge of putting on their ties. At 10:00 a.m. we left for the courthouse. We had invited several friends and were delighted to see our neighbors and four of my co-workers. A friend of ours videotaped the ceremony. One of my co-workers also taped the ceremony so we had two versions. We sat in the hallway waiting for our time to appear in front of the judge. I was very nervous, but proud. The boys sat quietly and, amazingly, were quite patient.

Finally, it was our turn. When our attorney opened the chamber door all of us proceeded to go in. The judge was amazed at the number of people who came to witness the birth of our family. He asked my husband and I a few questions such as "Did we want to adopt the boys," "Were we prepared to provide for them until they were at least 18," and "Were all the records in order." He then asked the boys "do you want these two people as your parents?" When they answered "yes" he said "in front of all these people who am I to say no. You are now officially a family." He then read off the boys' new names. Upon his request, we changed Wayne's first and middle names. We changed our second son's middle name, and of course all three received a new last name. We changed the names so each boy would have a family name for their middle name. They chose which male relative they wanted to be named after and this made them feel part of their new family. After this was done, everyone clapped and shed a few tears of happiness. As we walked out of the chamber Chris said, "Mom, now I know no one will ever take us away again!" I reassured him that he was right and he was our son forever.

We waited in the hallway for our attorney to bring us the certified paperwork. While we waited my co-workers gave us all a T-shirt designed just for our new family. My husband and mine read "Anyone can be a father (mother) but it takes someone special to be a daddy (mommy). The boys' shirts had a picture of a dinosaur with "I am the big brother tyran- nosaur," "I am the middle brother tyrannosaur," and "I am the little brother tyrannosaur." The back of all ours shirt had our last name. The boys also received some toys to take to their new home.

Our attorney returned and presented us with the official signed and sealed documents. He then pulled three bubble gum cigars out of his pocket with "It's a boy" written on the wrapper and gave them to my hus- band. It was the perfect ending to the morning. I thanked my co-workers for sharing in our happy day. "After going through the two year process with you, we would not have missed it for the world" was their response. I was very proud to know others shared our excitement.

When we got back to our house, we changed our clothes so we could leave that evening for our 3-day drive. While we changed clothes our neigh- bors sat up a table in the middle of our yard. On it they laid a cake and gifts. They also had made a CONGRATULATIONS sign and decorated our street. It was a fun celebration for our new family. Having others participate in the court ceremony and throw a party to show their happiness for our new beginning was one of the most memorable parts of the day. It somehow anchored our belief that we did the right thing.

After saying good bye to other friends that dropped by that afternoon and going for pizza with one of my co-workers and his family, we left for our new home. Although I had made this trip several times before without any problems whatsoever, I expected this trip to be harder since we were traveling with a loaded U-Haul, towing a car, driving our other vehicle, and managing the boys. But, my expectations were far exceeded by the difficulties that we encountered.

We stopped for our first refueling and bathroom break. When everyone was situated in his or her places, I pulled out. About ten miles down the highway I noticed my husband was not behind me. I told myself he was probably taking it slow due to the terrain, so, I slowed my speed and kept going. After a few more miles I pulled over onto the shoulder and waited for him to catch up. When he did not show up after 15 minutes I decided to double back and find him. Well, it wasn't until I reached the gas station that I found him. He hadn't even left the ramp of the highway. When he told me he had filled the truck with diesel instead of unleaded gasoline I became very agitated. But when he informed me that it would be the next morning before a mechanic could get to us and it would cost nearly all of our travel money, my agitation turned to bitter exasperation. On top of that, we had to pay $100.00 for a tow truck to move the U-Haul just down the ramp! In the meantime I had to do something with the boys. They were already tired from the days' events and there was not a hotel to be found. Fortunately I found some blankets and laid the boys on the seats and floorboards of both vehicles. My mother and I sat in the cafe and watched them. Several times through the night I had to go out and run the heaters because it dipped down into the 30's. Needless to say, my husband and I did not have an enjoyable first night as official parents. To tell the truth we avoided each other like the plague!

The next morning we were able to get the vehicle situation corrected and it was around noon when we finally were able to get back on the road.

We traveled the rest of the day and made up some lost time. Deciding we all needed a good night's rest we drove until we came to a Motel 6. After all, they promise to "leave their light on" and provide us, the boys, and our dog with a comfortable night's sleep. After the boys were tucked into bed, my husband and I knew we needed to clear the air between us. We sat in our vehicle and talked for a couple of hours. During our conservation my husband was able to admit to me the reason he had been inattentive to several things the past couple of months. He told me that with all the stress of the boys, finding a job, moving, and the adoption, he had not had the time to grieve for his grandmother who had passed away three months earlier. In addition, our adoption of the boys was causing him to relive issues of abandonment by his own birthfather. His birthfather had left his mother before he was born and never claimed my husband as his son. He told me "I love Dad (his stepfather) and as far as I am concerned he is the only father I have. But I am afraid the boys will not think of me in the same way and will someday reject me for their birthfather." I was astonished with his statement and now understood why he had been acting so unusual. For the next hour or so we discussed his feelings. When I asked him what his Dad would tell him about his feelings he answered "He would tell me it was okay to feel this way and he would always be there for me if I needed him." It was as if hearing himself say this put his perspective in focus. He smiled and said, "I guess that is all I can do for our boys too." We ended our conservation with a hug and we both felt much better.

The next morning I woke up with a sinus headache and was so sick I was not able to move without becoming nauseated. My husband and mother decided we better stay the rest of the day and head out the next morning. This would give everyone a chance to rest and allow me time to feel better. I did not mind because I was past the point of caring whether we were behind on our travel schedule. I believe this was intended to happen so I could get some rest. With all the stress and demands I had been handling alone, I was worn out. This was a way for my body to let me know I needed some rest from the past six months. By the next morning, I was refreshed and felt much better. We headed out.

It took us two more days to get to my parents' house. We stopped one more time and slept for a few hours in our vehicles. This gave us the second wind we needed. During these two days we had tremendous problems with Wayne. It was as if his misbehaviors before finalization were an omen of what was yet to come. Of course we had the usual bickering and whining from the other two boys but that was something we had expected. Wayne, however, was exhibiting behaviors that were very obstinate and strange. Once again, though, we attributed it to the adoption and move. We figured he would calm down once we were settled into our new house.

My husband and I went on to our new city and began looking for a house. The boys stayed with my parents. We were only gone for two days but during this time the boys caused a lot of trouble. Led by our oldest, they were getting into the neighbors' cars and rolling down the windows. They also climbed over the neighbors' fences and went onto their property. My dad warned them several times not to do this but they continued. When they were caught dumping trash out of garbage cans they received a severe lecture. When we returned we were told Charlie had hit the neighbor girl. Also, Wayne was setting up Charlie and Chris for punishments. He then would play their rescuer and try to gain favor from all sides. He was using his manipulative ways more frequently and was becoming more difficult to control.

When we returned to my parents' house, my husband sent all three boys to the backyard to discuss their misbehaviors during our absence. Wayne sarcastically snipped at me so my husband turned to confront him. Wayne immediately punched himself in the face, causing a bloody nose. He then ran into the house to tell my parents that my husband had done it. Although we explained to them what he had done, and that he had done it several times before, we could sense their skepticism. After all, if there was one thing all three boys were good at it was convincing others they are victims of wrongdoing. They were experts at playing the victim. Ironically, upon our return, my mother made the comment to me "I hope they want to come back again since I had to yell at them so much. Your Daddy had to lecture constantly and I had to swat Chris on his backside. I wondered many times since that day if she had forgotten about her experience with the boys and her exasperated statement.

Chapter 6

False Hopes

We had located a house during our house-hunting trip and were now ready to complete the final phase of our move. We drove to our new home the next morning and, once we arrived, we unloaded the U-Haul. My husband and I were still receiving a cold shoulder from my parents so we directed our concentration on the task before us. Once we arrived at our house we immediately began to unload the truck. We wanted to get the house in order as soon as possible and restore some normalcy to our lives.

The following morning my mother appeared at our door. We had stayed up very late unloading our belongings. Therefore, we were still asleep when the doorbell rang. When my parents entered, they told us that my Uncle wanted to use the truck and he would pay for the extra mileage. My husband had no problem with that but what really upset him was being prodded to get up and load something into their car. Before we could fully wake up, they were driving away. The boys looked at us as if to say "What was all that about?" We talked to them and asked if they noticed any difference in their grandparents. They did not hesitate to tell us "they weren't nice to you and they treated Dad like dirt." We explained that they were upset about the bloody nose incident. The younger boys let their older brother know that he had caused this problem with his lie and they did not like it.

The boys were up and dressed for school early the next morning. Charlie was nervous and scared, but our youngest was "ready to go." Our oldest began acting shy and bashful. When we asked if he was nervous he snapped "No" and proceeded into his room. After the boys were in their places at school, my husband and I spent the day establishing utility services and buying groceries. While out, we ran into my family and were invited to dinner. When we arrived for dinner everyone ate and, afterwards, the kids were sent to a room to play. At this point my Uncle stated "things need to be set straight." As we went around the room and discussed the events of the weekend, my Dad was astonished to find out that Wayne had a history of self-inflicted nosebleeds. He immediately apologized for his reaction to my husband and I. We were relieved to set the facts straight with him. As for the friction with my mother, it was something I had grown accustomed to. We had clashed ever since I was a child so I knew it could not be resolved in one sitting. I told my husband that she would have to realize that I was now an adult and mother with decisions to make and feelings of my own. The best way to deal with her, I told him, was simply to stay away for a while. With the responsibilities we now faced, we knew we would need to concentrate on our family.

The first week in our new home was rather hectic. We tried to establish a routine quickly because I only had one week before I was scheduled to start my new job. Therefore, I spent the week trying to get life in some kind of order. My cousin's son spent a lot of time with our boys and this helped eased their transition. Wayne was continuing his erratic behaviors but we were too busy setting up residence to realize he was steadily declining. Within a couple of weeks, he had reached a point where we could no longer control him and we had to reach out for help.

I had returned from a 30-day personal vacation. My new job, realizing the strain I had been under the last several months offered to let me start work the next month. I was very emotionally drained and began to experience physical fatigue. The month away allowed me to visit my best friend, go fishing and camping, and get some much needed rest. My husband held down the fort while I was gone. The night before I left, I wrote a letter to each of the boys explaining why I needed some time alone. In each letter I explained which behaviors they needed to work on individually, and as a team. I told each one that I loved them but I needed to spend some time by myself so I could be strong for them. I sealed each letter and put their names on them. I then asked my husband to give the boys their letter after I left. Before the boys headed off to school I gave them a big hug and kiss. I assured them that I would call while I was gone and that I WOULD be back after I visited my friend. I asked them to be good for Dad and help him by doing their chores. My middle son seemed most distraught but an extra hug and an "I love you" from me seemed to calm his fears. They all three waved as their school bus pulled away.

During my vacation my husband kept me abreast of the problems at home. Along with the minor, everyday boyhood antics, Wayne was displaying even more severe behaviors. They had escalated to a point where my husband had to keep a constant watch over him. In addition, Chris' teacher had called and suggested we have him evaluated for Attention Deficit Disorder (ADD). She said he was having extreme difficulty paying attention in class. He was out of his seat more than he was in it and was constantly bothering his classmates. None of her normal discipline measures were producing positive results with him. She also explained that his work was far below his grade level but she felt that he was quite capable of doing the work. "A child with ADD", she informed us, "is usually very intelligent but they are unable to attend to a task long enough to complete it. Therefore, their grades are far below a child with other disabilities, such as learning disabilities, for example." Charlie, on the other hand, was doing very well with his schoolwork. He was not exhibiting the behavioral problems he had in the past and his teachers were very pleased with his adjustment.

When my husband related the boys' progress to me, I asked him if he wanted me to come home. I was very grateful when he told me to finish my vacation and we would deal with everything when I returned. Although I appreciated what he was dealing with, I was more appreciative of his insistence that I not cut my plans short. Our give and take relationship was the aspect that kept us together. Even with all that we have endured since becoming parents, we were constantly asked, "How do you mange to remain married?" Sure we deeply love each other but just as with the boys and their behaviors, IT TAKES MORE THAN LOVE! A total commitment to each other, our marriage, our sons, and a strong faith in God definitely top the list of attributes required to remain intact.

The boys attended therapy once a week. They were counseled individually and as a family. At the last session, my husband recounted, Wayne displayed even more erratic behavior. When the therapist called him for his turn, he hid behind a chair and no amount of coaxing drew him out. My husband told the therapist to leave him there and continue with the other boys. Once Wayne heard this he came running out from behind the chair and pushed his way into the therapist's office. When my husband turned the focus on someone other than Wayne, he immediately knew he could not get any more attention from hiding. He then tried to shift the blame for his actions by telling the therapist that we did not allow him to participate in school activities. The therapist immediately picked up on his attempt at gaining unwarranted attention and confronted Wayne with the truth. When he realized his ploy did not work, he backed down, admitted it was a lie, and became silent for the remainder of the session.

In addition to this kind of behavior, Wayne also caused problems with the other boys. One of my cousins stayed with the boys while my husband worked. Wayne refused to mind and continually got into the snack drawer for food. My cousin warned him several times to stay out of the drawer but he continued to disobey. When all of the snacks suddenly disappeared, my husband decided that instead of spending money to take the boys to the fair, he would use it to replace what our son had eaten. This, of course, made the other boys angry and they began to spill the beans about other antics Wayne had pulled. For instance, my husband was shocked to find countless food wrappers hidden behind some tall grass in our backyard. Wayne had also, in addition to taking numerous snacks from our kitchen, had been stealing food from kids at school. However, he had been steadily losing, not gaining, weight. Ironically, the entire family had recently complimented him on his appearance because he had shed some unhealthy pounds and had toned up. By the time my husband found the empty wrappers, I was on my way home from my vacation. We decided to wait until I got home to take action on this newest behavior problem.

On the very day that I returned home, we received a call from the special education teacher at the boys' school. She informed us that Wayne had charged two lunches in the cafeteria plus eaten his lunch from home. Knowing about the other missing and stolen food, I told her that I was becoming very concerned about him. She agreed and suggested we increase his therapy sessions. She referred us to some therapists she had worked with and I contacted them. We eventually changed to a therapist she recommended because we did not feel the boys were benefiting from the one they had been seeing. Our new therapist was very impressive. She seemed more astute on the problems we were facing. This eased our frustration a bit because Wayne's behavior was continuing to deteriorate. I was receiving daily phone calls from the school about his conduct. He was stealing from the kids at school and starting fights on the playground. He was also pulling annoying stunts to get attention. The nurse told us that he had gone to her and told her that "my Dad pulled my ear off and it was bleeding." She told him there was nothing wrong with his ear but he continued to believe there was blood. This incident caused me to wonder if he was out of touch with reality. I had a hunch that he was confusing his past with the present. His psychiatrist later confirmed my suspicions.

His schoolwork and grades began slipping at an alarming rate. Part of this was due to his hiding books inside his school texts and reading them instead of doing his work. We also had this problem with him at home. If we could not find him, he usually was hiding in his closet and reading books. Furthermore, he refused to do any of his chores. Instead, we would catch him reading. However, he was using reading to close out the world.

During the course of all of the problems with Wayne, I made an appointment to have Chris evaluated with his pediatrician. After she concluded her tests, she agreed that he showed indications of ADD. Her recommendation was to start him on Ritalin and observe his behavior for the next few weeks. She informed me that it would take that long for the medication to reach its full effect and we could adjust the dosage as needed after that. Along with the Ritalin, she suggested we have him tested for hypoglycemia. I told her that he was terrified of needles and it was nearly impossible for me to hold him still while the technician drew blood. Hearing this, she decided to wait two weeks before running the test. This would allow the Ritalin time to take effect and hopefully calm him enough to have his blood taken. She made the appointment and said she would call as soon as she received the results. Until we knew for sure, she told me to take him off sugars and feed him several small meals a day instead of three full meals. Crackers, starches, and protein were the best types of snacks for him she said. After I left her office, I took Chris shopping and stocked up on "his special food." By designating the food this way, he felt important and gave me no problems about his diet.

Two weeks later, I took Chris in for his 6-hour blood test. It was not the most pleasant adventure I had ever been a part of but at least we *both* survived the day. I had to hold his arms and legs while the technician drew the blood. The more he squirmed and kicked the longer it took for the technician to get the sample. Needless to say, our son, the technician, and I all looked as if we had been in a bar room brawl at the end of the day. We were all covered with bruises, I was very stiff and sore, and I could barely move the next morning. Two days later, the doctor called me with the test results. Sure enough, our son was diagnosed with borderline hypo-glycemia. At least this and the ADD, I told my husband, accounted for some of the lack of self-control, wiggling, immaturity, and poor school performance.

The week before school let out for the summer, I received a phone call from the boys' principal. She stated that Wayne had numerous library books checked out but had never returned them. I searched his room and had no problem finding them hidden in drawers, under his mattress, and in his closet. I had no sooner taken care of this problem than I was con-tacted about a cafeteria bill that he had charged. Thinking this was the same as the one I recently cleared, I explained that I had already paid the charges. Although, it was true that I had paid the previous charges, these had accumulated since then. I was informed that he had been eating lunch during every lunch period. He simply ate, went outside, waited for the next lunch bell, and then went through the line again. He continued this cycle until all the lunch periods were ended. Furthermore, the lunch he was tak-ing from home was not even making it to school. Charlie told us that he would get in the back seat of the bus and eat it as soon as the bus pulled away from our house. Still, he was becoming very thin and haggard look-ing. It was then that I knew something had to be done to get him some help. After discussing it with our therapist, she immediately referred me to a prominent child psychiatrist. Without any delay, I called. I talked to the doctor for nearly an hour and she said she wanted to see our son "as soon as you can get him out of school and to my office." In an eerie way, I was relieved because she confirmed that he was as unstable as I had expected.

My husband came home from work and we got the boys from school. We drove directly to the psychiatrist's office. After her evaluation, she decided to put him on medication and monitor him for a few weeks. We had hoped he would be hospitalized but she explained that she would have to monitor him first unless he was displaying suicidal or homicidal behavior. He was out of the room at the time she discussed this with us and we told her that we had not seen anything like that. She gently told us that it would not surprise her if he were secretly trying to harm himself. I was terrified and it immediately dawned on me that somehow this was related to his tremendous weight loss despite the increased food consumption. She concurred with me and suggested "we watch him very closely because these types of kids are very adept at hiding their actions."

Although hesitant to admit to her that I had become fearful of what he might do to any of us, I related our schedule. I informed her that we suspected that he was wandering around the house at night so we had arranged for either my husband or myself to be awake at all times. My husband did not get home from work until 2:30 am every morning. I had been staying up till my husband arrived home from work. I then went to bed for some sleep and he stayed awake. After a few hours of sleep I got up so he could go to bed and the cycle began again. To our astonishment she understood our fears and commended us for the precautions we were taking. She conveyed only praise and positive reactions for our attempt to keep everyone safe from Wayne's deviant and dangerous behavior. This was encouraging because I was beginning to think I was overreacting. But, hearing the possibilities of what could happen, from a well-known child psychiatrist, assured me that I wasn't.

Our newfound confidence quickly waned when we discovered our car had been towed while we were in her office. Being new to the city, we were unaware of the parking regulations and had no idea of what to do next. I looked at my husband and burst into tears when I suddenly remembered "Today is our anniversary!" We were at a psychiatrist's office to get some help for Wayne and now we were stranded in downtown without our car. To top that off, it cost $100.00 to get it out of the police impound and we had not caught up financially from our move. My husband hugged me and tried to calm my grief. I remember telling him "Please wake me up, this has to be a horrible nightmare."

Wayne started his medication the next day. His doctor had also prescribed several tests at the medical hospital to monitor his physical adaptation. At home we implemented a new procedure for his eating. After every two bites of food he had to put his fork down and talk. I told him I did not care if he only said his name but he had to say something. Although it took quite a while for him to finish his meals, I stayed with him to ensure that he followed the procedure correctly. We hoped this would slow his eating because he continually shoveled food into his mouth if he was not stopped. Also, we did not allow him to go into the bathroom for at least 30 minutes after he had finished his meal. We suspected that he had been using the excuse of needing to use the bathroom as a means for purging his food. Once we implemented this routine he began to put on some recently lost weight. This confirmed our belief about the cause of his dramatic weight loss. I remained in constant contact with his psychiatrist to report his progress. His behavior continued to decline each day so she recommended that we increase his medication for two weeks. At the end of this time she said she would reevaluate him and admit him to a psychiatric hospital if he showed no improvement. During the interim she arranged for several more tests to be done at the medical clinic. One of the tests I remember clearly was the blood serum test. I explained what they were going to do and asked him if he was nervous. He said no and that *he never felt pain anyway*. This statement puzzled me, but I assumed he was trying to cover his fear. However, I was perplexed to watch him as the technician drew his blood. He laughed about it and bragged about the attention he was receiving. As soon as we returned home, I immediately called his psychiatrist. She decided to arrange another psychological evaluation as soon as possible. Unfortunately, we had to wait a week!

The next morning our neighbor asked our oldest and youngest son to mow her yard. This was Charlie's job but he was visiting my parents for three weeks. I told the boys they had to give Charlie 20% of their profits as a finder's fee. They both agreed that was fair and pleaded for me to allow them to do the job. Thinking it was a good way to keep them occupied, I allowed them to do it. Chris pulled weeds around the house. I stayed with Wayne while he mowed. About halfway into the mowing, he suddenly stormed off and I had to chase him. Once I caught him I made him finish the job. He never gave me an explanation why he took off so I let it go. I was exerting all my efforts on surviving that week and decided pursuing the matter was not important at that time. That afternoon, I told the boys they could play in the garage. We had a play area arranged for them with their toys, coloring books, and their pool table. I went into the house for a few minutes. When I returned Wayne was reading a book. Chris then told me that the book was his and Wayne had taken several from his room. Sure enough when I searched under Wayne's bed all of the books were there. I could not figure out how he got them there since I was watching him constantly. Somehow, though, he had managed to get them.

After dinner, my husband and I worked in the garden until he had to leave for work. We had the back door open so we could watch the boys while they did the dishes. I reached down to pick a melon when Chris ran out the door crying. He said Wayne had dropped a glass dish and it broke. Immediately our oldest ran out and smugly accused him of lying. When my husband asked what happened we received a different story so we decided to drop it. Because of his behavior, we felt that Wayne had a reason for breaking the dish and we regretted not staying with them until the dishes were done. My husband and Wayne picked up the big pieces while I swept the floor. My husband then went to work.

I was totally exhausted that night and fell asleep in a chair about 30 minutes before my husband got home. When he got home I went to bed and he stayed awake as usual. The next afternoon I took our son to see his therapist. She assured me that his doctor was adamant about admitting him to the psychiatric hospital because he was becoming a danger to everyone, including himself. She encouraged us to hang in there a little while longer because help was on its way.

At dinner that evening Wayne told my husband that he knew when he got home the night before. My husband told him it was not possible because he was fast asleep. Our son argued and retorted saying, "it was midnight." I told him that at that time I was awake and he was asleep. He continued to argue and this further frustrated us. I began to believe he had faked being asleep and waited until I drifted off then roamed the house. The whole idea sent chills up my spine and my husband became even more afraid for everyone's safety.

I had one more day to get through before our son's evaluation at the hospital. My husband had to be gone the entire day and I was dreading what could transpire within those few hours. Oddly enough things went pretty well during the morning and afternoon. Unfortunately trouble was lying just ahead but I was not prepared for it. The day so far had given me a false sense of hope and I let down my guard. After dinner, the boys and I went outside to water the garden. I said something to my oldest son but he did not respond. I turned to him and was horrified to see him swinging large sticks at Chris. I was furious and, on impulse, I sprayed him with water. His face became fiery red. I was terrified but knew I could not let him see that. I told my youngest son to stay away from his brother. I then moved the hose to the other side of the garden. When I looked around again Wayne was using the same sticks to whack off the tops of sunflowers. I turned to check on Chris and found him using a stick to beat the side of the house. When I asked him what he was doing he replied "Well if he can beat things, why can't I?" I sent him to the porch so we could talk while I kept an eye on Wayne. I decided to leave him alone because, although he was destroying the sunflowers, it kept him occupied.

My youngest son and I had a long talk about good and bad behavior. I suggested he follow his Dad's example if he needed someone to imitate. He told me the reason he had been "acting wrong" was because he was confused and did not understand why his brother was acting so *"weird."* He also said he was scared because Wayne kept trying to hurt Charlie. He was afraid if he did not do what Wayne told him to do, then he would also get hurt. It was not until that moment that I realized the extreme danger all of us were living in. I just prayed we could make it through the night without any further problems so we could get Wayne to the hospital.

We met his psychiatrist at the hospital and she told us that she could not get him admitted until Monday morning. I was relieved that he would be admitted, but also regretted the fact we had two more days to wait. At least my husband would be off work and it was Father's Day weekend. We had plans to be with my parents, my sister, and her family. We were relieved because there would be more adults to help watch Wayne. I honestly do not think I could have made it through the weekend. "When will this nightmare end so we can be a normal family?"

Chapter 7

Faded Hope, Shattered Dreams

The expectation of getting Wayne the help he so desperately needed gave us a tremendous boost. When we left the hospital that Friday afternoon, we felt like a burden had been lifted off our shoulders. We had no idea, however, that our elation would be short lived. As soon as we arrived home we began calling our support resources. Our hope of brighter days came crashing down upon our heads when we were informed that none of them would pay for the hospitalization unless it was a life-threatening situation. I could not believe my ears. How much more life threatening could our son become? It seemed that our vigilant monitoring of him so he wouldn't hurt himself or others was contradictory to what the system wanted. They would not pay for his treatment unless he succeeded in harming someone! I could not believe what I was hearing! Rather than prevent Wayne from harming anyone, it seemed as if it would be better to allow him to succeed in doing so. I did not understand.

The rest of the afternoon was a flurry of frustrations. I explained to the worker at Medicaid that I suspected his attempts of suicide and bodily harm, but was unable to provide any tangible proof. I related the dangerous incidents that I had knowledge of but still received the same answer from them. I was very upset and decided my husband and I would somehow have to pay the bills in order for Wayne to get some help. Then we received a very disturbing phone call. It was the hospital calling to inform us that because Medicaid denied paying for services, and the fact that the hospital had yet to receive its Medicaid license, they were unable to admit our son. I was completely devastated. I did not know what to do or who to turn to. I called my mother and she told me that my Granddad had always said, "if there seemed to be no answer to a problem, then it was time to involve the officials we elected into office." I immediately pulled out the phone book and called our state senator. Once I explained the situation to his assistant, she did not hesitate to get right on it. She told me to hang tough and she would get us some assistance.

After talking to the senator's office I felt more assured of getting some help. While waiting for guidance from them, our doctor called and said she had been informed of the situation. She told us that she was going to contact a Medicaid facility and get one of their doctors to take over the case. By doing this, she said, maybe Medicaid would be more willing to pay for the services Wayne so desperately needed. She told us to go ahead with our weekend plans and she would contact us if anything urgent arose before Monday morning. Her assurance that by Monday morning we would receive assistance, one way or another, provided me, temporarily, with the fortitude I needed to last through the weekend.

I kept a close eye on Wayne for the next two days. It was easier on me having several other adults to help, but I was still very exhausted and apprehensive. My parents reassured my husband and I that we had done everything possible to obtain services for him. They said they did not blame us, nor should we blame ourselves, for anything he had done. It was time for the authorities to step in and take some responsibility. I told them that I was at the end of my rope and did not know how much more I could take. I was afraid that if Wayne did not get help soon he would find a way to seriously hurt himself or us. I personally proclaimed to enjoy time with Wayne for the next couple of days. Not knowing what lie ahead with him was tearing me apart.

Monday morning arrived and we were instructed to take our son to see a doctor at the Medicaid hospital. When we arrived, the doctor told us that since Medicaid had refused payment for services there was nothing he could do. He then made the statement "he looks like a normal kid to me." My husband and I were furious at his remark. Not only did he say it in front of our son; he also had no idea what had been going on. The message the doctor sent to our son was "you are okay and there is nothing wrong with your behavior!" We had a difficult enough time trying to deter our son's actions. Now, a doctor is telling our son he is fine which further complicated our situation. Instinctively, I even began to feel myself resenting our son. I postulated he was "acting this way purposely" just to disrupt our lives. But, rationally I knew this was not the case and his behavior was a result of the horrendous abuse and neglect he had suffered prior to coming to us. Looking at it this way, at least, gave me an outlet for the blame. Having persons in which to direct my emotions helped me focus on the business at hand, helping Wayne.

When we returned home from the doctor's office we immediately began calling everyone involved with our predicament. Once we called our psychiatrist and told her what had transpired, she became even more determined than ever to secure help. She agreed that, as unsettling as this was for us, the continual changes were also unhealthy for our son. We had prepared him to go into the hospital that morning. However, when that did not take place he became very agitated. She pledged to have a solution by the end of the day. We then informed the senator's office of the latest development and they also declared to open some channels.

Within hours, our doctor called and told us to have our son at the hospital at 9:00 am the next morning. When I questioned the costs, she informed me that the hospital had agreed to eat the costs themselves because of our son's condition. They said it was time to get him help and she would bypass the system. We were totally astonished, but very grateful. The hospital called several times that afternoon for information. They wanted to have as much of the paperwork ready as possible so there would not be any more delays.

We explained the news to our son and told him he would be okay. Charlie was still with my parents so we spent the evening with our oldest and youngest sons. We did not think Chris fully comprehended what was taking place but he dispelled any doubts we had when he told his brother "I know you think we are putting you in the hospital because we don't love you but you are wrong. We are putting you there because we do love you." That was all the explanation Chris needed or wanted about the event. For only being seven years old, he had witnessed far more than other children his age. It was his positive attitude that helped me get through the rough months that followed. Despite of his own behavioral problems, I will always be grateful for his spirit and *"matter of fact, this is the way it is"*, disposition.

The following morning we were at the hospital at 9:00 am sharp. For the next several hours we processed paperwork, met with our psychiatrist, toured the facility, and talked with our son's day nurse. During her admittance evaluation, our son validated our suspicions of suicidal attempts. Although I had suspected it for quite some time, to hear him actually confirm his attempts was terrifying. In that instance reality hit. The bond I wanted so badly to establish with him was not going to occur with *any amount of love*. His psychiatrist, knowing this latest information hit us square in the heart, eased our pain by assuring us our son was where he needed to be. She told us "now we can give him the in-depth help he needs." She also told us that the hospital had, ironically, just received

Medicaid acceptance and approval for a seven-day stay for our son. She said seven days was not enough for the intense therapy that he needed, but at least it was a break and she would push for more. My husband and I knew that our persistent phone calls to the senator had paid off. We acclaimed this as a personal triumph and knew our determination had once again beaten the odds.

Before we left the hospital we sat down with our son's day nurse. She needed historical and behavioral information for her records. The more information I revealed to her, the more alarmed she became. She told us that she had worked with troubled kids for several years but she had to admit that our son was in "lethal condition." That term, I told my husband, described our son's condition perfectly. It is a term I will never forget as long as I live. After she had the information she needed, the nurse inventoried the items we had brought from home. I signed for the items, then our son was searched for contraband items. After this was completed, my husband, Chris, and I said our good-byes and we left for home. I had to fight back the tears of sadness as I hugged Wayne, yet, in a paradoxical way, they were also tears of gladness. I was anguished at leaving him at the hospital, yet, also relieved that he would be getting help and I would be getting some much needed physical and emotional repose. I realized I would still have to battle for additional funds and hospital days, but I also knew one of our biggest hurdles had just been cleared.

The drive home was a quiet one. My husband knew to leave me alone because I was mourning what had just occurred and also preparing my strategy for the battles that lie ahead. When we got home, I began making my pre-decided phone calls. The first person I contacted was the boys' adoption case manager. I filled her in on what was happening and she became very upset with the handling of the financial assistance by the adoption support agency. She told me this was the very type of problem that prompted her to make this agency's funds available to us. She told me that she was going to investigate the problem and would call us later. The next call I made was to the senator's office. They informed me that they had contacted Medicaid directly and passed the director's name and number on to me. This confirmed by belief regarding the sudden approval of seven hospital days! Several minutes later, I received a call from our local adoption support worker. She said she had been informed of the problems and alerted us to the availability of an appeal process. If Medicaid refused to pay the billing, we could initiate the process. I told her that the senator was involved in the case and she thought that was an excellent idea.

I had no sooner hung up the phone from talking to the worker when the phone rang again. Thinking it was someone involved with the finances, I answered with hopeful anticipation. However, it was a call that I could never have imagined in my wildest dreams. The call was from the hospital's physician. She had just completed our son's physical and was calling with the results. Nothing could have fully prepared me for the information she was about to relay. Her findings and diagnosis horrified me. To keep from falling apart, I had to remind myself that I had done everything in my power to prevent the self-mutilation she was describing.

She began by telling me Wayne had pushed his right testicle up into his body. When I inquired about possible long-term damage, she said she was unsure if there would be any permanent damage. She was holding out hope that as time passed the testicle would drop back into its proper place. Next she told me that he had fluid in his ears. I told her about his head banging and she said that was a common behavior and resulting injury. However, she felt that she could treat it and his allergies with medication. Before she told me the worst finding, she said that she found evidence of many self inflicted wounds on our son. She proceeded by saying "I am telling you this because of what I found in your son's mouth. All his gums, around every tooth, had been cut. Your son told me he waited until you went to bed one night, climbed above your refrigerator, and got one of your kitchen knives. He then used it to cut his mouth!" I was in such a state of shock and self blame that I could not speak. I am sure she felt my despair because she said that kids with such severe problems as Wayne "know when and how to harm themselves so the injury will not be noticed." She assured me that it absolutely was not our fault. After the knife cutting news, the rest of what she told me seemed trite. Besides his medical condition, she informed me that he was having trouble distinguishing the past from the present. Also, she said he admitted to her that he had been purging his food after every meal. When I told her we had expected as much, we immediately put a stop to him going into the bathroom right after he ate. She said "that was very insightful on your part and you should be proud of yourselves for protecting him as long as you did." I have often reminded myself of her accolade when everyone else was accusing us of not doing more for him or the other boys. Despite the eerie feeling I had after hearing her results, she, paradoxically, provided us with the first tangible glimpse into our son's mental functioning.

The following morning I received a phone call from the head nurse. The progress report she read to me did not contain any brighter news than what we had already been told. She told me that our son was under 24-hour visual contact because he was inflicting harm upon himself. He was pulling out his fingernails and eyelashes, poking his eyes, and bruising himself by biting or hitting objects. She said that he also was "acting good." He was in full honeymoon mode but they expected this. In the kids' minds, they were trying to convince the doctors and nurses that "they are perfectly fine and it is the family that's crazy." However, despite his acting, the staff was already seeing very severe repercussions of the past abuse and mental instability. She told me to hang in there and reassure our family that Wayne was getting the help he so desperately needed.

Later that afternoon, the adoption support agency from the state where we adopted the boys called and told me that they would be picking up all costs after Medicaid stopped payments. She informed me that their state senator had become involved and had approved the expenditure. I had to chuckle to myself when she said this because I knew I had finally found an avenue that provided us with the assistance we needed. I wished very intensely that my Granddad were still alive so I could thank him for the advice of going to our elected officials when all else failed. In addition, I was very thankful that I had inherited my Granddad's determination and spunk.

I received one phone call after another that afternoon. Everyone I had previously turned to for assistance was calling to apprise me of the "good news" about the financial coverage. I can't remember any other time in my life when I was complimented so much for having a stubborn determination. It was so nice to be lauded instead of criticized for the determination and stamina that I had bestowed upon me. I will always be grateful for that fact. There IS a reason for everything and now I had to place my family's future and our son's well being in the very hands that had brought us this far.

Wayne stayed in that hospital for nearly three months. During his stay, at least one other member of our family accompanied me to visit him every day. We missed approximately only ten days due to his loss of visitation privileges or obligations with our other two sons. This was not an easy time period and definitely not one that any of us would want to relive. But, we did learn more of what Wayne was capable of doing to himself and us. We witnessed first hand many psychotic, frightening episodes. Not having him at home, or the responsibility that accompanied his presence, provided us with a much clearer perspective on the situation. This is not to say it was any less painful but it did convince us that we had to do what was best for every member of our family, not just one member. A calm immediately settled over our other sons' behaviors as a result of Wayne being out of the home. It was also during this time that both of them began telling us things their brother had been doing to them without our knowledge. Through their continued weekly therapy sessions, we were able to keep them and the chaos of their behaviors at a controllable level.

Every visit with Wayne was different. We never knew what to expect and learned not to anticipate what would transpire during the visit. There were occasional and sporadic times when he seemed very happy to see us. Unfortunately these times were few and far between. On many visits he would either ignore our presence completely or simply sit and stare at us.

As bad as those visits were, several others were even worse. For instance, on our first visit Wayne described in detail how he had gotten the knife and cut his gums. Hearing the lengths he pursued to accomplish this feat was almost more than my husband, youngest son, or I could handle. However, we had prepared ourselves to listen to anything he said without showing any anger or emotions. We had readied Chris to listen to anything his brother said and told him that we could talk about it later. I was very glad we had done this prior to our first visit because he was able to act like a real trooper by saying "we all love you and that's why you're here." He waited until we were driving home to talk about his pain.

The first thing he asked me on our drive home was "how could he hurt himself like that." I was able to use this as a bonding discussion with him by explaining that sometimes when people keep all their feelings inside without talking about them, the feelings can talk you into doing very strange things. I also let him know that the reason he was doing well was because he talked about his feelings. I was certain he understood what I was telling him by his reply. "Mom," he said, "there is one thing that I have been keeping in for a long time. You told me during one of our talks that Dad was a good man to follow. I was afraid to be like Dad because no one ever told me Dad was good and not like the *other man*." Unsure who he was referring to I inquired "what other man?" He responded "you know, that *birthfather man*." Suddenly it occurred to me that the boys had never been taught that not all men did bad things to kids. When he thanked me for telling him that, I knew he and I had just taken a giant step in strengthening our mother and son relationship.

The next day my husband and I visited without Chris because we felt he needed a break from the ordeal of the past few months. The visit turned out to be very unpleasant and I was grateful we had not taken Chris. When we arrived we first met with the social worker of the hospital. While we were discussing our son's case, the nurse walked in to tell us our son had written a no harm contract with the staff because he was continuing to inflict injuries upon himself. She then left to get him ready for dinner since we had made plans to eat with him that evening.

After our meeting we walked into our son's unit and were immediately stopped by the nurse and told there was a problem. Our son was sitting in a chair crying, poking his eyes, and saying, "I don't want to eat with you." I went to him and asked if it was because of our "two bite" rule and he said no. I asked "are you mad at me?" and he said no. I then asked "are you mad at dad?" and he still said no. "Well," I told him, "you are going to have to tell us because I can't keep guessing." He began to blame his brothers for his problems but the nurse told him to "talk about yourself." He finally said he was mad because we didn't believe him about the broken dish and he got in trouble. I reminded him that none of the boys got in trouble, we simply cleaned up the mess. He made the comment "I had a big piece of glass in my leg." I was shocked and instinctively retorted "No you didn't." When his nurse confronted him about it, he hesitantly admitted that he had lied to her and his doctor about the incident.

In his very next breath he snapped "I don't like it when you tell me it wouldn't hurt to smile." I related to him that my mother used to tell me "it was hard to stay mad when you smile." His nurse suggested that was only a Band-Aid solution to a problem. However, when I explained to her that I only said it when he sulked every time we were having a fun family activity, she immediately understood and supported me. Instantly he became very sweet and *invited* us to eat dinner with him. I remember my husband looking at me as if he wanted to say, "what just happened here. One instant he is harming himself and lashing out at us, but the very next instant he is nonchalant and wants us to eat with him." As difficult as it was for us to switch our emotions to match his, we did it to keep the peace. During dinner we noticed that he ate at least four times as much as any hungry kid his age would eat. We were concerned about it since that was one of the behaviors we had to watch. His nurse informed us that they knew about it and were recording his eating behaviors and food intake. She told us that they were allowing it so they could gain more insight into his total behavior pattern. In addition, she guaranteed that they would not let him continue if it became a risk to his health. After their logic was explained, we felt better knowing that he was indeed being monitored very, very, closely.

After dinner was over, my husband and I attended another meeting with the psychologist. Expecting to hear positive details about our son's prognosis, we were completely dumbfounded to hear that, in all truthfulness, the prognosis was "not good, at best." "These kinds of kids never fully recover from the abuse" was more than we could comprehend. We thanked him for his honesty about our son; yet, we still had hope that he would recover with *just enough love*. We were not ready to let go of our dream. It took many more extreme and bizarre episodes to finally convince us that there was nothing else we could do for him. One such episode was the day the hospital social worker called to say we owed the hospital $265.00 for one of their steel bathroom doors. She told us that our son had become angry and *broke the door, a steel door!* I remember asking myself, "If he can do that to a door, what is he capable of doing to us?"

For the next three weeks, Chris continued to go for visitation with his brother. I was beginning to see the toll it was taking on him and became very concerned for his well being. Ironically, though, those three weeks laid the foundation that he and I would stand upon in overcoming future crucial periods. One instance in particular alerted me to the serious effect the stress was having on him. We were heading for the hospital for our daily visit when he said, "I'm just so frustrating with him." I asked him to explain what he meant and he told me he wanted his brother to get better. I tried to comfort him by telling him that was what the doctors were trying to do. It wasn't until several months later that I realized he only accepted my explanation that day in an attempt to pacify me.

When we arrived on the unit, Wayne grabbed Chris and squeezed him to the point of inflicting pain. Chris asked, unsuccessfully, several times to be put down. I finally had to pull him off because Chris was crying from the pain. Subconsciously, I think I knew at that moment that our family would never be together as a whole unit again. Still, I held on to the belief that Wayne would magically be cured if we just *loved him enough*. Once again, I was ceding to my heart and not my head. Every incident after that one succeeded in chipping a larger hole in my "it will be okay someday" attitude.

When Charlie came home it helped to ease the strain on Chris. There had always been a deep animosity between the two older boys. Finally, we witnessed how deep the animosity really was. We told Wayne that Charlie would be with us for our next visit. He smiled and seemed very happy. I asked him why he was so anxious and he said it was because he had been thinking about him and the good times they had had together. He told us he would start letting his middle brother play games the way he wanted. This, he said, was the reason they fought so much. I was not convinced this was the only cause of the fighting, so I delved deeper into his statement. He blurted out "I am mad at him because of what happened in the past. He told them (the birthparents) to beat me up all the time." I explained to Wayne that it was not any of the boys' fault for what happened to them. I told them that it was the birthparents' fault and there was nothing the boys did to cause it or could have done to stop it. He seemed skeptical but replied "anyway I have a soft doll I can hit when I get mad." We chose not to further pursue the discussion that day.

The next day Wayne had made a complete reversal in his attitude about his middle brother. He told us "He is my enemy." I was very confused and asked him which day I was supposed to believe. Yesterday, when he missed his brother, or today, when his brother was "his enemy." He wavered several times then began pulling out his eyebrows and inducing himself to vomit. He then said "I threw balls at the wall today and he was the wall." It quickly occurred to me that we were not going to get anywhere like this so I made a pact with Wayne. I told him that I thought I knew why there was so much friction between him and his brother and if he would tell me I would let him know if I guessed correctly. He accepted this as a detective game and it didn't take very long for him to "guess the reason." By using this strategy, he felt he had control of the situation. It also allowed us the opportunity to piece together his *clues* and recognize the root of his anger. In his mind, he thought his middle brother told the birthparents to beat and neglect him so they could have sex with his middle brother. In addition, when he heard his middle brother's crying, he felt guilty for not being able to rescue him. Once again, we reminded Wayne that it was not his fault and that none of the boys deserved the treatment they received. Unfortunately, we were not able to pierce the thick scars he had around his heart.

Although numerous incidents happened during Wayne's stay at the hospital, one in particular has stuck in my mind. We had been informed one morning that the nurses had found vomited food particles in several places on the unit. They were certain it was our son but were unable to catch him in the act. At the same time, he had also gained eleven pounds over a period of three days. His heart rate and cholesterol count had become dangerously high from the weight and his mouth was full of sores from vomiting stomach acid. They immediately instituted a strict diet and daily exercise schedule for him. Both of our other sons, my husband, and I visited that night. When we walked into the unit, the nurse pulled us over to the side and informed us that our son had a terrible day. He had the assumption that he could choose his food that day but a technician told him he had not earned that privilege yet. Wayne then began yelling at the technician. The technician sent him to the quiet room until he calmed down. Once he was calm, the technician told him that he would have to write a paper about his behavior and what he learned. Well, he refused and said he did not have to do it. The technician told him if it was not done before bedtime, there would be a consequence. Also, he was not allowed to stay up late to get it done. I told the nurse that if it was not done then our consequence would be no visit the next night. She appreciated our support and thanked us for working with the staff.

Our son, with an overseeing technician, was doing his exercises to an aerobics tape. Charlie joined him so we watched and waited until they finished. After they were done, we complimented both of them; Wayne for working hard and Charlie for joining in and encouraging his brother. The technician then told Wayne to tell us about his day. Of course, he steered away from the quiet room and paper incidents. We asked him about it and he said he was going to write his paper an hour before bedtime. I asked, "what if we do not leave by then." He did not answer me so Charlie talked to him and asked why he got angry in the first place. Wayne snapped at his brother and said, "because I want to choose my own food." My husband, the technician, and I then explained that we do not always get what we want and every action had a consequence. Charlie then asked, "what is the point of your paper?" When he ignored his question and continued to talk about food, the technician and I both said, "that was not his question." Then Charlie asked, "what will be your consequence if you do not do it?" Still, he did not answer so Charlie told his brother about a consequence that he had received that week when he misbehaved. The technician asked, "Did you learn anything?" to which Charlie said, "Boy did I. I learned not to do it again and that my behavior was wrong."

Thinking his brother would open up since he heard about another persons' consequence, Charlie then asked, "what should your consequence be?" Wayne smugly looked at him and said "Oh I will get to sit in the quiet room for a while—no big deal!" At this point my husband explained that a person does not always know what consequences their actions will bring. We then informed him that our consequence for him would be no visit the next night. The next fifteen minutes was like a scene out of a demonic movie. Our son turned and looked at us with a face that made me shiver. He growled "Get out of here, I never want to see you again." He also told Charlie "you haven't talked to me so I won't get mad at you." Charlie said, "I've been talking since we got here and if Mom and Dad aren't visiting neither am I."

Immediately, the technician told Wayne to take a shower and go to bed. He refused until he received a snack. The technician told him "no you are going to take a shower." Our son laid on the floor, crossed his arms and retorted "you will have to drag me." When the technician told him "no I won't" the nurse came over. Wayne covered his ears when she began talking to him. She continued talking to him and he turned his back to her. She then said "you only have two choices: 1—go take a shower and go to bed, or 2—spend the night in the quiet room. (The quiet room was a room with four walls and nothing else. There was no furniture or blankets.) In an instant Wayne got up, smiled sweetly, hugged us, and asked me to bring him some long sleeve shirts. Before I realized it I had said, "No, I don't think I will." His nurse replied "after the way you just treated your family, your mom doesn't need to do anything for you and I don't blame her. We will adjust the temperature instead." We left the hospital that night emotionally exhausted. "At least," we consoled ourselves, "we do not have to endure this again tomorrow because the paper did not get written and we are going to stick to our consequence of not visiting the next day."

On our drive home, Charlie and Chris discussed the visit. They were very angry about the way Wayne had treated all of us. We listened as they vented their frustrations. When they told us they did not want to visit Wayne again, we reassured them that time would change their minds. In the meantime, we told them that we would not force them to visit for a couple of days.

Chapter 8

Letting Go

With each passing day, our family began to lose hope that Wayne would ever come back home. This doubt was intensified during one of our last visits to the hospital. Wayne became extremely agitated while talking to my husband and middle son. I had stepped out for a few minutes to make final arrangements to transfer him to a long-term residential treatment center (RTC). When I walked back into the room, he immediately lashed out at me. He accused me of things that his birthmother had done to him. He said he knew that he was going to the treatment center and that he never wanted to see us again. He told all of us not to ever come back and see him because he hated everyone. Thinking he was lashing out due to the transfer, we reminded him that he wanted to go. He said, "I control my body so I don't have to talk to any of you." The frustration that had been building inside me took over. I told him "we are leaving and I do not know when we will visit again." His nurse then spoke up and said "Because of your actions you will now have to pay the consequences of your statements, even if that means no family visits until you are discharged." We did not visit him the rest of the week.

The following week we transferred our son to the treatment center. Although it was located four hours from our home, it was the only placement that had an opening at the time. Our son had lost the weight he gained while in the hospital and was in much better physical health. His doctor was comfortable with his physical condition and discontinued all but his anti-psychotic medications. Although we were not enthusiastic about this temporary RTC placement, we were relieved that he had a place to meet his needs until something closer to home had an opening. Sadly, our hesitations about that RTC were confirmed when, within two weeks, the center had allowed our son to gain 30 pounds. When I reported this to our son's psychiatrist, she expedited his admittance to our preferred treatment center. Once placed in the RTC located much closer to our home, she promptly initiated measures to restore him back to a good physical condition. In spite of the fact that this delayed starting the work on his psychological problems, it turned out to be a blessing in disguise. It allowed time for his "honeymoon period" to fade and they were able to immediately observe his true behaviors.

Our family continued to expect the *miracle cure* to take place in Wayne so we faithfully attended every scheduled visit and therapy session. We adhered to the myth that the magical remedy door was just around the next corner so we, therefore, refused to give up. Even the diagnoses of Multiple Personality and Antisocial Personality failed to fully persuade us. Once again, we could not face the fact we could lose Wayne to the world of the mentally unstable. There had to be a pill or surgery that would take the nightmare away. Even our son's deteriorating condition failed to convince us of the impending results.

We watched him become increasingly dangerous to himself and others. We passively waited, during the therapy sessions, when he ran out of the room and locked himself in bathrooms. We scolded him for attacking other residents and vomiting on them when he was angry for not getting his way. We listened as he displaced, onto us, his anger of the past in the form of very derogatory and hurtful remarks. We restrained our reservations of doubt concerning his stories of blood rituals, self-mutilation rituals, and bloody animals; which the doctors suspected were indications of cult involvement by the birthparents. Even with our hesitation to accept this account, I began researching the practices of cults and familiarized my husband and I with their activities. The information I obtained did help in explaining our son's bizarre and deviant behaviors but, at that time, we did not fully accept it as a factual occurrence in our sons' lives. Wayne stayed in the RTC nearly 4 months. The visits were always stressful on us. Thinking we had to endure the turmoil to be good parents, we continued to revolve our family's life around Wayne's world. We still could not let go of our dream of having a "normal" family. We persisted in our self-deception that we could *love our son into a cure*. It wasn't until Wayne's behavior became a detriment to our other sons' emotional, mental, and physical well being that we answered our wake up call.

Due to financial restrictions directed by Medicaid, the hospital was required to discharge our son two days before Christmas. It came as quite a surprise to us but we had noticed some positive changes during the last family therapy session and were optimistic. We mistook our son's acceptable behavior of the prior week as an indication that our love had, indeed, conquered his emotional instability. Furthermore, the spirit of Christmas clouded the reality of the permanent damage to his mental functioning. At the time, I believed his improvement was unfeigned. In spite of our hope, it was less than two weeks later that we ultimately had to accept the fact that neither he, nor anyone else, was able to control his behaviors. Prior to this time, my husband and I believed that he purposely behaved in abnormal ways and allowed ourselves to become pawns in his world. Therefore, we tried to change our selves and our other sons to accommodate the psyche of Wayne. We were in the "we must be causing him to behave this way" mode of thinking.

Christmas and New Year's went smoothly, at least as far as we knew. The only significant aberration during the two weeks was Charlie's begging to let him move into the bedroom with Chris. At the time I thought he was asking because they had shared a room during Wayne's absence so I encouraged him to stay with his older brother. Therefore, when our sons started back to school after the holidays I had a renewed sense of hope that we had actually overcome the adversities of the past. That is until the third day of school. The special education teacher called to say that Wayne had once again stolen food from the cafeteria. He then went into an aggressive rage when confronted. She told me he had calmed down but she was concerned about the strangeness that eluded from his facial expressions. I told her that I would immediately contact his psychiatrist and discuss the incident. She suggested we talk to him about it and see if he could tell us what triggered his behavior and reaction. I told her I would call back the next morning with the information. That phone call never came.

My husband and I talked to our son that night but he denied that the school event ever happened. We probed several times but he emphatically denied the event and began accusing us of trying to get rid of him. I knew at that moment that he was beyond any efforts of help we could provide for him then, or in the future. So, we dropped it and decided to let his psychiatrist handle the situation the next day. We went about our evening routine. Our youngest took his shower and went to bed. Wayne followed him. Charlie seemed to be taking a long time in the bathroom so my husband checked on him. He had locked the bathroom door and would not come out. We thought it was just another one of his misbehaviors so my husband got his tools and began taking off the knob. I was talking on the phone and did not get involved until I heard a bloodcurdling scream from Chris.

I saw my husband run into Chris' room. He instantly came back out to get me. Chris had vomited all over his room and was standing on his bed screaming "He's (Wayne) going to kill me, He's going to kill me, He's going to kill himself and everyone! Dad I am scared, Mom please, I am scared". As I ran past Wayne's room I opened the door and saw him sitting on his bed smiling; it was a type of evil smile I had never observed before, one that sent fear throughout my entire body. I held my youngest son while my husband cleaned up his room. Our middle son then charged out of the bathroom and sat beside me. He was trembling and cried, "that is why I locked the bathroom door. He has been throwing things at me every night but you wouldn't let me change rooms." I held them both and assured them they were safe and nothing else was going to happen to them. I struggled to push back my own sadness, anger, frustration, and guilt so I could comfort my two younger sons. After my husband cleaned the room, he called 911 for help. They referred us to the mental health crisis line. He called and to our amazement, the 911 operator had already alerted them to expect a call from us. They had Wayne's records and said "get him in the car and get to our hospital as fast as possible." My husband loaded up Wayne, secured the child safety locks on our vehicle, and drove straight to the crisis center emergency hospital—the same hospital he had been admitted 6 months earlier!

While my husband was gone, I rocked our other two sons and was finally able to calm their fears. Chris said "Mom don't let him come back again." Charlie agreed with our youngest and begged me not to let his brother hurt us anymore. As difficult as it was for me to admit it to the boys, I told them that their brother would probably never live with us again. Secretly, I had to accept the fact that I had to give him up in order to try and save the other two. When the boys felt secure enough to go to sleep, I made them a pallet in my husband's and my room. They were out like a light and I sat up waiting for my husband. When he returned he told me that Wayne was admitted instantly. My husband began to cry and said "Honey, we have to let him go. We can't help him and I do not want to lose the other two." I knew he was right. It was the most agonizing decision we had been forced to make up to that point; even more so than our decision to adopt the boys in the first place. We held each other and cried before we succumbed to exhaustion and fell asleep.

The next two months were pure agony. We were back and forth between hospital visits with Wayne and therapy sessions for Charlie and Chris. We discussed with the doctors, at length, our decision to terminate the adoption and our parental rights to Wayne. We contacted two attorneys for legal advice and many psychological experts for diagnosis and prognosis advice. We wanted to exhaust all avenues of doubt before we made a decision as crucial as termination. They all conceded that our decision was the best for our family, but unfortunately, they also painted a bleak picture of successfully accomplishing the task. The first attorney told us that the state in which we were residing was not lenient and was very uncooperative in predicaments such as ours. He was not a specialist in this area of law and referred us to an attorney who was. The second attorney said termination was possible and, although he appreciated our situation, it would cost at least ten thousand dollars to fight the state.

When the second attorney confirmed the first attorney's information, and revealed the costs involved, I began to cry uncontrollably. My mother was present for both meetings with the attorneys and heard the same information as I had heard. When I began to cry she said "Well what are you going to do?" At that moment I had no idea, so when she posed the question, all of the emotions I had been pushing back came to the surface. I walked outside to think and pull myself together. I then went back in and asked the attorney straight out "What can my husband and I do to get out of this?" He told me that if we could not afford to hire an attorney then the only suggestion he could give us would be to go to the hospital, put in writing that we would not bring our son back home, and leave the rest up to the system. The system—not a pleasant alternative. He told me the hospital, by law, was required to report my husband and I to the child welfare authorities who would, in turn, charge us with abandonment of a child. When I explored the ramifications of this he said that DHS would use every tactic in their power to scare us into changing our minds. He further stated that they could file legal charges, threaten to take away our other sons, garnish our wages for Wayne's support, draft child support documents against us, and force us into long term therapy in an attempt to "resolve our issues with our son." I was dumbfounded. "Our issues". We had done everything possible to help him. His behavior and psychological damage were NOT our issues; they were a result of his past, a psychological problem that, as the doctors had explained, would probably prevent him from functioning appropriately in a family atmosphere. The attorney suggested that if we could not afford legal fees, our best alternative was to work with the authorities. However, if they were unwilling to work with us for the good of our family, he cautioned us not to let them manipulate our lives or our other two boys with scare tactics. Furthermore, we were told by the adopting state that our adoption support contract released us from any financial obligations if the boys were placed outside of the home.

When I told my husband the news he agreed with me that we would work with the authorities as much as possible and exhaust every avenue available to find a placement for our son then pursue termination of our parental rights. We felt that if we held fast to our decision, our marriage, and our two sons, we could survive whatever would be thrown at us. As we were warned, within two days we received the first of many threats from the system. We were called into the child welfare office and told that if we did not agree to their terms, they would make our life difficult. It did not matter to them what we had done to help; all they were concerned with was another kid in their system. They told us straight out that they did not want another child straining their resources. To us, they had drawn the battle lines. To their downfall, albeit, they did not realize they were going up against two people who were learning the hard way not to be pushovers in the face of tribulations. We would not sacrifice four lives for the sake of one life, a life with only dim hopes of existing safely in a family. *Our love may not have been enough to make our son well, but it was enough to let him go and provide a chance of getting the help he needed for the remainder of his life.*

After many threats and attempts to dissuade our decision, the authorities slowly began to accept the fact that we were not going to bow down to their demands. We were not going to sacrifice the rest of our family to ease the pressure they were exerting upon us. They were going to accept responsibility for this child if we had to go all the way to the Supreme Court. We felt that if they needed someone to prosecute for the child's condition then they should seek the two "thugs" who subjected our son to the horrendous abuse in the first place. It was due to their actions and neglect, not ours, that propagated his condition. We just happened to be the ones who got involved by loving and trying to help him. Despite our efforts, he was too damaged. Nothing else we could do would reverse his psychological or behavioral capacities.

By the time the authorities began to accept our stance, Wayne had been transferred to a state psychiatric institution. Several staffings (meetings) between the doctors, social workers, child welfare authorities, and I occurred before the child welfare officials realized it was their office fighting the rest of us. The last staffing my husband and I attended was also attended by the governor's advisor on these types of cases. We later learned that the advisor had become involved because of the letter, sent by our son's psychiatrist, to the governor. It was not until this staffing that the child welfare authorities acknowledged they had to accept responsibility for this child. After the governor's advisor supported our decision to terminate for the sake of our family, the child welfare representative, ironically, told the governor's advisor "we are willing to start Managing Conservertorship action for him right now." That was all I needed to hear. I knew it was the first step in terminating the adoption relationship. It suddenly occurred to me that, just as before, Granddad was right—when all else fails, the elected officials will get things done.

My husband and I had no idea how or why the governor's advisor became involved, but when we left that day we thanked her for supporting us in our desperate plight. She smiled and responded "we are quite aware of the efforts you have exerted to help this boy and we knew it was time to step in and let you concentrate on your other boys." Her confirmation of our fruitless efforts felt as if someone had lifted the heavy and painful burden off our shoulders. We instantly knew we had made the best decision for our family, individually and as a whole.

We questioned our second attorney about the staffing results and the child welfare representative's offer. His reply erased all of our lingering doubts. He divulged that we received the best solution without hiring expensive legal assistance. He acknowledged that, if it were him, he would complete all the necessary paperwork required to change guardianship and custody and then move out of the state. By doing this, he claimed, the state would be forced to follow through on their proposal, freeing us to concentrate on our *two* remaining sons. In addition, he also forewarned us to prepare for more threatening harassment from the child authorities because they had a reputation of not giving up easily. We heeded both of his suggestions because our priorities had shifted to our two remaining sons and their well being.

Chapter 9

Please GOD Not Another One

My husband and I both applied for, and secured, jobs out of state. We enrolled the boys in school and bought a new home. My new job required a 2-week, out of state, training period. During this time, my husband stayed with our sons and acquainted them to our new surroundings and routine. He attended school during the mornings and worked part time in the afternoons. This allowed him to be at home with the boys after they got out of school. We explained to the boys that their new school friends did not have to know anything they wanted to remain private. They seemed relieved to know they had a fresh start and they would not be ridiculed about their older brother. The school year began just like that of any typical, American family. The boys became involved in sports, 4-H, and Cub Scouts. Both of them seemed to progress quite well, considering the turmoil our family had just experienced.

We immediately started both boys in therapy with a therapist I knew from my hometown. We hoped the therapy would ease the transition and stave off any problems before they occurred. We made a weekly trip for the sessions. After each session I took the boys to see my parents before we headed back home. The boys looked forward to their weekly visit and this caused my husband and I too feel confident that the worst was behind us. Therefore, when Charlie began to show signs of having adjustment difficulties, we were caught off guard. However, since we anticipated some transitional problems we decided not to pressure him about his misbehaviors. Instead, we chose to ride it out and see if his conduct problems diminished. We also believed his participation in football provided him with an outlet to release his pent-up anxieties. The aggressiveness of the game fulfilled his need to attack something other than his family members and schoolmates. However, he only allowed himself to develop friendships with just a few of his teammates. Since he normally was very outgoing and sociable, my husband and I were somewhat concerned about his withdrawal. On the few occasions we did inquire about his lack of new friends, he stated "I can only trust a few people." This seemed like a perfectly logical explanation at the time so we did not press the issue further. With therapy and time, we rationalized, he would return to his usual vivacious personality.

In contrast to Charlie, Chris did not exhibit any transition problems. He and his dad became involved in Cub Scouts and he appeared to adjust quite well. He confirmed our belief that he was more relaxed now when he told us "I hope my brother is okay but I am sure glad he is not with us anymore. He scared me and made me feel sick all the time". We acknowledged his feelings but also told him that it was fine to still love his brother. "Just because he does not live with us anymore", we told him, "does not mean that you have to forget him". He readily accepted our explanation. We hoped our positive attitude about his brother signaled that we still cared for him while not dictating how either of them should feel.

By the middle of his second month in school, Charlie's behavior began to rapidly deteriorate. It was during this period that we experienced our first runaway episode. My husband and I were preparing dinner and thought Charlie was in the backyard playing with the dog. However, when we called the boys for dinner, only Chris came to the table. We inquired about his brother and he replied "Oh he ran away." Simultaneously, my husband and I replied "He did *WHAT?*" "Why didn't you come tell us." "Because", our son defended himself, "he told me not to." My husband went one way, I went the other, and we both frantically searched the neighborhood. Within minutes my husband arrived with Charlie. He was sitting at the school. We asked him what in the world he was doing and he nonchalantly replied, "I was thinking." We explained that it was wrong to leave without telling us and he acted surprised. We decided not to elaborate on his runaway and justified it as "it must be one of the things he was never taught." We opted instead to let his therapist work with him and discuss whatever motive compelled him to run.

Through therapy, Charlie soon related that he was upset with us for leaving his older brother. We had always been open and honest with the boys, so we decided to tell him what had occurred during his absence that summer. We also told him all of the *scary* things the child welfare people were saying to us. Once he understood more of the predicament we were faced with in order to protect him and his younger brother, his anger towards us subsided. However, the school soon notified us that he was becoming very aggressive towards other children as well as his younger brother. We wondered if he was still struggling with the facts about his brother. With more intense therapy our son began to confront his feelings not only about his brother and the fact he tried to hurt/kill him, but also about his birthfather and the sexual abuse he inflicted upon our son. The most notable feelings he was disclosing were anger, confusion, and depression. Working through this in therapy indicated to us that he was processing his feelings and progressing well. The phone calls from school tapered off so we felt assured that he was benefiting from the therapy. Boy were we wrong!! It only took a few more weeks for us to discover he was a powder keg, ready to blow with the slightest of triggers.

Several weeks passed and as far as we knew no major catastrophes arose. Both boys, especially Charlie, seemed to be doing better and this delighted us. Considering the tumultuous times we had overcome, we were not sure how to react but we definitely enjoyed living a normal family life. We continued to provide them with the therapy sessions because the boys completely trusted and believed in our therapist.

Trust had always been an integral part in our family. Without it we would have surely separated during the trying times. With the therapy showing positive results and no problems arising at home or school, I slowly began to entrust Charlie with more and more responsibility and privileges. His previous misbehaviors were fading and I soon found myself letting down my guard. After I completed my entire out of state training, he began asking us to take him out of the after school child care program. He told us the older kids at school were making fun of him for still going to a "day care" and he felt he was old enough to come home by himself. In addition, my husband had just been offered longer hours at work, so the timing was perfect to give it a try. After we discussed the requirements and practiced his routine, including walking from the school and home several times, we decided to honor his request on a trial basis.

Our garage was a second play area for the boys and was well equipped to occupy our son for the 30 minutes or hour he would be by himself. We locked the door to the house but put the remote phone in the garage in case of an emergency. Our garage had a keyless entry security pad mounted on the outside. To ensure that he did not lose the code, I did not write it on a piece of paper or in his notebook. And, to ensure he did not forget it I did not rely on him to commit the code to memory. Instead, I wrote the code on the inside waistband of all his underwear. He thought I had lost my marbles but as I told him "at least this way I know you will not show your friends or any girls." He was at that age that *no one* could see his underwear or he would "die of embarrassment." The final requirement of the trial period was that he had 15 minutes to get home, get in the garage, feed the dog and start his homework before I called to check on him. I had convinced him that I knew exactly when he got home. Therefore, when I called he had to tell me, to the minute, the time displayed on the digital clock as he opened the garage door. In all actuality, I had no idea what time he arrived home, but he believed I did and this tactic worked for my purposes.

We continued to send Chris to the after school program. To our amazement he did not raise a ruckus about it because he enjoyed the activities at the program. We were relieved he did not throw a tantrum. It would not have done him any good though, because in our opinion, he was too immature to even give it a second thought.

Things went well for the first few weeks. Charlie accomplished his tasks with no problems whatsoever (at least none that we knew of). A short time later, my husband received an offer for a job in the town where the boys' therapist and my parents were located. Despite the fact we had only been in our new home less than a year, we felt it would be better for the boys to be closer to family. The boys begun to tell us that they did not like living that far away from their therapist or grandparents so we perceived the job offer to be a blessing and my husband accepted. He stayed with my family until we could sell the house. Once again, I stayed with the boys by myself. We decided to let the boys finish the school year instead of uprooting them during the middle. However, if caring for them plus working a full time job became too much of a strain on me, our alternate plan was to transfer Chris to a school by my parents. This would allow my husband to care for him. I would keep Charlie with me until the house was sold and school was out. Things were going so well, or at least I thought they were, that I did not give much thought to having both boys with me. After all, I told myself, we were only alone during the week. Either the boys and I spent the weekend with my husband at my parents, or my husband would come to our house. And with our weekly trip to the therapist, we were only alone for two consecutive days at the most.

It wasn't long until Charlie began, once again, to exhibit behavioral problems. Thinking that he was doing well, it came as quite a surprise when I started, and once again to receive phone calls from the school. I soon learned this was not a sudden onset of misbehaviors. Charlie, they told me, had been involved in many incidents of trouble but the school did not inform me. I was not pleased with the school for withholding this information. I explained that if they would have contacted us sooner, we might have been able to curb the misbehaviors through therapy. As it was, the school waited too long and our son's behaviors were indicating he was nearly out of control. He was regressing to the very behaviors he displayed during the first year after the adoption. In addition to frustration over his misbehaviors, I was devastated; all I could imagine was losing another son! I felt my heart could not survive another loss. Now to learn the possibility existed, regardless of how remote, was more than I could bear.

I still thought about Wayne and fantasized about the kind of family we had hoped for. So to learn another one of our sons was behaving defiantly and aggressively caused me to become very frightened. In fact, it was very poignant that the week prior to the school's phone call, my husband had taken me shopping for my birthday. I had asked for a mother's ring after we adopted the boys so my husband decided it was time for me to get one. The ring was only a material object but to me it symbolized and confirmed that I had earned my title of Mom! Sadly, my joy plummeted to heartache when the jeweler asked "And how many children's stones do you need?" I had not thought about the number until he asked. This turned out to be a very agonizing decision for my husband and I because of the situation with Wayne. We debated whether or not to include his birthstone. On one hand we wanted to, but on the other hand, we did not think he would ever return to our home. We decided this must be a family decision so we discussed our dilemma with the boys and took a family vote (something we had established from the very beginning). The boys suggested we buy a ring with space to add a stone later if their brother ever returned to our family. We all voted to go with their suggestion. All of us, in our own way, still hoped he would someday be "fixed" and return to our home

Charlie, the school reported, was disobeying his teachers. His assignments were not being turned in and his homework was not making it back to class. He was hitting the kids at recess and in his classroom. He then would run out of his room. The kids, in return, did not want to be around him and were excluding him from their activities. The more aggressive he became towards them, the more they would outcast him. To top that off, he had stolen lunch money from several of his classmates. When they reported it to their teacher, all of the others in class responded "Ask him (our son) about it. He steals all the time." When the teacher asked him to step out into the hall so she could talk to him, he adamantly denied taking the money and immediately began accusing his classmates of setting him up. This, we learned, was a typical reaction of abused children and our son was very good at it. He could convince just about anyone, except me, of his innocence. Therefore, when his teacher said, "let's go call your mother and tell her about this" he immediately confessed to taking the money. Sure enough, when his teacher checked his desk, he had stashed almost ten dollars in it. It was after she found and retrieved the money that I received the phone call. My son was the first to speak. He told me about stealing the money, and then his teacher related all of the specific details. I told her we would contact his therapist about his spiraling conduct and then get back in touch with her.

After this call, I contacted my husband. He made plans to come home for the upcoming weekend. We discussed our son's consequence and then called his therapist. We decided that for the next week, I would come home early from work and transport Charlie from school. We grounded him from his garage privileges. In addition, his teacher suggested we consider taking him out of football. She realized that it was a stress reliever for him, but his schoolwork was in poor condition. She felt he needed to spend time making up his grades or she would be obligated to hold him back a year. Since he had already repeated a grade, we agreed that he needed to spend his football time doing schoolwork.

I waited for my husband to get home before breaking the news to our son about football. When his dad arrived we drove to the football field. We accompanied our son onto the field and listened as he spoke to his coach. His coach agreed that we were doing the correct thing and told our son that he would have to explain to the team why he was not allowed to remain on the team. As a mother, my heart went out for him as he stood in front of the team and confessed to stealing the money. But as a mother who only wanted the best for him, I stood firm in the fact that he had to face the consequences resulting from his behavior.

He, outwardly, straightened up that week so the following week I allowed him to return to his schedule. I noticed he appeared happier and felt that we had triumphed over the misbehaviors one more time. I have since learned that when things seem to be going well, they can, in reality, be at their very worse! A couple of days later I was fixing dinner when Chris ran into the house and said, "Mom, he ran away." I turned and said, "Who ran away? What are you talking about?" He cried and said, "He packed his bag and took off down the street." When I checked Charlie's room, his clothes and gym bag were gone. I immediately called my husband and he said he was on his way. I then grabbed a flashlight and Chris and drove around trying to find Charlie. I searched for two hours without any luck. I then decided it was time to call the police. By the time an officer showed up to take the report, my husband had arrived. We described the situation to the officer and he quickly alerted the police. They checked a ten-mile radius around our house but found no trace of our son. Just as they were about to call in additional officers, a man drove up with our son. He was a father of one of my son's schoolmates. Our son had gone to their house and asked to stay the night. He told them he was going to "get up the next morning and be on his way."

The father talked to our son and convinced him that he should let his parents know he was safe. Our son agreed and by the time he arrived at our house, he had decided against running away. I thanked the father. He said he was glad to have been able to help. The officer then discussed with our son the seriousness of running away. He told our son, "we all care about you and there is nothing that your mom and dad won't do to help you with your problems. You just have to let them know instead of trying to solve things yourself." Our son admitted that he was very scared and, of course, *promised* to never do it again. The officer told our son he would let him off this time but, if he ran off again, they would have to impose serious consequences. My husband stayed home that night and drove back to his job the next morning. He explained to our son that he could not continue making this drive every night or he would lose his job. He suggested our son talk to his therapist before he did something that would cause himself serious trouble. Our son thought that was a good idea and he agreed to do it.

The next week I began noticing a rank-smelling odor in the house. My first thought was a mouse had crawled up in a hidden spot and died so I searched the entire house. Not finding anything, I told my son to clean the doghouse. This still did not take care of the odor. Every evening, I continued to clean different areas of the house. Despite, the sparkling clean house the smell was becoming more offensive. I tried to combat it with air fresheners and potpourri. This, however, just masked the odor until time to spray again. It took me a week to finally discover the source of the ever-increasing nauseating stench. I was gathering up the week's laundry. I decided to strip all of the beds and wash the sheets. Charlie's bed was the last one to strip. When I reached down to pull his sheets off I was almost knocked over by the rank fumes. I immediately realized I had found the source of the odor.

His sheets were dripping with urine. I looked down the wall and saw that the sheet rock was yellow from urine. I pulled his bed out from the wall and the carpet was soaked. I yelled for my son to "get in here NOW!" He must have known I discovered what he had done because he took off out the door. I did not have time to chase him at the moment so I waited for him to come back. He finally came back an hour later and had the nerve to deny he knew anything about the urine soaked bed, wall, carpet, and pajamas. I lost my cool and shouted "get a bucket of hot, soapy water and the scrub brush then get your little butt back in here." I must have caught him off guard because he wasted no time getting back. I had him pull up the carpet and throw away the entire pad underneath. The urine had permeated the concrete floor so I had to bring fans into the room to dry it out. His mattress was absolutely ruined. I made him carry it to the dumpster and throw it away. He followed, to the letter, my every directive. He had never seen me this angry and, if nothing else, my anger prodded him into action. I knew he had done this in his foster home just after his placement, so I was at a loss as to why this behavior suddenly reappeared. I goaded him for an explanation but he only replied "I don't know how it got there." I decided right then and there to leave it up to our therapist. Experience has taught me that it is impossible to fulfill the parental role and therapist role at the same time. They only conflict and further anger all those involved.

With all of my energy focused on keeping Charlie out of trouble, Chris began to exhibit misbehaviors again. His teacher called me to let me know he was having difficulty paying attention in class and his work was slipping badly. His normal A level work was becoming C and D level work, that is, if he even completed it in the first place. In addition, he was verbally lashing out at his friends and becoming very isolated. I explained the situation with his brother and the difficulty we were having with him. I also notified her of the strain he had faced the previous year. To make matters worse, his dad was away at work during the week and our son was only able to spend the weekends with him. This was especially hard, I explained, because he and his dad shared a special relationship since the first day they met. Just as Charlie and I developed closeness, so had Chris and his dad. After explaining all of this, I asked his teacher what she thought of our alternative plan of sending him to stay with his dad. Without hesitation, she said, "I think that is an excellent idea. From what you have told me, it sounds like he needs time that is all his, away from the effects of his brother." To hear his teacher express support for our plan convinced me that the change would not have any ill effects on him. If anything, it would be a positive move. Chris had always been very needy and wanted constant attention. When he did not receive, what he considered to be enough attention, he would misbehave. For instance, he had twice taken rocks, sticks, and keys and scratched the sides of two of my vehicles. At other times, he would destroy his clothing, toys, or other household items. And, of course, there were the crying and whining episodes that could last for hours.

After talking to his teacher, I felt her approval was the cue we had been waiting on to initiate our alternate plan. We only waited this long for fear Chris would view the move as a negative event. To our surprise, however, when my husband and I told him, and promised that he and his dad could transfer to a local Cub Scout troop, he was ecstatic. Any lingering doubts we had vanished when he instantly went to his room and packed his bags. Our son was not the only excited person; my husband was almost beside himself. He missed the time they spent together. When I saw the two of them so happy, I was convinced we were doing the right thing.

Chapter 10

Priorities

With just Charlie to care for, I had more time to devote to his needs. Although he was out of football, I planned many activities for the two of us. For example, we played catch with any ball we could find around the house, watched movies, took both of our dogs for walks, and any other mother-son activity that arose. Since our house was on the market, we also started packing items that we did not often use. Unfortunately, these happy times did not last long. The final straw occurred just two weeks into our time together. Abruptly, my plans were changed. I was taking my morning shower when the water turned ice cold. I went out to the garage to check on the hot water tank. I thought that maybe the temperature needed to be turned up since we were running the dishwasher and had started the laundry. Unfortunately, I was not prepared for what I discovered.

The pilot light was out and the gas valve was turned all the way up. I reached around the back to turn the gas off and found Charlie's homework, papers, and books stashed behind the pilot opening. I was terrified and at the end of my rope. Our son could have blown up our house!! I immediately grabbed all of it and opened the garage door. Next, I ran into the house, threw his things on the kitchen counter and opened all the windows. After I had the house as safe as I knew how to get it I yelled, "Get your little butt in here this instant." I knew he had seen me wildly running around the house so when he casually sauntered into the room, my exasperation level was over the top. I calmly (as calmly as I could in this situation) asked him where his schoolbooks were. Naturally he lied and told me they were at school in his desk. Each time I repeated my question my voice became harsher. By the time I asked the question for the fifth time, and received the same lie, I lost my composure. I told him "go to the truck and wait for me until I leave for work." I was so upset that it never occurred to me that he would not be there when I walked out. I should have known that HE WOULD RUN!! When I discovered he had taken off, I contacted the police one more time! Due to our son's habit of running away, and our good relationship with the police department, they were very empathetic when I called them for yet another runaway episode. They were also very frightened when I reported what I discovered with the hot water tank. I informed the Captain that when my son was found, I would be heading directly to a psychiatric hospital.

After calling the police, I immediately called our therapist. He told me to drive directly to my parents' house and call him when I arrived. In the meantime, he was going to call the hospital and let them know I was coming. He had previously discussed our son's case with the assessment workers so they were aware of his problems. They had told our therapist that when another episode occurred to contact them and they would assess our son upon arrival. I called the police back and told them that our assessment appointment was a definite go. The time of the appointment depended upon finding our son and making the two-hour drive.

However, when our son was found, I was fearful that he would try to escape during the drive. The police officer suggested I restrain him in my vehicle. I admitted to him that I had planned, but was hesitant, to ask them the very same question and was relieved to hear that I, as his mother, had the authority to restrain him for his safety. The officer then described some plastic rings that they used for restraints and referred me to the automotive shop that carried them. He told me they would let me know as soon as our son was found, but, if I found him first, they directed me to call them for assistance.

Thirty minutes later my phone rang. It was my son's school principal. The principal told me that a teacher had found our son hiding in a bathroom stall at the school. I told the principle to hold my son in the office and the police and I was on our way. When I arrived at the school, I gathered both of our boys' school records and turned Charlie over to the police officer. The officer escorted him to my vehicle and put him inside. I then got the plastic rings I bought and tried to restrain him. Unfortunately, I bought the wrong kind so the officer was kind enough to show me what to do. He then activated the child safety lock. After thanking everyone for his or her help, I turned to get in my vehicle. Before I left however, both of the police officers had a "talk" with my son. I am not sure what they told him but it must have scared the devil out of him because his face was as white as a sheet. With a nod from one of the officers, I started my vehicle and headed directly for my parents' house.

When I arrived, I left Charlie in our vehicle because I was afraid that he would try to run again. I, then, called my husband. He said he would be there in about 20 minutes. I sure did not want to be accused of "mistreating our son" because I had enough to worry about at the time. I did not have the time or stamina for any additional worry anyone could cause, especially someone without a clue of the circumstances, so I took a snack and glass of water to our son. I asked him if he needed to go to the bathroom. He said he did so I escorted him by the arm to the bathroom then back to the truck. Since the truck was more confined and was equipped with safety locks, I felt he would be safer there than out in the open where he could get away from me easily. I called our therapist and informed him I was there. I told him I was waiting for my husband to arrive and then we would head for the hospital. He told me everything was set and the hospital was ready for us. When my husband arrived, we drove to the hospital. We spent the rest of the day in our son's assessment. Four hours later, the assessment worker approved our son for day treatment. I was told to bring him back at 9:00 the next morning to admit him to the program. Of all days, I laughed, "Tomorrow is my birthday!"

My husband was not able to get off work the next morning. He and I, due to the boys' misbehaviors and subsequent mandatory hospital stays of the past two years, had either placed our jobs in jeopardy or lost our jobs due to excessive time lost. We decided that this time we had to give his job top priority; we just could not afford to lose another one. Therefore, my dad offered to accompany me to the hospital in my husband's place. I knew I needed someone with me in the event our son had any intentions of running. I was glad my dad went because he had never experienced first hand the emotional pain of placing a child in a psychiatric unit. I felt the experience would impress upon him the extent of what I had endured and he would better understand the lengths I had gone through in my attempt to help the boys.

We arrived at the hospital at 9:00 sharp. My son was not a happy camper and he conveyed, by his behaviors, the attitude *"I can con my way out of this just like everything else."* Little did he realize that I could see right through his cunning and manipulative ways. I was not going to allow him to weasel his way out this time. He had finally reached a brick wall in his life and that brick wall was me, his Mother!

After we checked in, we took a seat and waited for the assessment therapist. While we were sitting there waiting, a line of patients, obviously heavily medicated, passed in front of us. I will never forget the look on my dad's face. He looked at me as if to say, "Whoa, this is serious business!" I smiled at him knowing that the worst was yet to come. He had not sat through admittance yet. During the admittance process, my dad witnessed the seriousness of our son's emotional instability. Driving home that day he remarked, "Wow, that was something else!" I was emotionally drained but responded, "Yeah, but I am not losing this one. It may be a long struggle but my determination is stronger than the abuse or sorry excuse for humans that did it to him. If he leaves my life" I told my dad, "it will be by his own doing, not mine." My dad put his arm around me and said, "You're right honey and Happy Birthday."

Later that afternoon, my dad was outside working on his motor home. My husband went out to talk to him and happened to look down at the front bumper. When he did, he was shocked at what he found. Stuffed inside the grill were numerous, waded up papers. After he pulled them out he was devastated to discover they were more of Charlie's homework assignments. They were some of the very assignments that his teachers had informed us that never made it back to school! My husband and I were certain our son had been hiding them there every weekend. I showed them to my parents and the hidden assignments seemed to confirm all of the problems that, until now, we could only describe. Now, there was concrete proof of the psychological condition of our son. "It is one thing to hear about the boys' problems", my mother said, "but it is another thing to see evidence that actually confirms it." At that instant, I felt acquitted of any suspicions and doubts my family might have had about the way my husband and I dealt with the past two hellish years.

My husband and I spent that evening discussing what we were going to do when our house sold. Since the day we began dating we dreamed of building a log home in the country. It seemed now was the perfect time to begin searching for some land. We decided to buy a travel trailer and live in it until we got the land ready to build the house. Besides that, we realized we had to work for a year or two to save enough money to begin building our home. We were also extremely tired of moving and wanted a place where we would enjoy spending the rest of our lives. Not only did we move frequently with the Air Force, but also since adopting the boys, we had moved twice. We wanted this move to be our last. The previous two moves were for the best interests of our sons, but we had reached the point where we had to begin thinking of ourselves. We did not realize it at the time, but that decision was the one, which finally put our priorities in their rightful order. We realized we had to place our marriage and happiness before our boys' problems if we were going to survive the next 10-12 years as their parents!

Over the course of the next several weeks, I commuted from work to my family at least three times a week Not only did I need to work for the income, but I also had to keep the house ready for our Realtor. This was a very tiring time, but, the day I received word that our house was sold, I caught my second wind. My husband and I had already located 20 acres of land ideal for our dream home. The only thing holding up closing on the land was the closing on our house. In addition, we also needed to put a down payment on a trailer. Everything was tied to the closing on our house. Once that took place, all of the other transactions were set in motion. Three weeks later we moved onto OUR land.

Meanwhile, my husband and I chose to take Charlie out of the hospital. The staff had come to a standstill with him. They were concentrating on a behavior modification program. However, I felt, from past experiences with him, that it was fruitless until our son dealt with his background and the feelings associated with the abuse. Our private therapist was in complete agreement with us so we immediately reinstated his therapy sessions on a twice-weekly basis. With only a month left in the school year we felt comfortable that Charlie would do okay. We enrolled him at the same school as Chris. Between the therapy sessions, installing water and electric lines on our land, mowing waist high grass, and preparing to move our trailer to our land, the boys were too busy to even consider causing trouble. That month, in comparison to the entire time since having our boys, will always stand out in my mind as wonderful and exciting. The happiness we shared, and the teamwork we displayed, convinced me that *this is how a family is supposed to be!!*

Chapter 11

Here We Go Again

School was out for the summer and we wasted no time moving to our land. My husband had invited my parents to move with us. They enjoyed staying in their motor home and wanted to get out from under the responsibilities of a house. Without the financial obligation of a house, my dad wanted to look for a less physically strenuous job. With only a couple of years left before he could receive his retirement, he wanted to find something to tide him over. Then when he received his retirement my parents planned to do a lot of traveling. By moving with us, my dad had the opportunity to accomplish all of this. He also was very excited about helping us with our land and log home.

My mother was excited about the prospect of spending time with their grandsons and having my sister's girls out for overnight visits. My 5-year-old niece was very thrilled to know she could spend lots of time with her "boy" cousins and her Auntie. Our boys doted on my niece and they were like the three musketeers. When the boys donned their overalls to work on the land, my niece wanted some of her own. She was determined to keep up with them. If nothing else, she was instrumental in keeping the boys in line—they could not let a girl show them up or, heaven forbid, outwork them! Needless to say, that was one of our happier periods.

Six weeks after moving, our family, my parents, and my niece vacationed at Branson, Missouri. The week was very relaxing and fun. Considering the stress my husband and I had endured the past two years, we were extremely pleased to be able to enjoy ourselves. We hoped that the hardships and deep sadness, which resulted from the boys' misbehaviors, were behind us. Although we had gained enough wisdom to realize the years ahead would not be trouble free, with guarded enthusiasm, we hoped that the worst was over. Any emotional scars the boys still carried, we told ourselves, would be mild in comparison to what they had already worked through in therapy. We loved the boys and further convinced ourselves that love would see us through any problems yet to come! However, if anyone had told me of the downward spiral of hardships that were going to commence the very next week, I would not have believed them. Thankfully, we were able to enjoy a fun vacation before the bottom, again, dropped out from under us.

We arrived home from vacation and were preparing to build a storage shed when my husband's parents called. They were on vacation and had stopped in town to see us. We were quite surprised and glad that they could spend the night before heading back home. Later that evening, I commented to my husband that the boys were behaving 'too' well. We knew they were trying to impress their grandparents, but little did they know, we saw right through the act. Yet, none of us had any idea that two days later their actions would bring a parent's or grandparent's worst fear.

My in-laws left the next day. A longtime friend of my family was building the shed and since my husband had to work, I was helping with the construction. We spent the first day pouring the foundation. During breakfast the next morning, my dad asked the boys which one of them had locked all of our dogs in their motor home. Neither one of them admitted to it but this was not unusual so I let my dad handle the lecture. After the boys and I went outside, I asked them again and reminded them that God knew the truth so if they were not being honest, someday it would come out. They both continued to deny any wrongdoing so I dropped the subject. In the meantime, the boys gathered their buckets and were going to spend the morning picking sand plums while I worked on the shed. My mother told the boys that if they picked enough plums she would make them some jelly. They were very excited and immediately disappeared into the plum patch. About 30 minutes later, I walked over to the patch to check on them. I walked all around the patch and yelled for them but they did not answer. I figured they were exploring the woods so I went back to the building project. I checked again about an hour later thinking they must be getting thirsty but still could not find them. Since we had been on the land for less than a month, I assumed they were just being boys and exploring the entire woods for the perfect spot to build the fort they had talked about so fervently. I figured they would come strolling back when they got hungry. The only thing that confused me was the fact that they had not delivered the plums before taking off. "They probably planned on bringing them with them when they returned", I assured myself.

By lunchtime, there was still no sign of the boys. I asked my mother if she had seen them but she said no. I once again walked into the plum patch. This time I found the buckets the boys had taken with them that morning. There were only a few plums in the bottom. The first picture that came to my mind was that they had eaten all they had picked! I laughed at the mental image, yet, I was becoming perturbed at them for being gone so long. It had been three hours since I had last seen them that morning. I began searching the woods and walked along the creek bed but still saw no sign of them. After searching for nearly 30 minutes, I decided to wait a while longer. I just *knew* they would come straggling home at any moment. After all, they never made a point to miss a meal! We wrapped their lunch and left it in the refrigerator. My parents went to run some errands and I stayed with our friend to work on the shed. A couple of hours later, we decided to take a break because it was getting very hot. Still there was no sign of the boys. Now I was getting worried!

Since we were in the country, our neighbors were spread far apart. I contacted some of them to see if they had seen the boys but none had. I must have gone into overdrive because I walked the entire 80 acres. I was concerned that one, or both, of the boys had gotten hurt and could not get back home. In addition, it was getting hotter every passing minute and I knew the snakes would be stirring and would strike if the boys happened to disturb them. Our friend also joined in my search as well as all of our neighbors. I called my husband at work and told him the situation. He told me to keep looking and if the boys did not show up by the time he got home he would also begin searching. After searching for another hour, I was frantic and called 911 to report the boys as missing. A few minutes later, a deputy showed up and began taking information. By the time he completed his report, my husband had arrived home and he immediately began searching. It was 5:30 in the evening. The events, which occurred for the rest of the night and into the morning, were something I never dreamed I would experience. Of course, that is, until my life included the boys!

Within the hour, the sheriff's department had several teams combing the adjoining woods and farmland. They called for the search and rescue dogs and asked for a piece of our boys' clothing. Every time I turned around, more and more officers appeared. I looked around and saw nothing but camouflaged officers searching every inch of rock, tree, grass, and creek. Suddenly, I became numb and moved into automatic pilot. I answered the same questions over and over. What were they wearing? When was the last time you saw them? Where were they when you last saw them? Did they runaway? Do they have any hiding spots? Can they swim? Where do their friends live? "Friends", I answered, "we just moved here. They have not even been in school yet and the only people they know in this area are our neighbors and they have been looking for them too!" It had been over 9 hours since I last saw the boys. I sat down on an ice chest and broke into tears. All I could think of was "they have been taken. He (the birthfather) has found them and kidnapped them again." My sister and best friend comforted me and assured me that the boys would be found. I don't think I actually believed them but I tried to calm down. However, when I saw my husband break into tears, I was sure the boys were gone for good.

I don't know how many more people showed up to help in the search, but instantly I knew that there were hundreds. The next thing I saw was the police helicopter landing. My best friend told me they had been called because the road was jammed with cars. "Nobody can get in or out" she told me. Ironically, she knew several of the city police officers and they had taken the boys for a ride in the very same helicopter just months before. Now, the same police officers were combing the countryside for them. It was not too long after the helicopter arrived that the television reporters arrived. They asked for pictures of the boys so they could broadcast them on the ten o'clock news. I was hesitant, but, agreed to provide them hoping someone, somewhere had seen them and would call with information of their whereabouts. The boys' therapist had also arrived and he agreed to speak on the newscast. We were very leery of *who* would see the broadcast. Knowing the boys' past, we did not want to take the chance that anyone associated with their abuse or prior kidnappings could identify us. It was frightening that the boys' pictures were all over the airwaves; airwaves that I knew would be seen in the area where they had been taken into custody in the first place, three years earlier!

My husband and I had calmed ourselves down some and we felt we were handling our fear as well as could be expected. That is, until we turned on the television and saw the news. All the local stations were carrying our story. It wasn't until we saw the boys' pictures on the television screen that the reality of the ordeal overcame me. I was completely panicked. I could only imagine the worse, no matter how hard I tried to convince myself otherwise. My husband was also in his own sense of panic but he managed to hold me until I pulled myself together. As I look back on it now, I once again am reminded that being parents to our boys has taken *more than love*. Just as many times before, love was not enough to endure that night for we did not know if we would ever see the boys again. If we did, however, we were expecting to find them victims at the hands of fowl play.

Within minutes of the broadcast, the reporter who had become our liaison between us and the other media personnel rushed down the hill to notify us that someone had seen the boys. The man who called had invited the boys into his home when they asked for some water. The boys refused to go into his home, they only wanted the water. Soon, many other viewers began calling with sightings of the boys. My husband and I felt encouraged. Our worst fears had, at least, not come true. The boys had not been kidnapped! If anything, they were lost and could not find their way home. And considering their background, we knew they would not tell anyone or ask for help. They were afraid of anyone who (in their minds) would tell the birthparents. Even though this was a slim possibility, my husband and myself had similar thoughts before we knew the boys had been seen. Instantly, I realized what fear could do to a person's imagination. Even the most remote possibility seemed literally possible. For the next few hours, the search concentrated on the areas of their sightings. My husband, our therapist, and I, along with my best friend, jumped into our truck and began driving around yelling out the boys' names. I knew them well enough to know that they would not go to anyone yelling their names unless they recognized the voice. I told the police this, but they did not seem to accept my explanation. Then the scene turned ugly.

After my husband and I returned from searching the area, we were pulled into our trailer and further questioned about the boys' whereabouts. I was even told "You don't seem to be very upset, but, if they were my kids, I would be frantic." I just looked at the officer and thought,

"How dare you imply anything. My boys have been spotted alive. They were not kidnapped. I know they will be okay now because they have survived a hell of a lot worse than being lost." Instead, I remarked, "You do not seem to comprehend the fact that the boys were not kidnapped. I was frantic before the calls came in reporting they had been seen. Now that I know they are out there, I know Charlie will use his survival skills to take care of both of them. If anything, I am worried that they will run from the police since, in their view, 'the police always take them away.' Although we could still sense their skepticism, this ended their interrogation. Finally, two hours later, a call came across the police radio—the boys had been found. A patrol officer found them sleeping underneath a church porch. My husband and I hugged each other with joy. However, our joy was short-lived.

When the patrol car pulled up, we ran to meet the boys but the investigator, who had implied unconcern and wrongdoing from my husband and I, would not let the boys out of the car. He told us to go back to our trailer and he would bring them to us when he was finished talking to them. When my husband asked what the problem was we were told that Charlie was afraid to come home because he thought he was going to be in trouble. "Well dah," I thought to myself, "what kid wouldn't." Also, considering the life he lived before we adopted him, that was not an unusual assumption. Yet, the officer still did not seem to understand that. Instead, he continued to imply my husband and I had caused the boys to run away. Of all the people who helped us that day and night, and there were hundreds, it was too bad that one person had to cause such an unjustified rift.

When the boys were finally allowed out of the car, Chris, with tears running down his cheeks jumped into my husband's arms. Charlie hung his head and sauntered to me. When he reached my arms he too broke into tears and I felt his defensiveness melt away. After I hugged them both, I walked to the officer and thanked him but also told him that I did not appreciate his accusations. I suggested he educate himself on the erratic behaviors exhibited by abused children. I turned around and never looked back.

The boys told us they started walking the creek while picking the plums and lost track of the time. When the boys realized they were in unfamiliar territory they became scared. Also, since they were new to the area, they had no idea where they were or how to find their way back home. When I asked them why they did not ask someone for help, they said, "because you told us not to talk to strangers". Well at least they learned something from me!! Of all the times for them to actually heed my advice.

I needed to compose myself so I walked away and sat alone on the top of a hill. I sifted through the events of the day and began to wonder if we did the right thing by adopting the boys. My emotions were overwhelming and I could not face the boys until I had sorted out the magnitude of the day and the past two years. My husband realized I needed time so he watched the boys for me until the next night. By then I was composed enough to discuss with the boys the severity of the event. I told them it would be awhile before I could allow them to be alone. Until that time, they would need to be within my, or another adult's, eyesight at all times. I also told Charlie that I was having a difficult time trusting him because of his history of running. Although he adamantly denied this was a runaway attempt, but rather a simple case of getting lost, I still had that nagging feeling that there was more to it than that. Call it a mother's intuition, but something inside kept telling me to keep a close eye on him. As it turned out, no one knew him better than me!

Chapter 12

Lasting Effects

Two days later Chris came in for breakfast and informed me that Charlie was gone. When I inquired about his whereabouts, Chris said, "he took off this morning because he thinks you don't love or trust him." Damn it, not again!! My husband immediately jumped in his car and began looking for him. Luckily, it had been less than an hour since our son took off and my husband soon found him walking along the side of the road about three miles from home. When he brought our son back I sternly told him "I can not keep you safe if you keep running like this." I asked him what he thought he was doing and he told me he did not know. I then decided to try a different tactic with him so I told him he was not allowed to leave our property. However, I also said, "this is the last time we will chase you. If you make the choice to run away again, we will just call the sheriff and let them deal with the situation." I told him several times that I would not look for him or chase him down. I did this in the hopes that if he was doing it for the attention, he may think twice before deciding to run again. In addition, I fully intended to stick with my words. His running behavior was becoming more and more frequent. I knew that something had to be done if he indeed tried it again. In the meantime, I contacted the boys' therapist and informed him of the situation. He agreed I took the correct stance in telling our son he would have to face the consequences if he ran again. He also told me to stand strong and not give in to any attempts my son made to sway my word, in other words, "do not look for him."

The next few days seemed to go okay. I was beginning to think that my stance against the running away was sinking in to our son. That is, until Chris woke me up early one morning to once again tell me "he's missing." I asked him what he meant and heard my fears come to life. "He packed his gym bag and rode off on his bicycle. I tried to chase him mom, but he got away from me, so I yelled at him to come back home. He did not listen to me. He just kept riding and said he was going to kill someone. And besides that mom, the dog is gone. I think he took her and she is never coming back." I immediately walked outside and found that all of it was true. The bike, dog, gym bag, and Charlie were gone. He had done it again. This time, however, he had left me with a clue as to why he was running—he was going to kill someone!! I had a feeling I knew who that someone was but could not confirm it.

In the meantime, my mother took Chris and began searching for the dog. I called the sheriff's office and reported the runaway. I told them what had occurred this time and they notified all of the patrol officers. I was told to stay around the house in case he returned. If, on the other hand, he did not show back up by that evening, a deputy would come to the house and file another report. I once again called my husband and the boys' therapist. This time we all knew that when, or if, our son was found, his next stop would have to be another treatment center. Also, I told both of them of the statement he had made about "killing someone" and I said,

"I am sure it is the birthfather." This suddenly explained all of the run-aways and we realized our son's past had finally caught up with him. Sadly, he was not able to express his feelings about the abuse; he was the silent type. The more he denied it and stuffed his feelings inside himself, the more dangerous his behaviors became. This time, I assured myself, my husband, and the therapist, Charlie had done the one thing that would get him the intense help that he needed. I also reassured myself that "it was not me or my husband that was causing the misbehavior, rather it was the monsters of my son's past."

An hour later my mother and Chris showed up with the dog. We were not sure where she had been but they had found her not too far from home. She was walking back to the house and looked extremely tired. Chris cleaned her and gave her some food and water. This occupied him while I informed my mother of the situation. When Chris finally felt sure that the dog was fine, he asked me what was going on. I knew I had to make the situation as positive, but as truthful, as possible. One thing we had always been was truthful. It would do us no good to keep things from them or to lie to them. After all, they had already lived through enough lies before coming to our family. With this in mind, I told Chris that his brother would be okay and that this time he had done the very best thing he could do for himself. I explained that his brother wanted some help but did not know how to ask for it so he did what he knew to do, run away. This was his way of saying, "please help me feel better about myself and everything that has happened to me." Amazingly enough Chris said "I understand mom and that's why I talk so much, even when you get tired of me jabbering!" Well, I had to laugh because he had always been the one, out of the three, who would talk your ear off. His problems had never been in that area!

Later that evening, the deputy came to take the runaway report. We were assured that our son was being looked for, but also that it could take awhile to find him because he was adept at hiding. We informed the offi-cer that as soon as our son was found, we would take him to a hospital for evaluation and admittance. He agreed with us that we had done all we could and that it was time for more intense help. After he left we had as normal of an evening and night as possible for Chris. Although I was very concerned about Charlie, I had to hold my concern in check for Chris's sake. After he went to bed, I stayed up waiting for my other son. Sleep did not come easily although I must have drifted off because I suddenly opened my eyes when I heard a noise outside my window. I looked around but saw nothing so I went outside. I still could not see anyone or anything so I went back inside and prayed. I remember thinking "it is going to be okay because he is not very far away." I was confident that the noise I heard was my son signaling that he was all right. I can't explain it, it is just one of those mother's intuitions.

The next morning the phone rang and we were informed that our son had been found asleep behind an air conditioner unit at a ranch six miles north of us. The foreman had fed him and then called the sheriff. We were told to go to the sheriff's office to get him then take him to the emergency room for an examination. From there, we took him to the hospital's psychiatric ward for evaluation. He was covered from head to foot with poison ivy. Not much was said during all of this time. After all, it had all been said before and our son knew that he was headed to a hospital. When we left him hours later, the only thing I felt appropriate to say was "I love you." With this I turned and left. I knew it would do no good to prolong the leaving, and besides, I had to get out of his sight before I began to cry. I was fighting the thought of losing him, on one hand, and the determination that he was not going to leave us, on the other hand.

Over the next four weeks, my husband and I visited Charlie in the hospital. We tried to get him to open up about his feelings but most of the time he sat silent. The more I tried to ignore his pain, the deeper I felt it myself. One visit I remember vividly. The three of us sat at a table in total silence. My husband tried to engage our son in surface talk but he would not respond. Next, I asked him what he had been doing, still nothing. After 15 minutes of watching him stare off into the distance, we decided to leave. He still sat there. We informed the nurse that the visit was not going well because he would not talk to us. We told her if he decided to talk later, we would be at home. In addition, we were not going to come back for a visit because nothing was being accomplished. She agreed it would be best to leave. On the way home I told my husband it was very difficult for me not to take our son's behavior personally. He assured me that it had nothing to do with us and we needed to keep reminding ourselves of that fact.

Two weeks passed but we heard nothing from Charlie. We attended a meeting with his psychiatrist and immediately felt uneasy when asked what we had done prior to our son's onset of behaviors. We informed the doctor of the adoption and the abusive past. However, he did not seem to comprehend what we were relating to him and insinuated there was more to it. He told us that we had to attend parent-training classes. My husband and I looked at each other in disbelief. We informed him of the training we received before the adoption, the support group we had been involved with after the adoption, and the weekly therapy sessions we continued to attend with the boys. I remarked, "I could teach the classes with all that we had witnessed about special needs and abused children." However, he still wanted us to do more. My husband and I immediately decided to pursue another treatment center and psychiatrist, one experienced with these types of kids and that could better address the issues at hand. We did not feel that the current placement was working favorably for our son or our family.

I began to search for another placement and successfully found one. The psychiatrist had many years of experience working with abused children. Once he was contacted, he agreed to assess our son for placement in his residential treatment center. Since it was a Friday afternoon, the appointment was set for the following Monday morning. The next day the hospital where our son was still at called and told us they were waiting on us to come pick up our son for a day pass. We were taken totally off guard because there had been no notice. Besides that, there had been no contact with our son for the past two weeks. We informed them of this but it did not seem to matter to them. We also told them we were in the middle of putting up a fence and it would be difficult for us to come get him at the moment. Yet, the pressure was on for us to bring him home so I went to the hospital to get him.

When I arrived, our son did not say a word. He just looked at me and smirked. This irritated me. I looked at him and said "hurry up we need to get home and help your dad and brother." We got to the elevator to leave and a nurse stopped me and said I could not take him. This further irritated me because I had taken time out of our schedule to pick him up. She asked me if it would be better to wait until another day and I told her yes. She then said I needed to tell him that so I said, "I do not want to take you home today." He simply turned and walked back with the nurse. When I got back home and told my husband about the situation, he was glad we were moving our son to another place. We later learned that the nurse called the child welfare authorities and reported that I told my son "I do not want you." However, she failed to add the last part "...to take you home today" and that *she* is the one who told me to tell Charlie this.

We called our therapist and Charlie's case manager about the situation and decided to pick him up the next afternoon and bring him home for the night. This would give us a night to explain the change in treatment centers. My husband brought him home and we explained why we were moving him. Charlie told us he was glad because he did not like the one he was in. We had a nice evening with him, Chris, and my parents. It seemed as if our son was more relaxed after being told we were moving him. He talked freely that night and did not try to run or act up in any way. This helped confirm our beliefs that the hospital was not a good match for our son or our family.

Early the next morning I took Charlie to his assessment at the new treatment center. I was very impressed with the care and concern they displayed for both of us. Charlie seemed to fit right in and did not hesitate to tell the assessment therapist about his desire to "kill his birthfather."

Although it surprised me, the relief I felt from actually hearing him admit it was worth all of the problems we had in moving him. His admittance also confirmed my own beliefs that I knew him better than anyone else. Instantly, I knew that from now on I would stick with my gut feelings about the boys and not let anyone talk me into something differently. After all, when God gave them to us, he also gave us the knowledge and wisdom to handle their problems. Even if others did not agree with our decisions for our boys, my husband and I had to do what we thought was right. This is not to say we haven't made mistakes, we have. After all, we are only human and had to deal with extremely difficult situations. However, we always did what we thought was best. This has since been confirmed when the boys' psychiatrist told us, "there are no sure fire answers. What works for one kid may not work for another. Some kids make it and some kids don't."

When I left Charlie that day, he hugged me and cried. Although this tore at my heart, I knew it was a sign that we had finally found a psychiatrist and treatment center that held the same philosophy as we did. I felt Charlie was on the way to recovery. However, I had no way of knowing how long that recovery period would last.

Chapter 13

Season of Change

Since the day my husband and I first laid eyes on the boys, our lives had been in a constant state of change. The coming summer turned out to be no exception. With Charlie in the hospital, Chris, again, began to display his problem behaviors. They were the same problems we had already observed, but they were beginning to intensify. His behaviors were more overt than that of his brother. Although we never feared that he would run away because he did not possess the specific personality traits or characteristics, we also did not expect that he would steal or play with fire. Moreover, his lies were less convincing. Rather he told outrageous stories. We had learned how to swim through his stories to get to the crux of them. When we confronted him with the "point" of his story, he inevitably said, "well that's what I really meant." We worked continually on his communication skills but began to notice more and more elaborate stories. We also knew that he was attempting to gain attention through his stories. Chris had always displayed extravagant attention seeking behaviors and stories were one avenue he used.

Changing his processes of getting attention, we had learned, proved to be a difficult task. We not only had to teach him the correct way of getting attention, but we also had to alter his past learning because the measures he and the other boys had used to survive their past had become engrained into their personalities. Unlearning the wrong behaviors was much more difficult than learning the correct behaviors. In this aspect, I soon discovered that my husband and I were just as much victims of the boys' abuse as the boys themselves. Due to the hell we had endured because of the abuse, I could not understand how any grown adult could subject their child to it, whether they be birth, adopted, step, or foster. The effects of the abuse go much deeper than anyone could imagine. Once abuse has occurred, someone somewhere was forced to deal with its repercussions, for it did not stop with the child alone. Rather, behaviors, which result in response to abuse, spread like wildfire and destroy or damage everything in their path.

For this reason, and for the fact that I was unhappy in my current work, I made a decision to positively change my own direction. I resigned my job so I could go back to school. I wanted to study psychology. Ironically, psychology was my first interest in college. However, at that time, computers were the new and evolving field so I chose to pursue that educational area.

Because of the things I have witnessed, I have realized that a person must do what makes them happy. Working for money alone does not bring happiness and self-fulfillment! If we had not adopted the boys, I probably would have stayed in a line of work that was not my calling. However, some of us have to be hit over the head with reality before our eyes open to our purpose in life. Of course, I sometimes wish I didn't have to be hit as hard as I did, but then that was part of my personality also. My studies taught me that determination could be an asset when studying psychology. "Survival of the fittest" is a term that comes to mind and describes it perfectly! Problems arise when the behaviors used to survive become distorted and hurt others in the process. Things are not always what they appear.

A few weeks had passed since we changed Charlie's treatment centers. We had been informed that he was still in the honeymoon period, yet, his therapist was in no hurry to rush him through. She told me that she had already seen signs of his cunning and manipulative ways and he would soon let down his guard and exhibit his full scope of behaviors. In the meantime, Chris continued to misbehave. I was also feeling a growing sense of tension between him and my parents. Not only were there tensions between them, but I was too busy to notice other family problems. I was trying so hard to keep everyone happy and calm, that I was oblivious to the fact that tensions were rising between everyone in the family.

When my husband and I adopted our sons, I felt a great sense of pride and was happy to provide both sets of parents with grandchildren. This is not to say that we adopted the boys for our parents, rather that we were pleased to see them happy. After all, we told ourselves, we had provided them with something special—grandsons! Yet, it never occurred to me that it would be so difficult. The boys were not perfectly model children. Because my husband's parents lived out of state, the stress of the boys' behaviors did not affect them to the extent that they affected my parents. The toil of the boys' problems soon contributed to increased tension within my family. Soon, the toil became too much for my family. Whether they were protecting themselves from further pain of the boys' behaviors or just wanted to be free of the stress was uncertain at the time. Whatever the cause, it wasn't too long before they disappeared out of our lives and dismissed the boys out of their life.

Chris had begun to display covert behaviors similar to the ones Wayne and Charlie exhibited. We caught him playing with matches, telling boldfaced lies, and stealing. I usually could catch him and correct it on the spot. I had always been able to give Chris the "mother look" to produce appropriate responses and apologies. However, this seemed to be changing. He was still taking medication for Attention Deficit Disorder (ADD). However, what we had originally thought was hypoglycemia actually turned out to be symptoms of ADD and the medication only made it worse. He developed intolerance to sugar. If he consumed sugars while on the medication, he became very ill. We spent many nights trying to control the vomiting and headaches. His doctor informed us we could alleviate some of the symptoms by feeding him high protein snacks between meals and cutting out his sugar intake. We had already made this change the prior year so I continued to stock up on crackers, cheese, fruits, and nuts. I watched for sugarless candy and bought it for him whenever I could find it. Likewise, we had changed our family's eating habits to match his diet. When we had ice cream, for instance, I would buy sugar-free yogurt so our son could have it with the rest of us. We had previously explained the health dangers to our son and he seemed to be fine with the changes in his diet. After all, he did not like being sick. Furthermore, he enjoyed the extra attention he received from having "his own special food" to eat.

During the summer, Chris lost weight, but I contributed it to playing and working outdoors. He had never been a very big kid and now, because of his sugarless diet, I was fervently trying to increase his weight. It never occurred to me that he was stealing candy and becoming ill because of it. That is, not until I caught him red handed. My mother had returned from taking him to his therapy session. Just that morning, my mother had promised to take him and a friend to see a movie that afternoon. She also told him that in a couple of weeks she was planning to take him to an amusement park. He was very excited about the fun activities planned for that summer. It was while he was telling me about this that I noticed something stuffed in his pocket and asked him about it. He responded "nothing" and tried to hide it. I told him to empty his pockets. When he did, he pulled out five to six empty snicker bar wrappers.

"I found these blowing around the parking lot when Grams took me to my counseling session." I looked him squarely in the eye and said, "I want the truth." He began to fidget and I knew immediately that he was hiding something. The longer I "gave him the look", the more he stumbled on his words. I decided it was time for the "mother look." He eventually blurted out the truth through sobs and tears. As he stood there crying, I walked to my mother's cabinet, looked inside, and found a bag of snicker bars with several empty wrappers stuffed into the bottom. I then went back to my son. He must have known what I was doing because as soon as I opened the door he blurted out "I stole them from the cabinet and ate all of them then got sick." I called my mother and made my son tell her what he had done. She was furious with him. I told her that he had just blown his day at the movies. She abruptly told him that he may have also blown his trip to the amusement park but she would let him know later. I then had my son tell his friend why the movie was canceled. As he related what he did, she seemed disappointed but said that she understood. She was three years older than he was which proved to be an asset in this situation. She explained that all misbehaviors had consequences. He admired her opinion, so having to explain his action was just about as bad as losing the movie.

After his friend talked to Chris, my mother scolded him. The frustration she felt from the events of the past three years was evident in her voice. She could not understand why he continued to misbehave when "he had everything a child could want." I was as frustrated as she was so I let her release her emotions. After my mother left, I told my son to write a story about his misbehavior, after all he was good at stories and this provided him the opportunity to think it over! After discussing the incident with my husband, we decided he should do an extra chore. He had always exhibited a streak of laziness so an extra chore, in his view, was just about the *worst* kind of punishment. While Charlie enjoyed extra chores, because he hated to sit still, sitting was a reward for Chris. To him, having to exert any kind of energy was awful. Therefore, grounding did not work but extra chores did.

Our septic system installation was scheduled for that weekend. The workers had already informed us that the backhoe would dig up several rocks. They told us that the rocks would need to be picked up before we could mow the area or they would damage our mower. So, we told our son that Monday morning it was his responsibility to get a bucket and pick up the large rocks. When his bucket was full, we told him to dump them in a pile behind the dog's pen.

That weekend, my best friend offered to keep our son at her house. Both boys greatly respected her and she had a huge impact on them. She said that she would have a "serious discussion" with our son about his recent misbehaviors with the hopes that she could get through to him before they resulted in his own stay at a hospital. My mother stayed the weekend with my sister and I kept my niece at our house. My dad was in and out. The sand and gravel left from the septic system installation had to be moved before Monday morning. Since we had paid for all of it, the workers suggested we use it. We decided to place it around our patio. To do this, we had to move it one wheelbarrow at a time. Also, my husband wanted to finish the clubhouse that he and Chris had started building. Our son wanted it to resemble a log cabin so they used landscape timbers and stacked them for the walls. Everything was completed except the roof. Since our son was too small to help with the roof, I told them I would help finish it.

With everyone except my niece gone for the weekend, my husband and I had time to complete the jobs. We had to finish the clubhouse roof before we could move the gravel since the clubhouse sat on the edge of the patio. While my niece watched cartoons, we completed the roof. Afterwards, she played "grocery store" inside the clubhouse while we moved the gravel. I commented to my husband how different girls were from boys. She was content to play 'make believe' and never seemed to get bored. However, it was just the opposite with the boys. When they became bored, they involved themselves in mischief. Of course nothing was exciting unless it meant getting wet, muddy, or involved some kind of bug or critter. My niece, on the other hand, wanted everything to be spotless. For instance, when I played in the sandbox with her that afternoon, she made sure to keep the sand off of her clothes. I watched her and laughed at the mental image of our sons coming home many times completely caked with red mud, yet, she was worried about getting her clothes dirty with sand!

That evening we took my niece to visit Charlie. She loved her "boy cousin" and followed him around constantly. Because of this, I nicknamed her *Shadow*. She got a kick out of it, especially when Charlie began to call her by that name also. She made sure to tell all of us that was her special name. They had not seen each other in several weeks and were very excited. As soon as she saw him she ran up, put her arms around him, and said "Shadow's here." They were soon talking, giggling and playing together just as always. Even though she is nearly six years younger than he is, our son never grew tired of her. They indeed shared a special bond, one that had a very positive influence over him and that will never be broken. Even when my niece asked our son why he was at his "special school" (the reason we told her he was not at home) he protected her by explaining "there were some things I need to learn here that I cannot learn from regular school." She never questioned his answer.

The next morning, she played with her play dough and colored pictures while my husband and I finished moving the gravel. Later that evening, my parents came home and my friend brought Chris back. He helped us finish spreading the gravel while my parents took my niece home. My husband and I were both exhausted but proud of the end result of our work. The trailer, patio, and clubhouse looked like a scene from *Little House on the Prairie*.

Monday morning came early for our son when I got him up to begin his job. My husband and I knew it would only take a couple of hours to complete, but, we also knew he would drag it out in hopes that we would give in and let him off the hook. To his surprise, however, his ploy did not work. Not that he didn't try every trick he knew, it was just that he was unaware that he was wasting his time. It took him a couple of days to finally accept it, but once he did, it was amazing how fast he completed the task. It was still cool that morning so I decided to let him work on the rocks for a little while before fixing his breakfast. It was during this hour that the first of many devastating changes occurred.

I was working a crossword puzzle and drinking my coffee when my mother came to the door and asked what the plans were for the day. I replied "nothing, I am too tired from the weekend." She then came inside and demanded "what seems to be the problem." Grant it there had been a lot of tension between everyone the past few days but I attributed it to the problems I faced with the boys. I also felt that things would calm down now that Charlie was receiving treatment and Chris was receiving increased therapy sessions. However, it did not turn out as I had expected. I was not prepared for what was about to occur.

Although my dad was one of the most easy going men I knew, lately he seemed to be very edgy. I was not sure if it was the pressure of the boys or if he was having some problem. On the other hand, I could have been so absorbed in our son's problems that I could have missed something with him. Whatever the cause, he seemed to have become very unhappy and cynical. Knowing this, my husband and I were glad that we could help him. By inviting my parents to stay with us we hoped my dad would have one less worry. Anything that we were able to do to help, we did. All of this, combined with the problems my husband and I were having with the boys, was taking a toll on me. Unfortunately, I was not able to see this until emotions and situations were out of control.

I explained to my mother that the only problem I knew of was the hurt feelings and concern I was having about my dad. I did not understand what else we could do to help and asked her what else they expected from us. Immediately I was accused of being selfish and having ulterior motives for offering the assistance. She then asked me if we were upset with her and I told her no. I felt that I had made it clear what the problem was, but she was not content to accept it. Because I am not a morning person, I was not in the mood to continue the discussion. The more she talked, the angrier I became. I reiterated the fact that I was not upset with her, only hurt and confused about my dad. It seemed that the more times I told her this, the more irritated I became with her.

This continued until my mother retorted "well, we will just move." I looked at her and said, "I knew you would say that. You never listen to me, I only said I was hurt, I never said you had to leave." This went back and forth for several minutes and I finally said, "I do not want to argue with you so do what you want" hoping that she would leave and let me finish my coffee. Before long, many other ugly statements were exchanged. I felt myself losing my patience. I was growing angrier and angrier. I tried to ignore her, thinking, "surely she will leave." When she did not take my silence as a signal to leave me alone, and in response to her badgering, I cursed. When I did, I looked up from my chair and saw her coming at me. I was horrified. The next thing I knew a very nasty scene erupted.

I caught a glimpse of Chris outside, looking our way. I was appalled to know that he could hear what was taking place. I held my mother back but her arm slipped free and she slapped me. At this point I said, "you want a fight, is that what you want, then come on let's do it." I noticed the basket of dirty clothes behind her and decided to sit her down in them and walk away. My dad had always taught me that it was better to walk away from a fight than to do something you later regretted. I knew the pile of clothes should not hurt her so I sat her on the clothes. With this I turned and walked away, thinking, "this is unbelievable." To my surprise, she got up and came towards me. The entire time I was thinking, "This can't be happening, I must be dreaming." Finally, as quickly as it occurred, it was over. I sat back down in my chair and she began to look around. She informed me that she was looking for her glasses because I had knocked them off. I told her she had lost them, not me. Once she found them she calmly went to the door and said "Now can we forget this and go on?" I was totally dumbfounded. When I did not reply she said, "I'll be in my motor home when you are ready to talk." *"Ready to talk"*, I thought, it will take me a while, my entire world had just changed from bad to worse!

One thing I tried to instill in our sons was that they could tell me anything without fear. I told them that I did not have to agree with what they said, but that they definitely had the right to say it. The incident that just occurred between my mother and I was testimony to why I wanted them to be unafraid to tell me what they were thinking or feeling. "Every person", I told them, "had a right to their own opinion." After the incident with my mother, I felt even stronger about this belief.

I called my husband and cried uncontrollably as I recounted to him what had just happened. I was stunned when he laughed. When I told him that it was not a joke, he apologized saying, "you are serious, I thought you were joking. I'm sorry for laughing." He told me to take care of Chris and he would handle things when he got home from work. I got up, poured my son a glass of milk, and cut an apple for his breakfast. As I was carrying it to the door, my mother came out and said she was going to get her glasses adjusted and asked if I wanted anything from the store. I told her no. I called Chris to the picnic table. My mother said, "are the boys out of cereal?" "No", I replied. "They have plenty of cereal."

I stayed inside the rest of the afternoon and did some work on the computer. At lunchtime, I fixed Chris some peanut butter and jelly crackers, carrots, chips, and a glass of fruit punch. I only remember this because he commented on how much he loved the crackers and asked if I could fix him more. He then asked if he could take them in his lunch when school started next year. When I asked him why he said, "they are better than bread." Next, he asked me why I had bruises on my arm and face. When I told him I ran into the dryer door, he said "no you didn't, I heard the fight." I did not know what to say except that he did not need to worry about it and when dad got home we could talk about it. With this he said, "well, I have to get back to my rocks" and off he went.

My dad arrived home before my husband. Chris saw my dad pull up and ran to give him a hug. I then expected my dad to come ask me what had happened, however, he never did. My husband arrived home a few minutes later and I told him that I had stayed inside all day. I did not want another confrontation. He called Chris inside and tried to explain to him what had happened. He told Chris that mom and grams had an adult argument but he did not need to worry about it because everything would be okay. He then asked Chris if he had completed his chore. Chris said "well I should have been through but I've been taking my time." My husband told him that the sooner he got it done the sooner he could play. He responded "yea I know, it's my responsibility." Less than 10 minutes later, we heard my parents get in their car and leave.

After breakfast the next morning, our son headed out the door and told me he was going to "finish his chore" by lunch. I said that was good and also reminded him to take care of the dog. He answered, "I know mom and I give her water every time I get a drink then I spray her pen so she will stay cooled off." I checked on his progress throughout the morning. Most of the morning he sat and played in the dirt. I knew him well enough to know that it was just a ploy to get out of doing the task. When I thought of giving in and letting him off the hook, I remembered all of the training we had before getting the boys. We were told over and over "remain consistent in your discipline and always follow through." If we did not do so, we were told, these kids will wrap you around their finger, they are very adept at making you feel guilty for disciplining them. We were also told that giving in to their manipulations was one of the worst things adoptive parents could do because the kids had learned how to manipulate adults for their own desires. When we were first told this, I remember thinking that all kids were that way. However, it did not take us long to realize the value of those suggestions.

Abused children, we have witnessed, use the past abuse as an excuse to justify their behaviors. On one hand, they know when they are misbehaving and do so to test the parents' commitment to them. Yet, on the other hand, they quite often play the role of victim when being disciplined for their misbehaviors. It is their attempt to avoid facing responsibility for their actions. Helping them learn the difference between being a powerless, victim of the abuser, but a controller of their own actions, was one of the most important lessons they had to learn. Although they would always carry scars of the abuse, most abused children are capable of becoming responsible individuals. The difficult part for the adoptive parent was providing them with opportunities to distinguish between the two.

Needless to say, Chris did not finish by lunchtime. I called him in for lunch and told him that he would have to start on it later that afternoon. Until then, he wanted to sew up the tear in his overalls. When it cooled off outside he went back to work on his chore. A short time later, my dad came home.

I was washing the dishes when my dad brought in bags of food from their motor home. He laid them on the counter along with the keys to the car my husband and I had given to him a couple of months earlier. He informed me that they would be back the next day to get the rest of their things. I never turned around to look at him because I did not want him to see the bruise. The only thing I said to him was "okay" as he walked out the door. This was the first time in my life when my dad and I did not see eye to eye and work out a problem.

My husband arrived home as I was putting away the groceries. He walked in and asked me what was going on. I told him what my dad had said. My husband then looked out the window and saw Chris helping my parents carry their things to their car. This infuriated him and he immediately called our son inside. Our son informed us that my parents told him "your mom and dad have some problems they need to work out so we are going to leave until they do." My husband quickly corrected this falsehood by telling our son that we never told them to leave, they made the decision to leave. He also explained that we cannot control what other people do, we can only control ourselves. Chris then blurted out, "it is my fault they're leaving because I stole candy from them." We immediately rebutted this by telling him that was not the reason, even though it was wrong for him to steal. Through his tears, Chris said, "I'm sorry you got beat up by your mother, I should have stopped her because I am the one that she was mad at. But how come Gramps is leaving me too when I did not do anything to him? Isn't that the same as running away?" We did not know how to answer his questions. After all, how could we justify my parents' behavior when it was exactly the same type of behavior we had worked to change in our sons? The only thing we knew to do was emphasize the fact that, he alone, was only responsible for his actions but not those of others. We had no idea at the time of the negative impact that situation would have on Chris.

The next morning my parents came for the rest of their belongings. As soon as I saw them, I got Chris and we left. It is said that all clouds have a silver lining and this was no exception. He saved our aluminum cans and cashed them in at the recycling center for his spending money. We had told him that the more he collected, the more money he would earn. Since he had seen signs along the roads about adopting a highway, he asked if I would take him to pick up cans on the sides of the roads. I told him that when we had time I would take him. So on that day, I told him it was a perfect day for us to drive along the side roads so he could collect cans. He was very proud of his idea and was even more impressed when he turned his cans in and made nearly $10.00.

Both of our sons continued to pick up cans over the next several years. Once a week, my husband or I took the boys out and let them pick up as many as they could find. It has turned out to be a very prosperous adventure for them. Although it cost us more in gas money to drive them around than they earned, it was worth the time together and the lessons they were learning. Many positive rewards have come not only to them, but also to my husband and I as well through their "business" as the boys referred to it. For the boys, they love having their own money to spend. As for my husband and I, we have been stopped and thanked, by people driving by, for teaching our sons responsibility. Our friends have saved their cans for the boys as well as my husband's office staff and many people from the university, including the campus police department.

During one of our Saturday morning can adventures, a man stopped me and handed me two bright orange construction T-shirts to give to the boys. He said he was glad to see some responsible kids and wanted them to have the shirts so others passing by could see them. Another time, a man stopped just to give the boys a five-dollar bill. He had no cans to give them but wanted them to know that he appreciated kids who did something positive with their time. Even with all of the good that has resulted from the can activity, there have been a few criticisms. Overall though, the positive connotations far outweigh the few negative ones. These include, for instance, the night at a high school football game when a group of teenage boys handed our sons a five dollar bill for their work and for being good role models for others, the lost dog that followed them home resulting in a ten dollar reward from the owner, and the lost checkbook that they found and returned to the owner which landed them a twenty dollar reward. Best of all, something which could not be measured by a price tag, was the self-pride they have gained from doing the honest and correct thing.

One of the most fulfilling accomplishments they have received from their can business is their ability to buy things for the dog. They were making nearly $50.00 per month between them. They enjoyed being able to buy her special treats with their own money. However, one day the dog became sick from eating a toy they had left in her pen. I had told them several times to pick it up. Thinking they had picked it up, I never thought any more about it. That is, not until the dog began choking and collapsed. She had swallowed the toy and was beginning to have convulsions. Her subsequent trip to the veterinarian resulted in several medical charges. We informed the boys that part of the responsibility of having a pet was also to take care of it and protect it from such events. Chris decided that it was their responsibility to pay for the charges since they had not done what I had asked them to and the dog had suffered for it.

Charlie agreed. So, they (with the veterinarian's approval) chose to pay twenty dollars a month until their bill was paid.

Each month they asked for a ride to the vet's office, walked in with their bag of money, paid their bill, and waited for their receipt. Every time they visited the veterinarian, the staff complimented them for being responsible, young men. Not only did this event increase their self-esteem, but also it has provided my husband and I with a way of teaching them financial responsibility. (Of course they do not know that we paid "a little extra" on their bill each month) One Christmas, when they failed to pay their bill and were charged a late fee, they learned about the consequences of not meeting their obligations. It was interesting to watch them figure out just how many extra cans they had to pick up the following month in order to pay the late fee. Another lesson learned! What began as a diversion to a bad situation had indeed become a silver lining. Our life with the boys, it seemed, had been one silver lining after another! Of course, there were plenty of dark and stormy days in between.

Chapter 14

Full Circle

Charlie was still unaware of the events with my parents. We were scheduled for a group therapy session later that week and decided to tell him about it then. I had a feeling that he would be upset, but did not expect the depth of his anger. As soon as we arrived, the first thing he noticed was my bruise. When he asked about them, I told him that I would tell him after the session. After explaining how I received the bruises, I was unable to finish. My husband stepped in and told him the rest. When he knew everything, he screamed and yelled, "if they don't want anything to do with you then I never want to see them again." We had asked his therapist to remain with us while we told him and she immediately told him that is was good for him to let out his feelings. Once he calmed down he began to cry and asked, "will I ever get to see my cousin again?" This was a difficult question for me to answer, but, as always, I answered him as honestly as I could. I told him that I did not know, but that did not mean he had to stop thinking about her or stop loving her.

Charlie was different than Chris. He tried to develop a sense of trust in adults. However, when he allowed himself to begin trusting someone and that person did something to hurt him, he then became very indifferent towards them, which was very evident in this situation. That is, he was more upset about not seeing his cousin than about seeing my parents. In addition, he saw me deeply hurting and he could not deal with anything or anyone that hurt me; I had become the one person he could trust more than anyone else he had ever known. Therefore, he would go to great lengths to protect me. This soon proved to be the next large hurdle that we would have to overcome. However, we never could have imagined the extent of both boys' reactions.

Charlie began to show some progress in the hospital but still had many issues to deal with before he was ready to come home. Therefore, when his therapist called two weeks later informing us that the insurance had denied his claim for more days, we were apprehensive. She was in total agreement with us that he was not ready to be discharged, however, her hands were tied and there was nothing she could do to stop it. Furthermore, since it was late Friday afternoon, she had no way of contacting anyone for an extension. All we could do at that moment was pick up our son the next morning and bring him home. Hopefully, Monday morning would bring us an explanation and an extension for more days.

The next morning I headed for the hospital to get our son. His therapist told me that she had talked to him but he was not responding to anyone. She suggested I keep an eye on him the rest of the weekend and call her first thing Monday. As I drove home, our son gazed out the window not saying a word. I decided to let him be and not press him to open up. When we got home, I told my husband and younger son what the therapist had said. We all decided it would be best to give him some space. We were all fearful that if he became upset, he would run.

My husband and I were preparing lunch while Chris played in the clubhouse with his brother. Although we could hear them from the window, it suddenly became very quiet. Chris came running in and said, "he is banging his head with my toy box lid." My husband ran outside to the clubhouse and took the lid from Charlie. He then began banging his head on the wall. My husband held him until he calmed down and brought him in to eat lunch. He sat through lunch without touching his food and did not say a word. At the time, his not talking was the least of our worries so the three of us continued our conversation.

After lunch Charlie went outside and sat on the patio. I kept an eye on him while my husband and younger son played a game. I saw Charlie get up and walk around for awhile. When he walked up one of our hills and looked around, I became very apprehensive. I had a strange feeling that he was getting ready to run. Immediately, I called his caseworker and informed her of his head banging and his wandering around. During our conversation, my husband walked up the hill to get our son. By the time my husband reached him, he had curled up in a fetal position and was crying. His case manager told us to get him back to the hospital and she would send the assessment worker for an emergency admittance. When we arrived at the hospital, the staff was not surprised to see us. He was immediately admitted and was put on suicide precautions. We went back home and were relieved that he was in a secure environment.

Monday morning I received a call from the therapist and she informed me that his discharge had been a mistake. I said "no kidding" to which she responded "no I mean, it was a paperwork mistake, his file was mistaken for another child who was approved for discharge." Once her statement sunk in, I was terrified. What if our son had done something to harm himself while we had him at home those few hours? Would the fact that his discharge was a mistake make it any easier to accept? I calmed my frustration and was thankful that, at least, he was back where he needed to be. "After all", I assured myself, "his therapist was not at fault; if anything she had not wanted him to leave either." Fortunately, we had been quick enough to recognize the warning signs and were able to get him back to the hospital before he hurt himself or ran away. This was one time I was thankful for having witnessed his misbehaviors in the past; it alerted me to what might have happened when I saw his strange behaviors that Saturday afternoon!

Two days later Chris started school. I still had a week and a half before beginning my classes. I was very excited about my new direction and grateful for the time to myself those few days. However, I soon discovered that the quietude became an enemy because it gave me time to reflect on the event with my mother. It had only been three weeks and it was still very fresh in my mind. I was at a very low point. I tried to think of anything that I could have done differently that would have changed what happened. I knew we were both stubborn, but that did not entirely explain the incident. After all, we had clashed many times before, yet, we managed to remain friends. The only difference between the past arguments and this one was the fact that I had the boys. I decided their problems must have contributed more to the bitter scene than either one of us wanted to admit. However, at that time, I chose to stick by the boys because I honestly thought I could change them.

My grades and school honors were the first positive reflections of my strengthening self-confidence. However, it wasn't long before my new resolve was once again put to the test, for the boys were not grown yet! They were still children with problems from their past and now they had problems from the present. In addition to their existing behavioral problems, they were now experiencing another change, the withdrawal of my family. Life had indeed gone *full circle*.

Chapter 15

Repercussions

Within two weeks after Charlie was readmitted to the hospital, he openly disclosed, for the first time, his sexual abuse. Although this was a very positive step in his recovery, we were informed that once disclosure took place many deviant behaviors usually followed. Our son was no exception. He began to confuse the past and present, refuse his medications, act aggressively towards other children on his unit, and hide by curling up in a fetal position under sinks and counters. My husband and I were hurt to hear these reports, but, paradoxically, we were happy to hear that our son was exhibiting any type of emotion. We knew that he was finally dealing with the pain of his abuse and this was something we had waited on for two years. The only thing we could do was be there for him during the family sessions, which is exactly what we did. We had no idea how he would react each time we arrived, but we always hugged him and told him that we loved him. At first, he was unresponsive, however, this behavior slowly disappeared. The day when he returned my hug I knew all hope was not lost. I also knew that it would be a long road, yet, I was more confident that he would make it.

During Charlie's stay in the hospital, Chris began to again exhibit disruptive problems at school. For instance, he came home one day with a black eye. When I asked him about it, he told me that he was taking up for a girl because a bully was picking on her. When he did this, the bully hit him. I called the school to discuss the incident. The principal told me that she would take care of the situation. She then informed me that our son had been having numerous other problems in school. His teachers were reporting problems with keeping him focused on his work, doing his assignments, and obeying the rules. In addition, he had been getting into numerous fights. I told her that I would contact his therapist and increase his sessions. A couple of weeks later, his principle called us with even more disturbing news about him.

His class had gone on a field trip to a child abuse shelter at a local hospital. While the therapist was explaining the center's activities to the class, our son stood up and announced "I come from an abusive family." Of course those parents and hospital staff who were unaware of his adoptive status and the boys' backgrounds immediately thought he was talking about us. His teacher told me that she explained the situation to them but wanted us to be aware of the incident just in case there were those that she did not catch to dispel any rumors. Also, as she explained, she was not sure which kids heard it and "you know how kids are with their stories, they don't always have all the facts. If any of them say something to their parents it could cause some unnecessary trouble." I thanked her for alerting us to the situation and we immediately prepared for the worst. Ironically, just the week prior, we had been visited by the child welfare personnel.

Although the boys' "getting lost" episode had occurred four months earlier, the child welfare agency was just now getting around to investigating a report from that time. The allegations stemmed from the thank you letters Charlie had written to those who assisted in the search and the nurse at the first hospital. She had reported that I had told my son "I do not want you." Once our son told the investigator that I said "I do not want to take you home today", his response was "seems like you were set up" and it was dropped.

As for the thank you letters, Charlie wrote very poignantly. In nearly every one of them he wrote something to the effect of "I was stupid to get lost and not ask for help." He also thanked everyone for helping find him and that he now knew he could "trust the police because they are not bad people." I had read all of his letters before we delivered them but I did not censor what he wrote. My husband and I had decided never to do this due to the difficulty he had expressing himself. If we were to criticize his verbalizations or writing, he would shut down and the lines of communication would be severed. Besides that, we did not then, nor have we ever, censored anything our sons say. We believe they had a right to say whatever they wanted even if we do not agree with it. The only thing we required was for them not to be disrespectful when they voiced their opinions.

Well, of the numerous letters our sons wrote to those who helped, only one person called the child abuse hotline about Charlie's. We inadvertently were told who it was. It was one of the news anchors at a major television station. Even more ironic, this was the anchorman who had read portions of our son's thank you letter on the news the night our sons delivered them to the station. After we told the investigator this he smiled and immediately informed us that this allegation was a "file 13 report." We felt redeemed when he then told us "I wish there were more parents like you in this world. If there were, then there would be far less child abuse cases to investigate." It may sound smug, but, after he told us this, my husband and I looked at each other, smiled, and said "Ha!" I was once again convinced that right does win out over wrong! We also vowed to continue to act on our gut feelings when it came to parenting the boys.

Weeks passed and we did not receive any derogatory calls as a result of Chris' comment during his class field trip. We continued his individual therapy sessions and family sessions with Charlie. Life remained fairly calm during that time period. Although experience had taught us that the calm always preceded the storms, we had also learned to be thankful for, and cherish all the calmness that came our way. In addition, the holidays were coming and they had always been tumultuous with the boys. We therefore used this calm period to prepare for them. Once again, of course, we had no way of knowing just how tumultuous things would become during the next two months.

Charlie was discharged from the day treatment program three weeks before Thanksgiving. Since both boys seemed to be doing well, we made plans to visit my husband's parents for the holiday. It was a long drive (20 hours) but we enjoyed our holiday and trip. When we returned, we began preparing for Christmas. We used the weekends to clear trees on our land so we could begin construction of our house. Two weeks passed and no problems arose. However, this all changed one Sunday evening after we came in from cutting and clearing trees. We had just finished dinner; the boys had taken their showers and were doing the dishes when the phone rang. It was the child welfare department. They were on their way to our house. After I hung up the phone, we told the boys it was probably about the comment Chris had made while on his field trip. Chris said he would explain to them that he meant his birthparents so "don't worry Mom and Dad."

Well, we could not have been any farther from the truth. They were not there about our son's comment. In fact they knew nothing about it. They were there about allegations someone had made about us! It turned out to be allegations originating from someone who knew us well! This was to be the undoing of both boys. They changed from bad to worse.

Two investigators knocked on the door. After the boys finished the dishes they joined us. As the allegations were read off one by one, I began to realize who had made them. In fact, it was very obvious since some of the allegations regarded the brother we only had in our home for six months. Only a handful of people knew the specifics of that situation. My husband and I explained the ordeal with Wayne. We were relieved when the investigator told us that "unfortunately some of the older adopted children are too far gone and there is nothing a family can do to help them." Charlie then related some of the things his older brother had done to him and how "he scared me." The investigator told us not to worry about it because we had done everything possible and when the state took management of him they became the responsible party. This was a relief to hear because it was still a painful event for our family. We knew in our hearts, however, that he was where he needed to be and we had to go on.

Next, there was an allegation that we had made Charlie pick up rocks and did not allow him food or water all day long. However, Charlie was in the hospital when this event took place. Chris said, "I was the one picking up the rocks around our septic tank but I had plenty of water. My mom fixed me some peanut butter and jelly crackers and carrots that day and they were really good." When the investigator heard this he chuckled and said he was beginning to get the picture. He was further convinced when he read off the last two allegations. "It was also reported that you (looking at me) are an alcoholic and a drug abuser and that your house is very dirty." I was so dumbfounded when I heard this that I just sat there. However, the boys' reactions were perfect and could not have provided a clearer picture of us, even if we had planned it. They laughed so hard that they rolled on the floor and Chris said "are you sure you have the right house?" Once the investigator saw this he turned to the other investigator and said "did you note that reaction? It is obvious that these are nothing but false allegations." At this, I commented "and I could probably tell you who made them." He said, "from what you have told me I bet you would be correct." Before they left, they told the boys that they were very lucky kids to have so much land to play on and parents that loved them so much. "It is obvious that you are well cared for by the looks of your home and clothes." With this, they left and once again complimented my husband and I for the good job we had done with the boys.

After they left, I asked my husband and the boys if they realized who made the allegations. Chris said "whoever said it sure does not know us very much." I said "or maybe they knew us too well because how many people know about your brother." When I said this, all three of them looked at me and said "your parents!" I told them there was no way for us to know for sure, but I really felt they knew who made the accusations. Chris said, "it was all a lie, how can they lie about someone they say they love?" Charlie replied, "they don't love us!" My husband and I tried to reassure them that their grandparents did love them but sometimes grown ups did things that didn't make sense. However, the damage had already been done and the repercussions of this incident turned out to be very devastating. In addition to his other problems, Chris suffered over this and dealt with his pain by exhibiting more deviant behaviors.

Christmas had come and gone. We were into the middle of January. The boys and I had a day off from school. I told the boys they could play outside while I did my homework. It was a warm day, for January, so they were excited. I worked all morning and could hear them outside playing *king of the hill*. After lunch they headed back out to "finish winning their hill." Later that afternoon, Charlie stuck his head in the door and asked me if they could go play at their fort. I told him I didn't see any problem with that as long as they checked in with me every so often. Since I could see the tree that held their fort from our door, I felt it would be okay. A little while later, Chris checked in and said they were still playing.

About an hour later, my husband called to ask me how things were going. I told him the boys were playing and had done fine that morning. I told him they were at their fort and it was about time for them to check in again. He told me to tell them that he was proud of them for being good that day and that he would be home in a couple of hours. Not very long after I hung up, Chris once again stuck his head in the door. I asked him why his older brother didn't come also. He told me that he was checking in for both of them. I told him that would not do and he needed to send his brother to check in also. He yelled for his brother and I saw him emerge from the trees. I told both of them that their dad was proud of them for behaving so nicely. They thanked me and turned to go play. That evening, I was sure that the day had gone well and at dinner we once again complimented the boys for having such a good day. If we had only known that night what the boys had actually been up to that day, we would have choked on our words!

The next week was also very smooth. I told my husband that it was making me very nervous because I felt something was wrong. After all, the boys were behaving *too well!* We both held our breath because we were certain something was about to erupt. We just had no idea of what it would be. Knowing our boys, though, we knew to expect more than the ordinary male testosterone stunts!! The first clue to what lie ahead came on that Saturday morning. We had spent the morning cutting trees. My husband and I came in to make lunch while the boys took care of the dog. When lunch was ready my husband called for the boys. When his second summons did not result in the boys' appearance, he walked around to find them. While he was looking my instincts kicked in. "Where are they and what have they done now?" Within minutes my husband returned with the boys. They had walked off into the woods. When we questioned them about it, they told us some off the wall story about "exploring until lunch was ready." "It is starting" I told my husband. He knew I was correct and we watched their every move the rest of the weekend. Monday morning was a relief because it allowed us to let down our guard while they were in school.

The first part of the week was very quiet and I wondered if we had jumped to conclusions about "something about ready to happen." However, our expectations were justified by Thursday afternoon. Charlie's teacher called to inform me that he had been caught stealing a classmate's lunch money. When she confronted him about it, he fervently denied it. "Well of course he does" I told her. "This is not new and I bet you are finding yourself believing his denial." She told me that she knew he took the money and that, yes, if she did not know better, she would have believed him. She told me that she was going to turn the incident over to the principal and let her dispense his consequence. I told her that my husband and

I would support whatever consequence the principal gave him. We waited for her phone call.

The principal called the next afternoon. However, I was taken by surprise by all the news she had for me. Not only had Charlie been sent in for the stealing, she also had Chris standing in her office for misbehaving. "I knew it," I thought to myself. I took a deep breath and waited for her to finish. Charlie, for his stealing, was going to be given 30 minutes of community service after school for a week. Chris had misbehaved on the bus. He would not stay in his seat and disobeyed the driver when told to sit down. He also picked fights with the other riders. Therefore, the principal was suspending him from the bus for a week. She apologized because this caused us to have to take him to and from school. "Apologize to me" I said, "if anything we should apologize to you for all of the trouble the boys had caused at school." At this point I chuckled as I admitted "and we were grateful Monday morning when they went back to school so we could get some relief." After I hung up the phone, I called my husband to let him know that our hunches were correct; the boys had caused trouble. No sooner had I hung up from talking to my husband did I get a knock on our front door. It was our neighbor.

Our neighbor was there to inform me that he was missing some guns, a crossbow, and several arrows. They were in the trunk of a car parked behind his house. Since they had been out of town, I asked if maybe the person watching their place had borrowed them. He told me that he had already checked but the person had not. I told him that I had not seen anyone around the area, but I would keep a closer watch. I also told him that we did not have anything missing from our place. As he turned to leave he said "well I just wanted to let you know but I am not accusing anyone." He is such a soft spoken man that his comment did not sink in until an hour or so after he left. As I sat doing my homework, it suddenly occurred to me *"the boys took the guns!"* That explains why only Chris checked in twice the day they were out of school. Besides that, I thought, "the phone call from the principal was even more circumstantial evidence and the finger pointed directly at *the boys!*"

I immediately called my husband and told him about the latest. I asked him if he thought it was the boys, but, he thought there was absolutely no way and he tried to convince me that I was wrong. I told him it was just one of those gut feelings a mother gets and I was positive they were the culprits. I wanted so much to be wrong, yet, I just could not shake the feeling. We discussed what to do and decided to wait for a couple of days to see if the boys admitted anything to us before we confronted them. In the meantime, we also decided not to let them get out of our sight without letting them know we were watching them. With this my husband reassured me that everything would be okay and I shouldn't worry. That was easy for him to say because he did not have the feeling that I had; a feeling that grew stronger every hour. By the time he got home from work, I was so convinced it was the boys that I asked him to walk around our land and look while I made some excuse to keep the boys in the trailer. Whether he did it just to satisfy me or to prove me wrong, I never knew. However, his search turned up nothing.

The following evening my husband again searched but, once again, found nothing. Since the next day was a Saturday, we decided that my husband would take the boys out to collect their cans so I could search. I searched until they returned. I found nothing. The boys still had not said anything to us to make us suspect. Although I tried to convince myself that I had jumped to conclusions, I still could not shake that nagging feeling. My husband and I decided to get up early the next morning and search again. "By tomorrow morning", I told myself, "I would know for sure if it was our boys because we are going to comb every inch of the woods on our property." Until we knew one way or the other, my husband and I were too embarrassed to face our neighbors. We had not told them that we suspected our boys, but we presumed they suspected them. I wanted to be wrong, oh, how I wanted to be wrong!

We got up early to begin our search. We allowed the boys to sleep in their clubhouses the night before. After we got up, we called out our window and told them to get up. Chris did not come so my husband opened his door. When he did he got a surprise. Chris was starting fires on his bed. My husband immediately put out the fire and told both boys to feed the animals. He also told them they had lost the privilege of sleeping in their clubhouse. While the boys were feeding the animals, my husband and I started our search. We wanted to settle this once and for all, because, that evening was Charlie's birthday-Super Bowl party. If it was the boys who took the weapons, we wanted to know before we rewarded him with a party.

We walked the entire fence line around our place. We turned over every tree limb, dug through every pile of leaves and looked all along the creek. Within minutes I caught a glimpse of Charlie following us. I turned to my husband and felt my heart sink. "He's on to us honey. He knows that we know and he is trying to cover his tracks." We decided to split up knowing he couldn't follow both of us but would follow the one closest to their stash. My husband stayed by the creek. I walked into the cedar grove located just behind our trailer. Our son followed me!! He just confirmed my beliefs; "they were the thieves."

The branches of the cedar trees were low to the ground so I had to get on my knees to see under them. I kept watch over our son out of the corner of my eye. When I reached the second tree, he was right behind me. "It has to be here" I told myself. I looked under the branch—"Oh damn, a rifle!" My worst fears had just been confirmed. I yelled for my husband, then stood there and cried. Charlie turned around and tried to sneak away between the trees, however my husband got there before he could slip away. He shouted, "get over here NOW!" When our son came around the tree he nonchalantly said "Wow a gun, how did that get there?" His comment so infuriated my husband and I that we knew better than to say anything to him, we probably would have said something we would later regret.

My husband picked up the gun and checked it for ammunition. Thank God, it was empty! Just the thought of the boys carrying around loaded guns and what could have happened was enough to make me weak in the knees. My husband then took Charlie by his arm and parked him on the grass. He handed me the gun, told our son to stay put, and yelled for Chris. As he topped the hill and saw the rifle in my hand he immediately looked at his brother. They had been caught and Chris knew it. He had never been able to lie as well as his brother and my "look" immediately broke him. He blurted out "It was his idea" pointing to his brother "he told me to take them and we hid them all over our land." That was all it took, I burst our crying and had to walk to our trailer. I sat down in the chair, cried like a baby, and called the sheriff's office. My husband marched the boys home, placed the rifle on the picnic table, loaded the boys into the truck, and demanded "you will show me where you stashed the rest of them!!" While they were gone, the sheriff arrived; luckily it was our local sheriff, he had been involved with all of the other episodes our sons had pulled.

The look on my face must have told the story when the sheriff saw the rifle on the picnic table and my tears. He walked over to me and said, "they have gone too far this time." I told him the whole story and where we had found this rifle. I also told him that my husband had the boys out gathering the rest of them. He asked me what I wanted to do and all I could say was "put them somewhere besides here." He told me that unless the neighbors filed a report, he could not take the boys to juvenile detention. Of all the luck, our neighbors were not home. I began calling around to see if I could locate them, but I could not. About this time my husband pulled up. He had managed to gather another gun, the crossbow, and two arrows. There were two arrows and another gun still missing. This caused me to be even more terrified and determined to find a place for the boys. My husband and I absolutely did not want them at home. We had no idea what they had intended to do with the weapons in the first place and we were not willing to take a chance with our safety, their safety, or the safety of *anyone* else!

The sheriff placed both of the boys in the back of his car. He told them to stay put while he came inside with my husband and I. We spent the next hour on the phone trying to find a place for the boys. We were having a very difficult time finding a treatment center with one opening, much less two openings. The sheriff then called his supervisor for advice. He informed the supervisor that these were the same two boys who caused the massive search several months earlier and that Charlie was the one who ran away continuously. He explained how terrified we were to keep the boys at home and that we needed some assistance with them. The supervisor gave the sheriff the number to the juvenile office. He called and left a message for the juvenile officer to call us. In the meantime, the sheriff went out to talk to the boys. He told them that they had really gotten themselves into deep trouble this time and they were now going to have to pay the consequences for their actions. I could see them from our window. Chris looked like he had just seen a ghost. I could tell his conscience was eating him up and that he was nervous. Charlie, however, just sat there as he always did when he got caught. I thought to myself, "you won't be so glib when all of this works out and you have to go away for awhile." The phone interrupted my thoughts. It was the juvenile office. They told us that we would have to find a hospital for the boys because their hands were tied unless our neighbors filed a complaint. My husband called out for the sheriff to come back in. We explained to him what the juvenile officer had said. He told us that he would keep the boys in his car until we were able to locate a hospital. He was trying to find out from them what they had intended to do with the weapons but they were not talking. "That does it", my husband said, "they are going someplace even if it means we have to place them in separate hospitals located far apart." The phone rang again.

I answered the phone and was surprised to hear that it was one of the hospitals we had already called. The nurse told me, "I know we told you we did not have any beds but after talking to our doctor he told me to call you back and have you bring both boys here as soon as you can get here. He said we would make room for them since we are having a discharge tomorrow morning." I was ecstatic and asked who the doctor was. "It is the same doctor that Charlie had at the last hospital; he just moved here last month. Once we called him about the situation he wasted no time in approving the space for both of your boys." I turned to my husband and said "load them in the car they are both going to the hospital." Once we told the sheriff he was relieved, he too was very apprehensive about leaving the boys at home until we knew their reason for taking the weapons *and* all of them were accounted for. We thanked him for his support and help. He told us to hang in there and if there was anything he could do, just let him know. He then told the boys to "do what you are told to do" and he left.

We arrived at the hospital and once again had to relate the story. The intake nurse turned out to be the same one we had come to know at the last hospital. She had moved with the doctor. She was aware of Charlie's actions and agreed that we did the best thing by not allowing either one of the boys to stay at home. After finishing the intake paperwork, the nurse called a technician to come take the boys. Chris ran over to me and clung to me. Through every ounce of determination I could muster, I simply handed him to the technician, looked him straight in the eye and said "go on, go." After they were out of the room the nurse reassured us that we had done the best thing we could and that they would take care of the boys now. She told us to go home and enjoy the next few weeks by ourselves because "you deserve a break." We got back home around 10:30 PM. We were so emotionally drained that we went straight to bed. We looked at each other and knew we had done the right thing. All that was left to say was "I love you."

It was difficult getting used to just the two of us. It had been three years since we were alone. We were thankful for the time but also grateful that we had things to keep us occupied. I had school, my husband had work and we both had time to work on our land—we had 200 trees to plant.

Ironically, the tree seedlings became a symbol of our hope for the future. Not only would they improve our land, but as they became rooted and grew strong, so would the boys, we prayed. We supplied the *love*, but we knew that it would take *more* than that for them to become what God had intended them to become—the seedlings into strong trees, the boys into responsible men!!

Over the next two weeks we only heard from the boys once. We had become accustomed to the hospital routines, however, so we did not expect them to call more than that. We knew that they were angry with us for placing them in the hospital. What they could not accept was the fact that it was their behavior that actually resulted in their placement. It was easier for them to think of us as the bad guys than to accept responsibility for themselves. They were, as we have witnessed numerous times, playing the victim, a very typical trait of abused and neglected children. It, I believe, restrained them from moving beyond their past and was used as a justification for their misbehaviors. Once they overcome this way of rationalization, they have a chance at becoming responsible individuals. It took my husband and I several years to realize that we had to back away and not allow them to place us in the role of their martyrs. Putting the consequences of their behaviors back into their laps was the only way of keeping our own sanity. If we were to falter, and change their natural consequences, they would suffer in the long run. They had to learn that their actions would not be tolerated. However, as we had also learned, that little matter of loving our sons tore at our hearts and tried to work against logic.

Love, we had learned, was a great motivator of many bad decisions. It required a much stronger person to use love in the way that was constructive rather than destructive. As parents, we had to remain consistent in our love for the boys, in addition to insisting that they suffer the consequences of their actions. If we were to rescue them from their consequences, we realized, they would never have the opportunity to *"grow"* out of the victim role.

Our first family session occurred two weeks after the boys' admission to the hospital. Although the hospital staff had pressed the boys for the reason they stole the weapons, they had not told anyone. This made it difficult for my husband and I to attend the session. If the boys had stolen them to come after us, we did not know how to react to them. However, if there were other reasons, how could we deal with it unless they told us? We decided to ignore Charlie and press Chris for information. Chris could not hide the truth from me no matter how hard his brother tried to get him to do just that. Our plan worked.

When we arrived for the session, the therapist left my husband and I in the room while she went to get the boys. When they walked in Chris immediately ran to me and hugged me. Charlie sat down in a chair and looked in the other direction. Next, Chris told me "I love you mom. I really miss you and want to come home." I told him that I loved him too, but he could not come home yet. He then hugged my husband and told him the same thing. Charlie slowly walked to me and gave me a hug. It was very hard for me to do, but I sat there and did not respond to him. The therapist immediately noticed this and after everyone was in his or her place she mentioned it. I told her that I was having a difficult time forgiving Charlie because I felt it was his idea to steal the weapons and I could not figure out why he wanted to hurt us. This was just the prompt Chris needed to "spill the truth."

"We did not steal them because of you mom. Nobody is going to take us away from you and we were protecting us." I looked at him in utter confusion. "What are you talking about, I don't understand." He then said, "Grams tried to get us taken away that's why those people came to our house and said all those lies about you. Well after what she did to you and then lied about us, we were not going to let anyone take us away." Suddenly everything made sense. I glanced at Charlie. He was staring at the floor. I knew he had something on his mind so I stared at him until he blurted it out. Finally, he broke down and retorted, "nobody is going to take me away again. I stole the guns to keep everybody away and to protect us."

This was the break we had been waiting for. Now that we knew the reason, we were able to deal with it. We told the boys that they had nothing to worry about because no one was going to take them away. My husband told the boys that they did not have to protect us—it was our job to protect them. As he was talking to them I was thinking "what a thing for 9 and 10-year-old kids to be thinking about. They should be thinking about sports, fishing, and playing but instead they are only thinking about defending our family so they can stay safe. What has the world come to?" Chris came over and sat in my lap. He was trembling. I told him that he did not have to be afraid because we would not let anything happen to him. "I'm glad to hear it was not me or dad that you were wanting to come after." When I said this both boys began to cry. Charlie sat in his chair so my husband went over to hold him. He then broke into tears. Our poor therapist must have felt lost during all of this because she was quiet.

After the boys calmed down, my husband told them that neither of them could come home on a pass until the other gun and arrows were found. He explained that it was too dangerous to have them lying around in the woods. He told Charlie to draw a map to the places where they were hidden. My husband told the boys that all of our neighbors had been helping search for them and that the map should help us find the rest of them. At this point the therapist said our time was up and that we could talk more about all of this at our next session. We told the boys good bye and they left. We informed the therapist that we would let her know when we found the rest of the stolen weapons. Now that she knew why they had done it, she said she would begin working on their issues of insecurity and stress the importance of making good decisions.

The reality of what had just transpired began to sink in on the drive home. My husband and I were quiet at first. When I noticed him crying I said, "I'm sorry my argument with my family has caused so much trouble." He looked at me and told me not to apologize. "If anything", he said, "they should apologize to the boys for their actions. I do not understand how grandparents can do this to their grandkids and desert their own daughter for doing her best to raise difficult kids." It was not until our boys went to such great lengths to protect them from what they perceived as a threat, that I became infuriated. Knowing their background, how could this happen; it was totally inconceivable. Why did my family have to take out an adult problem on the boys; the grandsons that they wanted so badly?" Sure, the boys were difficult kids, but we had done the best we could. If my family could not deal with the boys' behaviors, why didn't they tell us instead of running out on them, I asked myself? Will they ever be able to trust anyone else again? I had no idea how to handle this situation or what to do next. I just could not comprehend it all.

Chapter 16

The Beginning of the End

We spent the next two days following the map. However, we could not find anything. Finally, in desperation, my husband called Charlie and told him to "walk me from our door to the place where the gun is hidden." It took several tries, but our son was able to describe the route we needed to take to walk directly to the gun. After my husband got the information we needed, we searched again. It was difficult but we finally managed to get to the creek bed where the gun was supposedly hidden. The rain and mud had buried it, but, we caught a glimpse of the butt sticking out of the mud. We had it. Now all that remained were the two arrows. It would take a miracle to find them. We searched, yet, were only able to find one of them. I guess half a miracle, with the boys, was better than none. We never found the other arrow. With the rising creek level, we comforted ourselves by believing it washed away or was so buried that it would not cause any danger to anyone. My husband called the hospital to tell the staff and our sons that we found the other gun. We never said anything about the arrows; we wanted to see if they looked for them.

We had previously returned the other weapons to our neighbor. He was very compassionate about the entire situation. We were very embarrassed about what the boys had done, but he reassured us that he would not hold us responsible. Now, we had to return a rifle that was full of rust. "I hope he is as compassionate about it now" I told my husband. Fortunately, he was. The only request he has was that the boys to work off the amount of money that it would take to have everything repaired. We totally agreed with him. Once released from the hospital, the boys worked for him until their debt was repaid.

Well, another birthday was upon me and I had to celebrate it around a hospital schedule. This time however, both of our boys were there so I went to dinner with my cousin and her girls. For some reason my birthday became a milestone marker. It was interesting to guess, if by each birthday, I would have a son (or sons) in a hospital. The day they were both home on that day would be cause for great celebration.

That weekend we visited the boys. We took our dogs and Charlie's rabbit. We were disappointed, however, when neither of the boys was responsive to us. We tried to find out why they were so quiet, but they would not tell us. So, we packed up the animals and told them that we were leaving. We told them we were not going to play their games and when they were ready to visit with us, they could call. If not, we would see them at our next session. We did not hear from them before the session. They told us they were waiting for us to call them. They did not believe us when we told them we wouldn't play their game. I guess they had to prove it to themselves!

For the next two months, my husband and I attended every weekly family session. Each session seemed to show improvement in Charlie's behavior. He was doing well at the hospital and began to earn weekend passes to come home. He also called home several times. The staff informed us that his doctor felt comfortable enough to discharge him. However, one week prior to his discharge, he experienced a major setback in his therapy.

Charlie had earned a field trip to the Omniplex science museum with his therapy group. While there he saw my mother and his favorite cousin. He called me that night with the following account. "Mom I wanted to kill somebody today. I was really scared and I wish you were there." I was taken completely off guard by his phone call and was in utter confusion about what he was talking about. When I asked him what he was talking about, he related what had taken place. "I went on a field trip today and I saw Grams there. She just stared at me." I asked him if he had said anything to her. "No, I was scared and I went over and stood beside one of the staff. She saw me but did not say anything. Then I saw my cousin, she smiled and waved at me but Grams did not." "Maybe she was not close enough to say anything to you," I said. "Yes she was mom and then when we got back on the van she was right by the window and just walked away. I wish you had been there mom, I was so scared." I told him that if I had known anything about it I would have gone with him. But since there was no way of knowing he would see her there was nothing I could do now. I told him I was proud of him for not making a scene and that he did the right thing by staying with the staff. I told him he should not say anything to his brother about it because it would upset him. I assured him that his dad and I would tell Chris about it instead. Our son agreed that it would be better if we told his brother.

After a two-month stay, Charlie came home. Unlike his brother, though, Chris was not doing as well. He was not participating in group, family, or individual therapy. He was sullen most of the time and continued to misbehave.

The first weekend Charlie was home, Chris earned a 6-hour pass. I spent most of the time with him because my husband was helping Charlie build his own clubhouse. Up to that time the boys had shared the one that Chris had built with his dad. We had decided that it would be best if they each had their own. While my husband and older son were busy building, I sat down and told Chris about his brother running into their grandmother. I explained to him that there was nothing to worry about, it was just one of those things that happen. I told him that his brother had done the right thing by not making a scene. "It is hard for someone to talk bad about you when you do the right thing. By behaving appropriately when he saw her, he did the correct thing and nothing bad happened" I explained. Chris was very "sad because I didn't get to see my cousin too." I explained that it was "okay to be sad but that things like this just happen without planning them. The main thing to remember was that his grandmother and cousin love you even if you don't get to see them." I did my best to downplay the event because I knew he would be upset. It was something that he would have to deal with himself and decide if he would let it continue to affect his behavior. All my husband, his therapist, and I could do was be there for him. Ultimately, he would have to be the one to work through his feelings. Unfortunately, it proved to be a tough road for him; one that never ended.

Although Chris was on restrictions most of the next month, Charlie, seemingly, adjusted well to home and school. We did not have any runaway experiences for an entire month. He was talking to me about his problems and staying out of trouble. My proudest time with Charlie happened that month. It was the month of the Oklahoma City bombing. Whether I will ever experience Charlie's true inner abilities to that extent again is unknown. However, I witnessed something special during that time, something I will carry with me always.

Along with the rest of the world that fateful morning, I was shocked to hear what had just taken place. I was washing dishes when I heard and felt the tremor. I thought it was a sonic boom and went outside to look around. Our dogs were pacing and howling, as I had never heard them before. Seeing nothing unusual, I went back to the dishes. It never occurred to me to turn on the television or radio. An hour and a half later our phone rang. It was the emergency response team from our son's school asking for blood. When I inquired as to what was going on, I was horrified to hear that the boom I heard, and the tremor I felt, was a bomb. I immediately asked if the kids at school were okay and then called the hospital to check on Chris. Both of them were fine. The teachers and staff were calming all of them and keeping a close watch on their behaviors. I called my husband and he met me at the blood donation center. After we were finished, he went back to work and I went home to watch the news coverage. I picked up Charlie from school that afternoon and took him to see our family therapist. The session had already been planned and I felt that it would be best to keep the appointment so Charlie could discuss his feeling about the bomb with his therapist. The session seemed to calm the fears he had as a result of the death and destruction of the bomb.

On the way home from the session, he told me that he wanted to do something to help the families since most of the city had helped look for him when he and his brother got lost the summer before. I told him that I would check around to see what he could do to help. He told me "don't forget mom because I really need to help the people who helped me." I promised him that I would do what I could and I was sure there was something he could do. The next morning I hugged and kissed Charlie twice before he got on the bus for school. I told him I would make some phone calls and let him know what he could do when he got home after school.

I made a phone call to one of the television stations that helped search for our sons when they were lost. Once I informed them what Charlie wanted to do they immediately referred me to the Red Cross station at the church where the victim's families were gathered. I called the number and left a message about what our son wanted to do and informed them that the television station had referred me. Within minutes a Red Cross volunteer returned my call. They needed some toys for the children of victims' families who were waiting for word of their loved ones. I told the volunteer that I would pick up my son and have him there that afternoon. She was very appreciative to hear that my son wanted to help repay the community that helped him. "You deserve credit for raising such a conscientious and respectful son." I thanked her for her comment and told myself "she's right, after all we had been through up to now, maybe we have made some progress and left a positive mark on our sons."

I drove to my son's school and got him from class. I told his teacher what he had been asked to do and she was just as proud of him. She began to gather some toys to add to his donation. I then brought him home so he could get the toys and cars that he wanted to donate. From there, we drove to the church. I told him how proud his dad and I were that he wanted to help others. He said, "I have to mom." When we arrived at the church we walked to the door. My son was very determined to get the toys to the correct people. He asked a National Guard sergeant where he needed to go. The guard directed him to the television crew. The crew then told him to get the spokesperson's attention and tell her who he was and what he was there to do. Once he did this, the spokesperson pointed him to the drop off door. She also told him, "you should be prepared to be mobbed by many reporters. There are reporters from all over the United States as well as other countries. Once they know what you are doing you will be asked to give numerous interviews. If you don't want to do it, just tell them." He told her, "I don't mind telling people why I want to help." After he told her this, she asked him, "do you want to go national and stand at the podium for everyone to hear." "Sure, where do I go", he asked her. She told him to stay where he was and she would arrange it. I was dumbfounded, he did a lot better than I would have done.

As we were waiting for her to arrange the news brief, reporters from Arizona, North Carolina, Ohio, and several others confronted our son. Each time he was interviewed he recounted the following, "I was lost last summer and all of these people helped find me. I want to show my respect for them by helping them now." After these interviews were concluded, he was escorted to the podium. When all of the reporters were in place, he once again told why he was there and why he wanted to help. He was asked numerous questions and he answered every one of them. Needless to say he was a real trooper; he did much better than his dear, ole mother, I was a nervous wreck but too proud of him to let it interfere with his good deed. Once his interview was over, he dropped off his donation and we walked to our truck. Before we got in, an Air Force sergeant ran up to our son and said "I just want to tell you that I really liked what you did. You did a nice thing and I'm glad to see that there are kids like you who do good things for others." Needless to say our son smiled from ear to ear. It was the perfect ending to what he had just done. As we drove home I again told him how proud I was of him. I asked him how he felt and he said, "like a good person." What else could I say?

Later that afternoon, I was called by the Red Cross and asked to help at the church after the memorial service Sunday afternoon. I told the volunteer that I would be happy to help and would be there immediately following the service. When my husband arrived home from work, he told our son how proud he was of his actions. My husband then called the hospital and arranged to pick up Chris for the memorial service. Chris told the staff that he was not going to go, but this was quickly remedied when his dad said "you have no choice in this matter, you are going." Grant it, he was not happy with the ultimatum, nevertheless he was with us on that Sunday. Midway through the service, he snuggled up to my husband. My husband reached his arm around Chris and held him close. For that one moment, we were a family once again. Even in the darkest hours, the smallest beams of light can glow like a bonfire. For this one day, I forgot all of the misery we had endured since becoming parents and instead reveled in the peace that only a greater power can bestow.

I arrived at the church and checked in. Because I was a graduate student studying psychology, I was assigned as a mental health escort to one of the families. Once again, the irony of life was lived out before my eyes. I was assigned to a family who had lost their daughter. Their daughter was my age and had been adopted at the age of three years old. I informed the family that I, too, had adopted older children. We immediately experienced a bond that only adoptive parents can know. I understood their feeling of loss and they understood my feeling of endurance. I admitted to one of the family members that they had given me more than what I could ever have given them—pride in my parenting skills.

Early the next morning, our son's principal called. She had been in Louisiana during the bombing coverage and was stunned to turn on CNN and see our son being interviewed. She wanted to compliment my husband and I on our job of raising him. "After all the criticism that you have faced because of the boys' behaviors, you can hold your head high and know that you have made a difference in their lives. Hold on to that pride during whatever life deals to you in their future." She also wanted to ask me about a phone call she had received from a children's television station in Missouri. They had read an article about our son in their city newspaper and had called her to ask permission to do a story on him and his desire to donate toys to the children. She wanted my input. I told her that I would discuss it with my husband and call her back.

My husband and I decided that it would further reinforce our son's positive behavior and, as long as it was a legitimate station, we saw no problem. I called her with our decision. She said that she had already checked out the station and yes, they were legitimate children's television station. They were produced by high school journalism students and only did stories on the positive behaviors of children with the intent of portraying positive role models for other children. I told her to go ahead with the plans and we would explain it to our son. Three days later, the event took place. Our son was more nervous doing this than when he appeared before all the reporters. However, he pulled it off like a champ and told me "I really like the way I feel when I do the right things and not the wrong things." I told him to always remember that feeling. I hoped, "maybe this will be the thing that turns him around."

That weekend, Chris was discharged from the hospital and placed in a day treatment program. He was continuing to have difficulty dealing with his grandparents' absence, an issue the doctor wanted to continue to work on over the summer. In addition to the day treatment therapy, we kept both boys in counseling with our family therapist. With school out and plenty of time on their hands, I wanted to keep them busy and OUT OF MISCHIEF so I planned many activities. We worked in our garden, played in the water, went on vacation, and began planning our house construction. Most of the summer went well. Of course there were the minor spats between the boys and the occasional mishap that resulted in a lecture or grounding, but nothing explosive. Charlie still ran off when he was disciplined or did not get his way but he only went as far as his fort. The times that he did this without letting us know, we would ground him for a week. He did not like not being able to be out of our eyesight and for that summer, this tactic worked well. After every grounding, he would inform us the next time he wanted to walk away. We did not have any of the all day or overnight runaways.

One interesting event took place that summer. We received a phone call from the social worker that worked our adoption. Her department had received a letter from the half sister of the boys. She explained that someone in the office had remembered she was the boys' case manager and passed it on to her processing. It contained a picture of their sister and her new infant baby along with a letter asking to contact the boys. I told her that I did not feel very comfortable about allowing any contact due to the fact that she had helped in their kidnappings while in foster care. She said she would send the letter to us and let us decide later. After my husband and I received it, read it, and contemplated what to do, we decided against any kind of contact, written or otherwise. Since we still honored our promise of not hiding things from the boys, we told them about the letter. We told them that we had already made our decision but wanted to hear their wishes. Ironically, both of the boys wanted nothing to do with the letter or their sister. They were still afraid of her. My husband and I were relieved that the boys had no desire to contact her, it made it easier for us carry out our decision. Either way, we were not going to allow any contact. However, we were happy the boys had come to the same conclusion.

I contacted their case manager and told her of our fears. I told her that I had a feeling it was just a ploy to find out where the boys were located. She admitted that she had not thought of it that way and that she would write a letter stating that we did not wish to return the contact. Two weeks later my suspicions were confirmed.

The boys' case manager called one morning to tell me that she had mailed a letter stating our wishes. She mailed it to the post office box the sister had set up for the reply. The PO box had been closed with no forwarding address!! A wave of fear rushed over me like a ton of bricks. We were right!! There is no telling what would have happened if we had not listened to that little voice telling us "this was not an innocent act." I knew at that moment that I would never doubt that voice again. The case manager voiced the same thought, "I will never doubt your decisions regarding the boys again. There is a reason I placed them with you and it is proven with every decision you and your husband make." After I hung up the phone I thanked God for giving me the wisdom to once again make the right decision.

All in all, the rest of the summer went fairly well. I wanted to believe the bad times were all behind us but was not quite comfortable enough to completely let down my guard. "After all," I reminded myself, "the boys were just now reaching the adolescent years; a time period that I was dreading with every ounce of my being!"

School started, and for the first time in two years, both boys started school on the first day. This in itself was a positive experience because neither one of them was in a hospital. My husband and I deliberately brought this to their attention. They had not thought about it, but were pleased with themselves when we complimented them for being able to hold things together. That fall, Charlie played football and Chris participated in his first year of wrestling. They both did well in school and at home. I was very involved in my studies and loved every minute of my schooling. My husband had been offered a great job with the city, a major boost to his self-esteem. In the past, his work had suffered because of the boys' behaviors. He and I both had lost more than one job when we had to take time off for the hospital visits, family counseling, and runaways. We were off to a great start!

By mid-fall we had completed the excavation work for our house. We also had done all of the landscaping and tree planting we could do until we finished the construction. Every spare moment we had we spent laying the concrete blocks and installing water and septic lines. All of this had to be completed before we could pour the foundation for the garage. The garage became our primary goal. We were going to live in it while we built the house. This allowed us to move out of our trailer. One of our goals was at last being realized. Just as we had when we first moved to our land, our family worked together as a team. It was a wonderfully exciting time to watch our plans come together in such a positive way. After much hard work, the day finally arrived to pour the concrete.

It began as a clear, warm morning. My husband and sons were spreading the sand and gravel. The pipes were all laid and we waited for the material from the building supplier. Of course, even the best made plans can have a hitch. We were by no means strangers to Murphy's law and we should have known that if anything can go wrong we would be at the top of the list. This project was no exception. How silly of us to expect everything to go right! The materials did not arrive until after the concrete trucks arrived. Because of this we could not pour the foundation wall for the house as we had planned. All we could do was pour the foundation for the garage, shed, and the boys' clubhouses. "Oh well", we comforted ourselves, "there had to be a reason and at least we can get the garage poured so we can get the building started." Then it happened—the nice and warm, sunny weather changed in the blink of an eye.... it began to sleet and snow!! Our well-planned out day was going down the tubes right before our eyes. However, just as everything else we had encountered the past few years, we were blessed with understanding people.

The concrete workers went way beyond their call of duty and assisted my husband in spreading the concrete. It was not as smooth as we had wanted, but hey, it was poured. "So what if it has little divots all through it where the sleet landed" I told my husband. "At least we have another reminder of our life, one that we can laugh about 20 years from now." To make matters worse, he had completely ripped out the crotch of his pants while laying the wire mesh on the sand. As he stood there, soaking wet and shivering from the snow blowing into a part of his pants that no man wants snow to blow, he smiled and said "oh yeah, I forgot that we don't have a boring life." "If nothing else", I told him, "this is something the boys will never forget, these are the types of experiences that childhood memories are made of." Heaven knows they could use a few funny memories to accompany the bad ones.

Thanksgiving consisted of building the garage and eating turkey. We were all tired, but, the end was in sight and this kept us going. The boys were real troopers, they helped as much as they could. Chris was up on the roof with his dad every chance he could get. I called him my little monkey. He was not afraid of anything. Just the thought of climbing on the ladder was enough to send me in a headspin, but not him. Probably more for my own assurance than his, I convinced him to tie a rope around his waist and anchor it to one of the rafters. He obliged my request even though he looked at me like I was some kind of overprotective mother. At least if he fell, I assured myself, he would not get hurt, he would just sway back and forth until one of us got him down. We had a nice break when we took a morning to attend his first wrestling tournament. He won his first match and we were very proud of him. However, his loss on the second match was the beginning of what was to turn out to be his turn at giving my husband and I more gray hair. For the next month, he turned into a holy terror. His happy and comical personality faded, his grades slipped, and he became one of the most oppositional kids I had ever met. Here we go down that all too familiar road again.

We informed the boys that Christmas was not going to be laden with gifts. All of the extra cash we had was going into completing the garage so we could move in. We explained that it was time for them to start realizing that we were not made of money and that we had provided them with abundant Christmas' up until that point. "You are old enough to understand the real meaning of Christmas. The real meaning does not mean getting every gift you want, it is being with family, giving to others, and remembering the gift that God gave all people. Gifts come in all shapes and sizes and this year your gift is our garage and the loft that we are building for you." Naturally, they did not understand or want to accept this, but as we told them, "that is the way it is."

By the end of that week, the very meaning of Christmas that we had explained to the boys was to be played out before us. My best friend and the boys' school provided our Christmas. My husband and I swallowed our pride the day that Charlie's teacher called and told us that the school had adopted our family that year. They had gifts for the boys and Christmas dinner for the family. They also had bags of groceries to stock our cabinets. It was a very humbling experience. My husband and I had never been on the receiving end and it proved to be much harder than giving. In addition, my best friend took me shopping for the boys. It was one of the most embarrassing events of my life. "I am not used to this and feel more comfortable giving than getting" I admitted to her. "Just as you have done for me in the past?" she questioned. She had me on that and there was no argument I could come up with that matched her statement. "For the last five years you two have done everything for the boys and now it is time that you allow other people to help you and let you experience some of the joy that you have given others. I will not take "no" for an answer so you take whatever you get this year and know that someone is looking out for your family." It is a Christmas that I will never forget. I guess you are never too old to add to your collection of memories!!

With Christmas behind us, my husband and I were able to concentrate on getting Chris some help. He was getting worse each day. He was destroying property, chewing on his clothes, and withdrawing into his own inner world. This was the last signal that we needed because he had always been very open and talkative. We called his case manager and she arranged an assessment for the second day of January. We knew he was going into the hospital. Although we had been through this before with the boys, this time felt different. Chris had never been in a hospital because of his own issues. After all that he had been through prior to the adoption, and afterwards with his brothers and my family, I felt an inner peace knowing that he needed time that was all his own. Sure it was a relief in the sense that we got a break from his behaviors, but it was a different type of relief than we had experienced before. We *just knew* that he would be fine. We never had a doubt that he would return home. Therefore, the day his doctor suggested otherwise by telling us to consider relinquishing his adoption, we were flabbergasted.

Chapter 17

Which One Now

January was unusually cold. Nevertheless, we spent our spare time working on the garage so we could move into it. We had numerous setbacks. The water pipes kept bursting. My husband would no sooner fix one busted connection than the next one up the line would blow. He spent two weekends going around in circles. During this time, we had to stay with a neighbor. Finally, out of complete frustration, he called the supplier. They sent a representative to inspect the materials. To my husband's credibility, it was not his fault. The supplier had sent the incorrect supplies. My neighbor and I both had to apologize to my husband for giving him such a hard time for "not being able to connect two pipes without problems." Luckily for us, he laughed with us after he learned of the real cause of the trouble. "I was beginning to doubt my own abilities", he told us. As it turned out, the supplier paid to reinstall the entire line, paid for the rental of the trenching equipment, put us up in a hotel for a week, and compensated us for the inconvenience. I guess good things do come to those who wait. But the wait can sure be a frustrating time and we, of all people, did not need any further frustration. Oh, but we had to remember who we were.

My husband had taken a part time weekend job to help cover some of the expenses. Since I had gone back to school and unable to work due to the boys' hospital stays, we had lost a major part of our income. It was Saturday morning and my husband had just arrived at the hotel room from his part time job. He was very tired so I told him that I would take Charlie home and get things ready to lay the new pipe. He said he would get some sleep and meet us in a couple of hours. While I was busy getting the heat turned on in the garage, our son again chose to cause problems. He ran away.

He had gotten out of bed in one of the moods that always preceded his bad behavior. He defied everything I told him to do and purposely did just the opposite. I had learned to confront him on the spot when he acted this way or he would continue to cause problems. I stopped him, let him know the ifs, ands, and buts about his misbehavior, and then told him to sit until he could change his attitude. He chose to go outside and sit by the dog. I kept a close eye on him because I had a feeling he would take off. Sure enough, when I turned my back for an instant he ran. I waited for a few minutes to see if he would come back on his own, but he didn't. I could not find our phone book and did not know the address of the hotel for the operator, so I went to my neighbors and looked up the hotel. I called my husband. I could hear the frustration in his voice when he said he was on his way. The frustration of not only being up all night and getting no sleep, but, also for another runaway was obvious in his voice. He told me to wait at the garage in case he showed up.

When my husband arrived, he told me that he had decided not to call the sheriff until that evening. "You told him that we were not going to chase him anymore if he chose to run, so we are going to stick with it." I agreed. We could not continue to allow him to have the power in these situations because he knew the consequences of his actions. Not only had we warned him, but also, so had the sheriff and therapists. We therefore, proceeded with our work; it was not until that night when we were ready to go back to the hotel that we called the sheriff to report our son as a runaway.

The sheriff we had worked with previously was off duty but the one that showed up was aware of our son and his behaviors. We told him all of the pertinent information. He then left to look for our son. He told us to stay there in case our son came back. He said, "I would not worry too much this time because he sounds like he is very resourceful and can take care of himself. He will curl up somewhere to keep warm." I replied, "Yes, he will crawl up in someone's barn and steal food if he has to." The officer then said, "you did the right thing by not chasing him because he thinks this is a game. As long as he can lure you to chase him, he will continue to do it to have the control." As he turned to leave, he told us he would call in an hour or so to inform us if he had located our son. My husband told the officer that we were staying at a hotel until our water line was repaired. The officer said, "Then if he does not show up in an hour or so, go ahead and leave. Your son will just have to pay the consequences of his actions." We thanked him and he left. We decided to wait the hour and then leave if our son did not show up.

An hour passed and the sheriff called. He asked if our son had returned. When we told him no, he said that he had searched the area but could not find him. I asked if it was okay for us to leave, he said yes. He also told us he would contact us the next day, but if anything came up before then to call the office and have him paged. With that we headed out the door to leave. I stepped out the door and stumbled over something on the step. It was a rock. Our son had written a note asking to come home and left it on the step. He was in his clubhouse waiting for us. "Waiting for us," I said to my husband. "I wish we had left before he had the chance to leave a note and let him suffer out the night alone in his clubhouse." My husband agreed. He sent me on to the hotel and said he would get our son and meet me there. He told me I probably did not want to hear what he had to say to our son. It was a father-son thing, he informed me. I knew by his statement that he was running out of patience with the running away and I also knew that I needed to stay out of this one. I never found out what my husband said that night but it must have been potent because our son did not run away for another four months!

On the way to the hotel I remember asking myself "how long will this continue to go on. How long do we have to live through the hell that the boys are dishing out." I had not reached the end of my hope. I was expecting the boys to change their actions because of our help. Soon after that night, I realized there was nothing we could do to make them change; only they could change their behaviors! They had to take ownership of their actions and take responsibility for them. As long as we took the responsibility for their behaviors, we would remain frustrated. We had to place their behaviors right back into their laps; this gave the responsibility back to the boys and forced them to deal with their consequences. We had tried everything else and I knew we had nothing to lose. I later explained this to my husband and he agreed, yet it was much more difficult to implement than to say. However, within a couple of months two major events, one with each boy, provided us with the opportunity we needed to carry out our new approach of dealing with their misbehaviors.

A couple of weeks later, we went furniture shopping. While we were out, my husband, older son, and I ate lunch. As we were sitting there discussing Chris, my husband said, "look who is walking in the door." I turned and saw my sister. "What should I do?" I asked both of them. "There is no way to leave without her seeing me." Our son said, "Mom just stay here and if she talks to you just ignore her." I told him that I would not ignore her, I would be pleasant. "There has to be a reason that we have run into each other after all these months" I told both of them. "Let's just do what we know is right and let God handle the rest."

My sister came around the corner and instantly saw me. "What are you doing on this side of town?" she asked. "We had some errands to run" I answered. Next she noticed my wrist in a cast and asked about it. "I broke it building our garage." "Oh, are you living in it yet?" she inquired. "Not yet, but we are just about to move in." I then asked when the baby was due. It seemed to take her off guard when I said "and it's a boy this time." She said she had about six weeks to go. Next, she asked where Chris was. I did not know what to say so I remained quiet. She asked again and my husband answered "he's in a hospital." She did not say anything so I asked her "do you want to know why?" She replied "I guess so." I told her why he was there—he could not accept the fact that he had no contact with my family. I told her that he also did not understand why she wouldn't celebrate her birthday with him anymore. "Well there is nothing I can do about it, I have to do what my husband tells me to do." I wanted to speak my opinion about that statement, but decided it wasn't worth it. Instead, I asked how my nieces were. I asked her to give them a hug for me and tell them 'hi' for me. With this she said good bye and left. When we left a few minutes later, I waved to her but she did not respond. I could not understand the meaning of this encounter. I only knew that there was a reason and it was meant to be. I was hurt that she did not seem more concerned about me but I let it go.

Within three weeks we had completed the water lines and installed the heater in the garage. We moved into the garage on Valentines Day because I wanted to wake up in my *new* house the next morning, my birthday! I woke up with a pride that only one can have after accomplishing a major goal. In addition, I came to the conclusion that I was going to cancel the therapy scheduled with Chris. I was not about to spend *another birthday* in a hospital with a son. My husband called our son's therapist and explained this to her. To our amazement, she was in absolute agreement. She told us she was glad to hear that we were making the boys work around our schedule and not the other way around. "Wow" I told my husband, "this stuff really works." For the rest of the day I did what I wanted to do, not what the boys wanted me to do.

We had seen Chris once prior to moving into the garage. All he did was try to convince us that he had learned his lesson and was ready to come home. What he did not realize was that my husband and I had become real pros at seeing through his bologna. When we told him that his ploy was not working, he became infuriated. He did not talk the rest of the session. We had already anticipated this prior to the session and told his therapist of our plan to get up and leave. She was in full agreement and played her part perfectly. When our son did not respond for 5 minutes, I looked at his therapist and said, "Well we are going now. I have homework to do and my husband needs to get back to work. We will talk to you later." She replied, "yes and I have some important things to do also." With that we told her good-bye and, without acknowledging our son's presence, left the room. As we walked out of the room I caught a glimpse of our son; he was sitting there with the most astonished look I had ever seen on his face. His look said it all; "hey, they just left me sitting here, now what do I do?" As his therapist unlocked the door she looked at my husband and I and winked. On the drive home I told my husband, "it worked." He smiled and said, "yeah, we did not allow him to have control of this session as we have done in the past. Whether we do the same in the next session will also depend on his behavior! The sooner he learns that, the better off he will be."

During the next session Chris tried, again, to gain the upper hand. However, we stopped him early in the session. It began just as the previous session; he said that he was ready to come home because he did not like the hospital. He told us that he would try to do the right things. He then asked me if he could come home. Before I could answer him, my husband shook his head and said "No." This angered our son and he glared at his dad. After he saw that my husband was not going to budge on this issue, he asked "why not." This was the opening my husband needed to set our son straight. "First of all", he began, "you know the difference between good and bad behavior. Secondly, you have used the same line for the last four years. You always say you will try. Then you go ahead and do what is wrong. Then afterwards you tell me you are sorry about what you did. Well, I will no longer accept your *trying*. You either choose to do the right thing or you choose to do the wrong thing, but you will not hide behind the excuse *I will try*. Now, if I know that there is something mom and I have not taught you and you make a mistake, then that is a different story. We will not get onto you for that; we never have and we will not start now. It is your choice." Our son was so livid that his dad had confronted him with the truth, which left him no room for hedging, that he got up and stormed to the door. I was so proud of my husband for finally standing firm with our son that I stepped in.

"Get your little butt back over here now and sit down", I demanded. His therapist joined in and said, "you are not leaving this room." If looks could kill, all three of us would have been doomed. Chris stormed back and slammed himself down in his chair. His therapist looked at me as if to say "go ahead, it's your turn." I looked our son square in the eye and sternly said "you do not have the authority to leave this room just because you do not want to accept the truth. Dad and I, or your therapist will tell you when you can leave. Now you are going to listen to me. I have put up with your little tantrums as long as I am going to. Dad and I have made as many changes as we are going to make. From now on you will abide by the rules we make. If you choose not to, then you will have to pay the consequence. There will be no more changes made for you. We have moved for you, lost jobs for you, protected you from your brother, and given up friends and family for you, but no more. Life does not revolve around you and it is time that you grow up and act your age. Your actions have hurt too many people. You are rude and do not care who you hurt as long as you are the center of attention. Part of the reason that your grandparents do not want anything to do with you is because of the way you treated them. You stole from them and you lied to them. Then you expected them to do everything for you while you continued to act the same way. You are mad at your aunt for not wanting to have her birthday with you. Well you hurt her feelings when she was pregnant. You smarted off *'you are fat and need to go on some walks'*. And, speaking of birthdays, the reason I did not come last week was because I was NOT going to spend another birthday in a hospital because of a son who could not act like a son. Finally, there is your dad. You treat him like he is dirt under your feet. He has taken up for you for the last time. Well, let me tell you one thing, mister, he is my husband and you will not treat him like that anymore. If you want to be a lonely person and push everyone out of your life than that is your business. But, when you try to split up dad and I, then, you have crossed the line. We almost divorced because of you boys, but we realized our marriage was more important than that. We will not ruin what we have because of you or your brothers. The end of the line has come and you are no longer the center of our attention." I then looked at his therapist and said, "we are leaving now and I will talk to you next week."

She escorted us out of the room and to the doors. While she unlocked the door she said, "Now we will see what he does with it. I'll keep in touch." With that my husband and I left. On the drive home I admitted that it was one of the toughest things I had done with Chris, but I knew it was needed. My husband muttered, "he did not say one word to me until I told him he could not come home. That was the final straw for me, especially since I had to take time off of work to attend his sessions." I had not noticed it until he told me but he was right. I felt more empathy for him than our son at that moment. My husband dearly loved our son and he was deeply hurt over his actions.

For the next two months Chris refused to talk to or see us. He would not cooperate with the staff members or his therapist. He told them that he never wanted to see us again. When his therapist called to tell me this I said, "I have told him many times that he needs to be careful what he asks for because sometimes he just might get it." "Yes, he may have to learn this the hard way. Do not worry about coming for a family session until he changes his attitude," she told us. "I do not want to waste your time or mine." We waited.

His therapist related something his doctor suggested which totally shocked us. His doctor suggested we consider terminating the adoption. "Do what" I asked. She told me that the doctor did not see any other solution to our son's opposition and defiance. The only other option the doctor could suggest was to find a long-term foster care placement for our son. I told her that I would have to discuss this with my husband and our other son. I also told her that we would want Chris' input before we could make a final decision. We had always asked for the boys input on major decisions, even if we did not agree with, or decide to act in accordance to, their wishes. She told me that she would ask our son what he wanted to do and get back to me. "By the way," I told her, "his birthday is in a few weeks so we will give him his wish about leaving him alone and see if he still feels the same way." She agreed that was a perfect thing to do. "We will also ignore his birthday and see how he reacts because he will be expecting the staff to do something. Time will tell."

His therapist called back within a couple of days and said that Chris "did not want to come home and he wanted to go to a foster home." I told her that my husband and I had not made a decision yet, although we had been checking into some options. We still had not talked to either of our sons and wanted to do this before we made any final decisions. "We will call Chris soon to confirm his wishes" I informed her. Later that week we did just that.

My husband called the hospital and asked to speak to our son. He used the speakerphone so we could talk to him at the same time. The nurse called him to the phone. But, when she told him that it was his dad, he refused to answer the phone. My husband told the nurse he did not care what our son wanted and that he wanted to talk to him. However, the nurse told him that there was nothing she could do. Before we could say anything, we heard our son in the background say "wait there is one thing I want to say." He shouted across the room "I'm fine with the decision, good bye." and hung up the phone. My husband was furious. He paced the floor and said, "that's it." I knew he was hurt and did not know if I should say something or remain quiet and let him talk. "If he won't even talk to us on the phone about a decision as important as this then he's outta here. I am going to find someplace for him to go. He is not coming back here and make my life a living hell anymore." Charlie, in his non-chalant way, said "what a dumb kid." I looked at him and said, "boy you have a lot of room to talk after all of your runaway stunts." He knew he had just stuck his foot in his mouth and said, "I know we have a good home." All I could do was smile and say, "what is that? What did you just say?" He hung his head and mumbled "you heard me mom."

After my husband calmed down, I told him that I would support whatever he decided. Frankly, I too was tired of the life the boys had brought to us. I knew it sounded selfish, but, we could do nothing more for Chris, it was all up to him now. "Honey" I told my husband, "we have done everything we can do and sacrificed everything we have to keep our family together. There is nothing left for us to do." We decided to let whatever happened with Chris, happen. If he was not going to work on coming back home, then there was nothing we could do to change it. I called his therapist the next day and told her to start looking for any placement she could find. I told her we had exhausted all of the ones we knew. Besides, his birthday was the next week. "It will be interesting how reality affects him" I told her.

For the next three weeks I kept in constant contact with his therapist. She was calling every foster care, treatment center, and boys home that she could find but was not having any luck. I asked her how our son was doing and she said "interestingly enough, his attitude about home has softened. He has been talking about missing the dogs and school." I asked her what he had done on his birthday. "Well, he was very quiet the entire day. He appeared anxious every time the door opened. It was as if he was expecting someone he knew to come in. We didn't make a big deal out of the day and I did not tell him Happy Birthday until he reminded me that it was his birthday. Then I just said 'oh that's right, happy birthday.' I then reminded him that he did not want to see you and you were abiding by his wishes." She said the anticipation on his face suddenly disappeared. "Reality hit home" she said. "I knew it" I told her. He did not think we would actually ignore him on his day. When he was reminded that he got his wish, it suddenly did not seem as big and brave as it sounded. I suggested "since we are all having a difficult time finding a placement for him let's ride it out for a while and see if he makes any change in his behaviors and attitude." She agreed to do this and call me with any changes.

Another week passed. It was a Friday afternoon and I was in town running some errands. A song came on the radio that Chris and I had claimed as 'our song'. I was suddenly overwhelmed with a sense of wanting to see him and give him a big hug. I decided to go to the hospital, surprise him with a visit, and see how he reacted. It had been two months since I had seen him. The receptionist paged our son's therapist. When she came in, I told her why I was there. "This is a great idea, let's go see how he reacts to you," she said. I was very anxious, but had already told myself that I was going to be calm, cool, and collected. I was going to approach him in a light hearted manner, a "I was just thinking about you and wanted to see you."

Chris walked in, saw me, and said "hi mom." I was completely surprised; I was not expecting the change that had taken place during the past two months. He had gained nearly 50 pounds, he was taller, *and* to top it off, eerily was a spitting image of his oldest brother. I had to take a double look to convince myself that I was looking at Chris and NOT Wayne, the brother we had not seen in years. "Boy, you have gotten big" instinctively rolled out of my mouth. "Yea, I've gained a lot of weight in here" he replied as I hugged him. His therapist jumped in, "we have been working to get some of the weight off of him because he has gained more than he should." I told him that I was glad to see that he had put some weight on because he was too skinny when he went into the hospital. "I know, but I need to lose some of this" he replied. We sat down.

"What are you doing here mom?" "I just wanted to see you. I had no idea when I left home this morning that I was coming here, but while I was running errands I heard our song and started thinking about you. I wanted to see you so I drove here. Nobody knows I am here, I did not even know myself until I pulled into the parking lot. So, here I am." The smile on his face seemed to confirm my belief that he would be receptive to me. I knew in my heart that he was not angry with me and I told him "I know you are not angry with me, you only want me to think you are. In fact, I don't even think you are angry with dad. It's just that we are the ones you are taking it out on. I know who you are really angry at and I think you do too, don't you?" He hung his head and was very quiet. "You are angry with your birthparents and my family." He looked at me and nodded his head. "I am also angry cause my aunt won't see me and she won't let me see my cousins either." At that moment I knew I had the opportunity that I had waited on for the past four months. It was an opportunity to discuss his feelings and behaviors.

"I understand how hurt you are over everything that has happened in your life. I wish I could change everything bad that has happened to you but I can't. Nobody can. If I could take it all away and start again with you as my birthson, I would do it in a heartbeat. I can't. There is nothing I can do to make it go away. It happened and now you have to learn how to deal with it. Everyone has had bad things happen to him or her. The only thing you can do now is figure out a way to beat it instead of letting it beat you. I know you can beat it because you are a very strong and smart boy. But, let me tell you one thing. You are not going to add dad and I to the list of people who have abandoned you. If you decide not to come home it will be because you abandoned us, not us abandoning you. I will not allow you to add my name to your long list of people. And, before you say it, I will let you know that, NO, it should never have happened to you in the first place. But, as I said, there is nothing you or anyone else can do to change your past. You only have two choices, accept it and go on or let it ruin the rest of your life. It's your choice, I can't do it for you." At this point he once again hung his head and mumbled something. Neither his therapist nor I could understand him so I asked him what he said. He mumbled "nothing, it doesn't matter." His therapist said "yes it matters it's just that we did not hear you, tell us again." He crossed his arms and became very isolate.

For the next five minutes or so, his therapist and I sat and waited. She looked at me and mouthed "what do you want to do?" I mouthed back "just wait." I knew that, with time, he would open up. He had never been able to close himself off completely and I knew he needed some space at that moment. Finally, he looked up at me. With fire in his face, he blurted out the words to the song *Love Will Build a Bridge* (a song by the Judds). When he finished I asked him "what did that mean?" Once again he said "nothing." I continued to ask him to explain it because I wanted to know what he was trying to say. After a couple of prompts he began to soften and he shouted, "it means that I love you." I said, "well why didn't you just come out and say it?" "Because I was afraid to," he cried. "There is no reason for you to be afraid to tell me that you love me because I know you do. He had a look of total amazement on his face when I said that. "I will always love you, it's your behaviors that I do not like. There is nothing you can do to make dad and I stop loving you, but, there is a lot you can do to make dad and I not love your behavior." With this he began to talk and the aura of defensiveness he had displayed a few minutes earlier faded.

"You know, I can't make you happy, only you can do that. There are a lot of things I can do for you but I cannot change your behavior and I cannot make you happy. Until you are happy with yourself everything else in life is going to seem bad. But if you are happy with yourself, then the bad things in life don't seem as bad, they just happen and then they go away." "That's right," his therapist said. I continued, "Let me tell you about a foster kid on your brother's baseball team. He is always happy. When I asked him why he is so happy he told me 'why not'. He is right. So you see, you can either be a happy person or a sad person but either way bad things can still happen to you. The trick to life is to decide which person you are going to be. Are you going to enjoy your life or let life enjoy you and beat you down? Only you can make that choice. Dad and I can help you but we can't make the choice for you or be happy for you." Our son looked confused and unable to grasp what I was saying. My husband and I had learned long before that day that we had to be blunt with our sons in order to get our point across. They had witnessed too much in their lives to tolerate skirting embarrassing facts. I decided to explain what I had just said as bluntly as I knew how.

"Let me explain it this way. It's kind of like when you get married and you have sex with your wife, only you can do that, dad and I can't do it for you. Sure, we can tell you how and get you books to help you learn how, but, we can't do it for you." Instantly, our son smiled and relaxed. "Oh mom," he snickered, "I get it now." He began to talk about how he had not been a happy person since his birthparents left him. "Is it sort of like a rat in a maze that has to find it's way out," he asked? "Yea" I told him "it's exactly like that." "When a rat gets caught in a corner it has to turn around and find another way to get out of the maze. So, I guess I have just been sitting in the corner waiting for someone else to get me out. But, I am the one who has to find my way out because nobody else can do it for me", he confessed. Both his therapist and I agreed with him. "And I guess I can be happy or sad but I still have to find my way out of the maze don't I mom?" "That's right. I will help you as much as I can, but, you have to make the decision" I told him. With this, I told him that I needed to get home before his brother got home from school. I told him I loved him and he gave me a big hug. "Thanks for coming mom, I love you."

As I drove home, I relived the events of the last two hours over and over in my mind. I was grateful for listening to the little voice in my head that morning when it told me to go see our son. I always obeyed that voice when it spoke to me about our sons and had never regretted it. This was no exception. Once again, I was led in the right direction; the thing I had to do now was leave the outcome to a higher power than myself. I stopped by my husband's office. I was very anxious to tell him about my day and the demeanor of our son when I left him. I knew that my husband would be intrigued but I also knew that he was still deeply hurt. Somehow, I had to convince him that there would be a positive outcome to this event. Sure enough, after I related the visit to my husband, he had a guarded optimism. "I have a feeling he will call us" I told my husband. "Let's just leave it up to him and see what he does with it" I urged. He agreed. I told him I would pick up Charlie and meet him at the baseball field. On the way to the practice field, I told Charlie about my day. He did not respond.

Chapter 18

Nightmares Aren't This Bad

The first thing I did when we got home that evening was check our answering machine. As I anticipated, Chris had called. When I informed my husband, he grinned. My husband wanted to have our family together, so, when it appeared possible, he was astonished. I played the message for my husband and Charlie. "Hi, it's me. I just called to say hi but since you aren't home I'll call you later." Privately and in our own way, the three of us fantasized about a future as a family. However, we did not realize it at the time that Charlie's fantasy differed from ours. I rationalized Charlie's solitude over this new development by believing he was protecting himself from a painful experience if his brother did not come home. Well, I was totally wrong.

Before the weekend was over, Chris called us back. He talked to his dad then asked to talk to his brother. Charlie was reserved afterwards, but I attributed it to mixed emotions. Never, in my wildest imagination, did I anticipate that Charlie was plotting revenge for losing his spot as the only child at home. I mistakenly assumed Charlie shared in our excitement of being together again. I was heartbroken when Charlie regressed back to his unruly behaviors. The lying started as well as the provoking, stealing, and running away. He initiated fights with other children at school and returned to playing the victim. Hoping to combat his problems, we increased his therapy sessions. However, this did not curb his misbehaviors. He knew what to say to please our therapist, that is, if he said anything at all. What he did relate, was muddled in half-truths or blatant lies. Money, once again, began disappearing from our home. Not only did our money disappear, but his piggy bank savings were also dwindling. When I confronted him, he told me that he needed it to buy pencils for school. I reminded him that his dad and I would take care of his school supplies, all he had to do was tell us that he needed something.

I also began noticing that he was not taking his lunch bag to school. When I asked him about this, he told me that he put his lunch in his backpack. I believed this the first time, but after he used this excuse several times, I began to have doubts. My doubts were soon confirmed when the principle called to inform us that Charlie owed money for several school lunches. When I questioned this situation, his principle was not certain what was taking place. She promised to check into it. After checking, she called to tell us that he had charged several lunches over the course of the two weeks, the same amount of time that had elapsed since Chris began to initiate contact with us.

In addition to charging lunches, Charlie came home one day with money he *"borrowed"* from his teachers to pay for his baseball fee. When he begged us to let him play baseball, we agreed on one condition. We told him that since we had paid for his entire football fee and uniform a few months earlier he would need to help with his baseball fee. We would, however, pay for his uniform. The baseball fee was sixty dollars. We informed Charlie that we would pay $50.00 of the fee but he had to save

$10.00 from his spending money to pay the rest. We told him he had five weeks to save the money and it would only be about two dollars a week. He agreed that was fair. Yet, on the day his part of the fee was due, he did not have the money. Therefore, when he came home with the money and told us that he had borrowed it from his teachers, we told him he had to take it back because he had not earned it. Furthermore, we told him that he had been given plenty of time to save the amount he needed. All of this, in addition to the lunch charge incident, convinced me that he was doing something with the money, we just had to find out what it was.

The next day Charlie left me a note saying, in addition to the teachers' money, he had taken some money out of his bank to pay for his lunch charges. I called the school to confirm that he actually had paid his bill. I was told that he had come into the office to pay his charges however, the amount he had taken minus the amount of his bill did not add up to the amount of change he brought back home that afternoon. My husband and I immediately queried our son about the unaccounted for money. He told us he did not know what happened to the rest of the money because "this is all of the change the lady gave me." We told him his story did not make sense, yet, he continued to hedge the issue. He then told us the cafeteria ladies made him eat two lunches. We knew this was a lie but decided to ask his principal anyway. Our suspicions were valid. She told us "we do not make children eat a school lunch when they have a lunch from home."

That evening I went outside to water my seedlings and flowers. My husband was nearby working on our mower. He called Charlie over and asked him point blank "why did you have lunch charges at school?" He replied, "I took a sandwich, an apple, and a juice for lunch but the cafeteria ladies *made me eat a school lunch too.*" I turned around, doused our son, and said, "why don't you try the truth for once." He then turned to run. I knew that if he was not stopped he would be gone and we would have to once again call the sheriff's office and report him as a runaway. I yelled, "come back here." He stopped, turned and looked at me, then turned back around to run. Although he was a few feet from me I reached for him and grabbed him by his arm. In the process we both slipped in the mud. Several things flashed through my mind. I remembered the hospital staff and the police officers telling me that we had the right to restrain our son from running. I also remembered the time my husband had to chase our son. I did not have time to think through my decision, I chose to restrain him from running. As I tried to hold him still, he twisted around and began to beat his head on the ground. Every time I tried to grab his arm he wiggled free. I looked up and saw my husband coming over to help. He knew as well as I that if Charlie got loose, he would take off running. I was not capable of catching him, but my husband was. Suddenly, Charlie stopped kicking and twisting. We were both drenched. I went inside to change clothes. Charlie got the weed eater out of the shed and mowed around the house. He never offered an explanation about the lunches or the missing money. Knowing it would be fruitless to try to get an honest answer, we did not ask again.

Later that evening, we noticed Charlie had a black eye from banging his head on the ground. We laid him on the sofa and put an ice bag on his eye. As he was lying on the sofa we tried to talk to him about his running behavior. We wanted to understand why he continued to run instead of facing his problems. As we had done many times in the past, we explained that running only made things worse. While we were talking to him he informed us "I am going to tell the school that you gave me the black eye when you punished me." My husband and I looked at each other in disbelief and walked outside. We knew him well enough to know that he could convince anyone of anything, anything that he wanted them to believe, that is. I remarked to my husband "boy, we are damned if we do and damned if we don't." He agreed and said "if we had only known what it was going to be like before we adopted them, we would not have done it." It was the first time he had ever voiced his regrets about the adoption. I knew that he was at the end of his rope. We decided that the best thing for us to do was to contact the sheriff and explain what had actually taken place and why I restrained our son in the first place. We were going to visit

Chris the next afternoon and decided to stop by our sheriff's house on our way back home.

The visit with Chris was pleasant. We talked about his progress and what his plans were. He told us that he wanted to come home because he realized that home was a good place. We asked him how he intended to carry out his plan and he said, "I already am. I am obeying the rules and talking to my counselor. I have some problems that I still need to fix but I am working on it." My husband and I both complimented him on his hard work and told him that we were glad he decided to be part of our family. Then, Chris, in his familiar and blunt manner, asked his brother about the black eye. He had never been one to mince his words. Instead, when he had something on his mind, he made no bones about coming right out and asking. "What is wrong with your eye? Did you get into another fight at school?" he asked. Charlie replied, "no I got in trouble." "Well, why don't you ask him to tell you the whole truth" I told Chris. "Well?" he asked as he glared at his brother. "Tell me, I'm listening." As my husband and I suspected, Charlie told about half of the story. Of course it was the half that depicted him as the victim.

"Oh stop it" Chris replied. "Why can't you ever tell what really happened. I don't believe you. I think you did something and you are trying to blame mom just like you always do. I know you and you know it." I decided it would be best to explain the incident to Chris because he was becoming upset with his brother. When I finished telling him about the things his brother had been doing for the past couple of weeks and how he actually got the black eye, Chris was furious. "I am really mad at you" he told Charlie. He looked straight at him and continued. "I am in this place and I am working very hard to come home. But you are home and you are working harder to get put here. I just don't get you. You know, if you don't make yourself happy, none of us can do it for you." I chuckled to myself. He was telling his brother the same things I said the day I unexpectedly dropped in for a visit. He turned and said, "Yes mom I heard every word you said that day and you were right. Boy was I acting stupid then but not anymore. Now", he turned back to Charlie, "you are doing the same thing. Mom and dad can't change our past; it is up to us to change our future. Do you want to change or not? If you don't then fine but I am coming home and you better get used to the idea." With this Charlie hung his head and remained silent. I could tell by his expression that his brother's words had hit home. The only thing I was not sure of was how Charlie would react; would he straighten up or was this the beginning of another episode from hell. I should have known it would be the latter of the two.

We left the hospital and told Chris that we would call him that week. He was not happy about staying, but convinced himself that he needed to stay a little longer to work on his problems. With that he gave me a hug and my husband took him back to his unit. While he was gone, Charlie was quiet as usual. I left him alone with his thoughts. We stopped by the sheriff's house and our son explained his black eye. The sheriff asked our son if he wanted to talk privately, but our son said no. With that the sheriff talked to our son about doing the right thing at school the next day when the teachers asked him about his eye. Our son said he would take care of it. Take care of it he did! He twisted his story around to make it sound as if I had hit him. When he did not show up after school, I knew that something bad had happened. An hour later, we found out that he had been placed in protective custody. I told my husband that it was he and I who needed to be placed in protective custody because being the parents of the boys had placed us on the endangered species list! Nevertheless, we were informed to show up at a hearing the next day and appear before the judge. It would be decided then what the next course of action would be; whether the state decided to keep him or release him to us. I honestly did not know what to expect or even what I wanted to happen.

My husband and I showed up for the hearing and waited for hours. When it appeared that it was our turn to see the judge, we were informed that no charges had been filed and that we were free to leave. We never saw the judge. We were told to get our son and go home. After all the anxiety caused by the past two days, I was confused. We asked the authorities if there was anything they could do to help us with our son. As before, we were told that unless we were charged with criminal actions, they could not intervene. Here we were again, unsupported with a very difficult child; a child that could cause major disruptions in our family when he did not get his way. We were told that if we did not pick up our son we would immediately be placed in jail. When we inquired about alternative plans for our son, the supervisor in charge called the police department and requested a police officer. Before we even made it to the door to get our son, an officer appeared to arrest us. We had no choice but to pick up our son. We took him home and waited for his next big episode. His next one, however, topped all others that he had tried.

That evening we called Chris to tell him what had happened. Since we had never lied to the boys or kept things from them, his therapist agreed this should not be the first time. We also felt that it would be best to tell Chris while he was still in the hospital. That way, he could process his feelings about his brother's antics with his therapist. When I told Chris about the incident he was furious. He could not understand why his brother would intentionally lie about the black eye and risk losing the family. "Mom I just don't understand. I am here and I want to come home but my brother is there and wants to be here. It just doesn't make any sense. Maybe you could swap us and let me come home." I explained that he was not ready to come home yet. However, in his mind, it did not add up. No amount of reassurance on my part was able to convince him that everything would work out for the best. "Well, I don't understand Mom, but, you are the boss. I just want you to know that I don't like it." I told him I knew it was difficult to understand, but he would have to trust us.

With Chris taken care of, I still had to face Charlie and the anger I felt about his lies. I was very upset with him and decided to tell him exactly how I felt. Instead of talking to him about his behaviors and the trouble it had caused, I chose to concentrate on my feelings. I explained how hurt I was that he would intentionally lie about me. Not only had his lies caused me great pain, but they also hurt his dad and brother. I explained how frustrated I was with him and that I was beginning to doubt that he wanted a family. He raised his head and looked at me. I knew him well enough to know that my statement had gotten his attention. Even though I wanted him to respond, I knew it would be fruitless to try and elicit one from him. I had his attention so I decided to keep the focus on my feelings. I told him that I loved him but right then, at that instant, I honestly did not know if I wanted to have him at home. I explained that I brought him home because I was forced to make a decision between him and myself. "You are here because I did not want to ruin my future by going to jail. While you are here, you will live by our rules. If you choose to break the rules you will have to suffer the consequences. You have lived with us long enough to know what the rules are so I will not accept any excuses. When you are 18 years old, you can leave home and make your own rules. When that time comes, then I will be glad to help you pack your bags. Until then, I am responsible for you and you will abide by the rules whether you like them or not. Now, you will eat your dinner, take a shower and go to bed. Tomorrow morning we will discuss how you are going to straighten out the mess you caused at your school. You caused it and you will take care of it." I turned and walked away. As I did, I suddenly realized I had taken a stance with Charlie that I never had, one that needed to be taken long ago.

The next morning I took Charlie for a psychological assessment. Upon their recommendation, we increased his therapy sessions. After monitoring his behaviors for a couple of weeks, it would be decided what action, if any, would be taken. When we got home, I told Charlie he had to call his therapist himself and set an appointment. I hoped that by having him do it, he would be taking the responsibility for his actions. After he hung up from his therapist, he sat down and began to talk. I was surprised because it was the first time he had initiated any type of conversation after one of his behavioral episodes. I decided to give him my full attention and let him lead the conversation. I was not sure what sparked him to do this, but

I was going to reinforce it as much as I could. For all I knew, it could have been one of his manipulative ploys. Whatever his reason, I gave him the benefit of a doubt and my undivided attention.

"I have an appointment for this week and two appointments next week. After that, my therapist said we could schedule the next ones. I have to decide what I am going to tell my school when I go back. I don't know what I should do. Can you tell me what to do?" I looked at him and replied "I have always told you to tell the whole truth no matter how hard the truth is for you. If you had told the whole truth in the first place you would not be in this situation. I have noticed that you only tell the part of the truth that makes you look good. But, that is just as wrong as lying. You know, I could have only told half the truth yesterday when I picked you up. I could have said that you started running away for no reason but that would only be half the truth. Yes, you started to run away but it was because you had been caught in a lie and did not want to admit it. Do you see the difference here between the whole truth and only half of it?" "Yes, but it is hard for me to tell the truth" he mumbled. "I know it's hard. It is hard for everyone, not just you. It was hard for me to admit that I did not want to bring you home. When I admitted that I was admitting that I did not want to deal with your lies. But, it was the truth and I told it. If I had told you that I had no problem about bringing you home, what would you have thought?" "I would have thought that what I did was okay." "Exactly! And if you thought it was okay then you would not have to accept the fact that you were wrong and have to face the pain that you caused our family. But, when I told you the truth about your actions, you had to experience some of the pain with the rest of us." "Wow, Mom I never thought of it like that. Tell me some more." While I had his attention, I tried to think of another analogy to get my point across. For some reason, I decided to use a color example to solidify our conversation.

"What if I told you something was blue? That would only be half the truth because there are many different kinds of blue. There is sky blue, navy blue, and royal blue. But, there are also many others types of blue.

So, if I did not tell you the whole truth, you may think of one kind of blue while I meant another kind of blue. The color blue is only half the truth; the kind of blue is the whole truth. Do you see the difference?" He nodded and said, "I think so. But what do I do about school? I only told them some of what happened and now I have to tell them everything." I told him that he would have to make his own decision. However, I also told him, "if you will tell the truth dad and I will go with you to talk to your principle. I have always said that I will support you in the truth. But, if you are not willing to own up to your lies, then, you will have to face her alone. That is your decision, not mine. It takes a stronger man to tell the truth and take the consequences, than to lie and look like the victim. But just remember every time you lie, you are hurting someone else. The hurt you cause someone else is just as bad as the hurt that have already lived through." "Okay, mom I will tell the truth. Will you go with me?" I told him I would, but, that I could not speak for his dad and he would have to ask his dad himself. He decided to ask him when he got home from work.

I could see the anxiety on his face when he asked his dad to go with him the next morning. "Well how do I know that you will come clean when you talk to your principle? If I take time off of work to go with you and then you do not live up to your end of the deal, I will be very upset." "I promise that I will tell the truth dad. It is going to be hard for me and that is why I want you to go with me. Besides, you will be right there and will know that I told the truth." "Well", my husband replied, "I will give you one chance." When our son thanked him, my husband replied, "that's okay, it's my job." This eased our son's anxiety and he laughed.

The next morning the three of us went to Charlie's school and waited to talk to the principle. When she asked my husband and I what she could do for us, I told her that we were only here to support our son. "He is the one that has something to say to you." With this, she asked our son what he had on his mind. He told her what had actually happened and she was very attentive. When he finished, she said, "my, that is somewhat of a different story than what you told the first time. You made it sound very suspicious

and that is why we had to call the police. But if you had told the police officer and me the whole truth you probably would not have had to spend the
night in the shelter. I am glad that you decided to tell me the whole truth."
Charlie looked at me and smiled. He turned back to his principle and said,
"that's the same thing mom told me." With this, he went to his class and
my husband and I thanked the principle for her time. We walked out,
hopeful that he had learned a valuable lesson. However, we also knew that
there would be other trying times. Experience had taught us that Charlie
went through cycles every three to four months. We hoped he stayed with
his pattern so we would get some rest before his next incident.
Unfortunately, this did not happen.

A month later school let out for the summer. I told Charlie that I would
take him on a trip around the civil war battlefields during the summer if he
could stay out of trouble. He promised so we made plans to leave the next
month. In the meantime, he behaved pretty well. Then we received a
phone call about Chris. He was being discharged from the hospital and was
coming home. He would go to day treatment every morning and come
home in the afternoons. He spent the nights and weekends at home. I reassured Charlie that his brother's discharge would not affect our trip. I told
him that the only thing that would change the plans is if he made some
wrong choices and began to misbehave. He was fine with this and promised to stay out of trouble. Things went smoothly, for about two weeks.

I was beginning to think that we were going to make it through the
transition just fine. Then, suddenly, Charlie resorted to his old behaviors.
I was extremely disappointed because I was looking forward to our trip. I
had to make a decision. Should I ignore his latest surge of misbehaviors
and still go on the trip or should I stick to my word and take the trip away
from him? I decided to let the first wave of misbehaviors pass and not
change our plans. To my disappointment though, Charlie did not have
the same idea. Everyday was a new adventure in the same old tricks.

After another week of lies, fighting with his brother, sneaking around
the house, and disobeying the rules, I told Charlie I was going to cancel our

trip. I informed him that he knew the deal, but he had chosen to misbehave anyway. I explained how disappointed I was about having to cancel our plans but that I made my decision based on his actions. He was furious with me. I expected him to be angry, but I did not expect his extreme reactions. When I turned my back later that afternoon, he ran away!

Later that evening, a deputy brought our son home. He ran to a neighbor's house and called the child abuse hotline. After the deputy talked to our son for awhile. He told our son that he was going to have to stop running. He also told him that he believed the "story" until he caught our son lying to him. This convinced him that our son had made it up because he was angry at having his trip taken away. He told our son it was his responsibility to talk to us because he made some very bad accusations. Of course, despite his promise to the officer, our son did not say a word to us.

For the next week, Charlie tried exceedingly hard to please us. We knew it was his way of making up, so, we let him continue. We also let him decide when he was ready to discuss his misbehaviors. A month passed and things went fairly well. We delivered phone books, which delighted him up because he loved having extra spending money. I thought we would make it until school started without any additional big incidents. However, it did not happen that way. Without warning, Charlie took off.

We contacted the sheriff. Around midnight the phone rang. Our son was found wandering the streets. The police officer took him to a youth shelter because he said our son was very angry and would probably run again if brought home. When the shelter called to ask us what we wanted to do, my husband told them to keep him there for the night and he would pick him up the next day. They agreed.

The next morning we picked up our son and, as usual, he made no attempt to explain his behavior. We told him we would not tolerate his running and if he did it again he would have to deal with the consequences. Also, as we had heard so many times before, he promised not to run again. By that evening, however, he disappeared. Some neighbors found him and brought him home. Unfortunately, they did not know us or our situation and our son convinced them he was abused. He was right about one thing. He was abused but it was by the birthparents not us. We informed the people of his behavior, but they did not understand. They left and we could feel their skepticism. We sent our son to bed.

In an effort to keep Charlie from running the next day while my husband was at work, I took his shoes and moved his clothes into my dresser. I hoped that by doing this he would not take off. After all, he did not have anything to pack nor did he have shoes to wear. However, when I checked on him he had wrapped his football pads around his feet and was holding a rope that he had tied into a slipknot. I panicked and took the pads and rope away from him then I called my husband. He called the sheriff and requested some help for me. When the sheriff arrived he talked to our son alone while waiting for a backup officer to arrive. I stepped outside to gather my thoughts. When the second officer arrived he went inside to talk to our son. Within minutes, both officers came outside and told me to go in and wait. I thought they were going to call for assistance. However, I looked outside and saw them looking around our yard and into our sons' clubhouses. I was puzzled. I could not figure out what that had to do with getting our son some help. The next thing I knew the second officer came into the house and took Charlie out to his patrol car. He came back in and told me that he was going to "force the authorities to do something about this." I was still confused and asked him what he was talking about. He told me "there have been numerous officers out here and we are beginning to think that there is something wrong going on here. We are not going your psychological route this time, we are going to handle it my way." I was astounded because this was the same officer that had caught our son in a lie. Now, he was beginning to believe that our son was telling the truth. "About what", I asked. He only replied, "stay here while I go to my car and get a form to take your statement." I could not believe my ears—what had our son made up this time? I called my husband and told him to get home ASAP.

In the meantime, the officer came back inside and told me to write my statement about what had happened. He also began to ask some very ridiculous questions such as "Is your son allowed to come into the house?" "Do you have running water?" "Where does he sleep?" and "Do you have a bathroom?" I stared at him in utter confusion. He was inside our house and could see for himself. I showed him the boys' loft, the kitchen, and the bathroom. He did not want to listen and told me he would be back in a minute. While he was outside, my husband drove up and asked our local sheriff what was going on. He told my husband that the other officer was in charge and he needed to ask him. So he did. My husband was told that they were going to place our son into protective custody and call in the child welfare authorities to conduct an investigation. My husband told him he could call anyone they wanted but they would not find anything wrong. He also informed him that the best way to help this situation was to assist us in finding help for our son or find the birthparents responsible for the damage. The officer did not agree and replied, "they (meaning the birthparents) are not here and you are." A few minutes later, this officer was contacted by his superiors and told to take our son to a shelter because there was no basis for protective custody. His superior, by the way, also had an adopted son with many behavioral problems, so, he was aware of the extremely difficult behaviors these kids were capable of exhibiting when they did not get their way. He assured my husband he would assist us because he understood and empathized with our predicament.

Charlie stayed at the shelter for three days. During his stay, a county health inspector and a Child Welfare caseworker came to our house. The inspector confirmed that, *yes,* we did have water, electricity, and toilet functions. The caseworker cleared us from any wrongdoing. We immediately searched for, and located, a therapist with experience working with Attachment Disorder children. We wanted someone who was aware of the bizarre and deviant behaviors they exhibited. We made an appointment to see her after we picked up our son from the shelter.

I had written a behavioral contract for Charlie. It listed behaviors that we would not tolerate and an alternative to each. Also, I listed consequences that would occur if our son broke his contract. I showed it to him and he agreed to the terms so he signed it. I gave a copy to his new therapist at the initial session. Our son seemed to take the contract seriously and honored its rules and consequences. It hung on the refrigerator and we were amazed at the changed behaviors he exhibited. It was as if seeing the expectations and consequences in writing provided the incentive to maintain his behavior. He managed to maintain his behavior until school started two weeks later.

For the first time in three years, both boys began the school year at the same school. Also, both of them, amazingly, were home for my birthday— I finally had the day I was aiming for. I just did not know that, unfortunately, it was the last.

During the following year, Charlie ran away only once and exhibited only minor behavioral problems. However, with the help of his therapist, he was able to stop himself before he caused any major episodes. We were so impressed with his improvement that we allowed him to have one wish. He wanted to have an animal for his 4-H project; so, we gave him our permission. He choose a llama.

The day he got his llama, he entered him in a show and won grand champion. Our son's face beamed with delight. His self-esteem shot through the roof. It was as if having a living and breathing responsibility provided a motive to stay out of trouble and not run away. He spent hour upon hour taking care of his llama. Soon, the llama and Charlie developed a bond with each other. The llama became very attached to Charlie and followed him everywhere. If he could not find Charlie, the llama would whine and cry just as a lost child cries for a parent. Charlie liked the "feeling of being wanted and needed" and announced this to everyone.

Next, I turned over the garden to Charlie. He enjoyed growing vegetables and melons. He especially enjoyed eating them. He tenderly cared for each of his plants. He sold some of his crop and made extra spending money. Because stealing had always been a problem with Charlie, I was glad to know that he was learning an honest way of earning money. He and I made jelly and pickles to enter into the state fair. He also continued to work to get his llama ready for the fair. He even landed himself a job at a horse stable for the summer. He fed and watered the horses and cleaned their stalls twice a day. Not only did he earn more spending money for himself, he spent some on his llama supplies, saved half, and always had a dollar in his pocket. When Charlie took the family for an ice cream cone with his first paycheck, my heart was filled with joy. He had come a long way since the first day I met him.

Things were going very well at home. I graduated with my Masters degree and was taking a summer off before starting a Ph.D. program. As a graduation gift, my husband gave me a horse. I had asked for one since the day we met and this was his chance to provide it for me. We also got an additional horse for him and for Chris to help with. Chris had become fascinated with horses since we enrolled in the therapeutic riding program upon his arrival to our family. The added responsibility of feeding and exercising both horses improved his accountability level, something we had battled since adopting him. To top it all off, both horses were expecting foals and Chris was thrilled to be able to witness the impending addition to "our family."

It had been three years since the boys had seen my parents. Although the stolen guns were meant to use against my mother and my sister in addition to the boys' birthfather, I felt the boys were past the anger when they began asking to see my family. They told us they wanted to apologize for their past bad behaviors. After discussing the pros and cons and considering the boys' currently acceptable behaviors, my husband and I decided to invite my parents to a cookout at our house. They accepted the invitation and the evening went very well. The boys were happy to spend time with them. Charlie showed off his llama and garden while Chris brought them up to date on his activities. Both boys played horseshoes with their grandfather and enjoyed the day.

The day was a success and I was extremely pleased. Experience had taught me how vulnerable the boys were. Although life was calm at the moment, this could all vanish quickly and without notice. Therefore, I had learned to enjoy the pleasant times, I never knew when or if it would the last. The rest of that summer consisted of many, many outings and activities. It was the busiest summer since becoming a family, one that I will always remember. Unfortunately, it was also the beginning of the end as a family.

Chapter 19

Three Strikes

It was August. School would be back in session in two weeks. Since the summer had gone well, I commented to my husband "I think we are going to make it through a summer without any major behavioral problems." Wrong thing to say.

I woke up to the frantic barking of our dogs. My husband had already left for work so I assumed the boys were playing with her. I looked outside but did not see them. I then called upstairs and told them to get up and feed the animals. They did not answer so I walked outside and called for them. Still no answer. The dog was still barking. I got dressed and went to the barn thinking the boys were feeding the horses and the llama. Still nothing. By then, I was becoming frantic. "Where in the hell are they now" I wondered. I took care of all the animals then went to the house and called my husband. It had only been an hour since he left home. He said the boys were on their way to the barn when he left so they may be in the woods playing. I told him I had already checked there but none of the animals had been taken care of and the boys were nowhere to be found. I also told him that I felt different about this time. It did not seem like Charlie's usual runaway pattern. For one thing, his brother was with him. Of the two, Chris was very lazy and would not run because he would be uncomfortable and have to work to eat. My husband agreed. What was going on?

The only thing I could think that may have happened dealt with an event the evening before that morning. We had called the horseshoe training facility to request a farrier for our horses. They sent one of their upper level students and his understudy to our house. After he finished working on our horses, I asked him his last name so I could write him a check. I was astonished when he told me, it was the boys' last name before we adopted them. "Couldn't be any connection" I convinced myself because we are in a different state. Yet, I could not shake the feeling because, after all, we were living in the state where the boys were found after a kidnapping. I decided to be cautious but not mention it to the boys. They were outside and did not hear the name so maybe this was just one of those ironic coincidences. Before the farrier left, he wrote his name, office address, and phone on a slip of paper. I placed it on the desk by the phone and forgot about it.

"Do you think the boys saw the paper with the farrier's name?" I asked my husband. "If they did, did they get scared and take off thinking he recognized them and would tell their birthparents? Or, did he recognize them and take them that morning after you left and I woke up?" My husband agreed. We were terrified and did not know what to do so my husband contacted a police officer he worked with and asked for guidance. The officer told us we needed to report the incident to our sheriff. My husband came home immediately and started searching for the boys while I drove around and looked for our local sheriff. When I found him I relayed the information and asked him what to do. He said we needed to go to headquarters and report this to an investigator because, he too, believed it was too consequential to ignore. I found my husband and we headed for the sheriff's department.

We arrived at the sheriff's department and asked to speak to an investigator. "Oh great" I whispered to my husband when I looked up and saw who was walking towards us. It was the guy who accused us of wrongdoing and caused so much trouble on Charlie's past runaways. When my husband saw him he sighed in disgust. We did not know it at the time, but we could have requested a different investigator. As it turned out, we should have done just that.

He began by asking us what we were doing there. We related the events to him. We also gave him the farrier's name and phone and asked that he call to check on his whereabouts. My husband had called earlier but was told the farrier had called in sick that morning. This terrified us and our imaginations were running wild. We thought that the investigator might be able to get more information than we might so we asked him to call. He then told us to stay seated and he would be right back. We thought he was going to make the call. When he returned he told us that he was going to take our written statements, but, he was going to separate us while we wrote them. He left to get the forms. I looked at my husband totally confused. "Why is he separating us, it makes no sense, we have nothing to hide" I said. My husband, as confused as I, was becoming very upset at the way this guy was handling the situation. If we knew we would be treated this way, we would have continued looking on our own. However, we decided to drop it because we were worried about our sons and wanted to find them.

After we wrote our statements the investigator told us that he was going to go with my gut feeling that something was wrong. He said, "nobody knows kids better than their parents." "Finally" I thought, "he is going to help us." The three of us went into a private room and talked. We told him everything we knew. He asked if anything had happened the day before other than the farrier's visit. I told him no and that neither one of the boys had been in trouble. It had been a very easy summer with only the normal boyhood reminders to take care of the animals, wash the dishes, and keep their room clean. The investigator told us to relax and the department would get right on the case. "I wouldn't worry too much about them because Charlie is quite the McGuiver. He will steal food if he has to and will curl up somewhere to keep warm. He could survive in the woods with nothing more than this pencil," referring to the pencil he held in his hand. He said a missing child alert was going to be sent across the national computer. He also told us he would be in touch with us and contact us immediately if he heard anything. Then, he gave us his pager number and escorted us to the door. We thanked him for his help and went home. We continued to search that afternoon but found nothing. As each hour passed we became more concerned that something bad had actually happened to the boys this time.

We called the investigator every two hours. Each time he said the same thing, "I have no news." We reported the name of every person we contacted; friends, neighbors, therapist, teachers, and principle. He told us to keep in touch. I was becoming very irritated because he did not seem to appreciate the efforts we were putting into finding the boys. My husband also was beginning to feel the same so we called the boys' therapist. She understood our fear and told us that she was available to talk anytime we needed. She also told us she supported us 100 percent and reminded us to keep the faith. Her reassurance helped ease our frustration.

Two days passed with no news. I was afraid the boys were long gone. We were asleep the second night when the phone rang. It was a police officer. The boys were sitting in front of him. They had been found roaming around a mall, 15 miles south of our home. My husband asked if they were hurt. The officer said they were fine, just dirty and hungry. "I am on my way and will be there in about 30 minutes" my husband told him. As we promised, we called the investigator to tell him the boys were found. He asked where they were. My husband, not thinking twice about it, told him and said he was on his way to get them. The investigator told my husband to wait until he called us back. My husband hung up. We were both very baffled why we had to wait. My husband waited 10 minutes then hugged me and left to get the boys. We did not understand why we were told to wait but felt very uneasy with the investigator. It was as if he had been pacifying us the entire time. We had done nothing wrong and were not going to be pushed around by him again.

My husband walked into the police station. He told the officer who he was and asked for the boys. The lieutenant came out and told my husband that he could not have the boys because the investigator called and was on his way. "For what?" he asked the lieutenant. "I don't know, but, he has jurisdiction and we have to wait" he replied. "Okay, whatever" my husband said. It turned out that Chris went to school with the lieutenant's son and they knew each other so my husband and the lieutenant talked for quite some time. About an hour later, the investigator arrived. He headed straight for the boys leaving my husband sitting. When he talked to my husband an hour later, he told him that he was placing the boys in protective custody because they asked for it, but, if they had not asked for it he was going to do it anyway. "Why, what is the problem" my husband asked. "They are accusing you of abuse." "And you believe it? If it were true, they would have said something to the other police officers. It is funny that they only said something after you show up and talk to them. In fact, the lieutenant knows Chris. I know him well enough to know that if it was true, our son would have told him, if for no other reason than to get attention" my husband asked. "Yes, I believe them" he said. "You will be contacted by the child welfare division regarding a court hearing. Until then you can't talk to or see the boys. And, by the way, I am now a full time investigator, not a part time patrol officer. I have a 40-hour workweek and a regular salary so I have more power. I am going to get to the bottom of what is going on in your house this time."

My husband was livid. What had the boys said this time? Here, we had been worried sick about them and their safety and they had turned and made more false allegations. When he got home and told me, he was more upset than I had seen him during any prior incidents. "We should have suspected that ... investigator would try to pull something. He is determined to find something derogatory against us, even if he has to invent it, just so he can add a star to his record." "We have done nothing wrong except love and try to help those boys. We have many people who can testify to that. And, our therapist will report there is no abuse of any kind occurring in our home, so don't worry honey" I told him. My husband responded "That sorry S.O.B. I would like to know what goes on behind his home doors and what he is hiding with his three kids."

Sure enough, the following morning, we received a call from the child welfare office. We were expected to show up for court. The judge would then decide what to do with the boys. When we asked what we were being accused of, we were told that the social worker would come to our house and tell us. Until then, we had to wait. Two days later, the social worker came to our house. He told us the boys said my husband beat Charlie for losing the kitten. My husband laughed because the kitten was sitting in my lap directly in front of the guy. "Your son has bruises on his backside." "How old were those bruises? He just had a physical for football the day before he took off and there was nothing there. He could have received those from his llama or during his overnight runaway" my husband said. The social worker did not have an answer for us but said that if we could get a copy of the physical it would be a good thing. My husband said, "I did get on to our son for not watching the kitten but I did not beat him and bruise his butt!"

Next, the social worker said Chris accused me of throwing him out of the truck and cutting his knee. I could not believe what I was hearing. I told the worker "our son was determined not to get out of the truck and water the dogs so I walked to the back to tell him to get out when he jumped, rolled on the ground and scraped his knee. I did not throw him. In fact, while he was rolling around on the ground making a scene, I told him "oh stop the dramatics and get up." The social worker said "that sounds more logical than his story and I noticed him picking the scab the entire time I talked with him." I told the worker that was not unusual and he always picked at himself to keep sores open and bleeding. I also provided him with the file of hospital notes, treatment center stays, and the boys' current therapist. He said he would call the therapist and get her report but from the history, it looked like the judge would see through the boys' story. "It sounds like they are trying to avoid taking responsibility for running. By making up their story they don't think they will have to pay the consequence and be punished. Also, it sounds as if the investigator wants to find someone to boost his career and he is using your family to do it." We were relieved to know that the social worker had been able to figure out what was happening. However, he turned out to be true to our former conclusion regarding the mentality of social workers. Experience had taught us that social workers were nothing but a bunch of overworked, underpaid clerical workers who knew nothing about Attachment Disorder children. Furthermore, we had only met one who understood the stories these kids were capable of concocting and the extreme problems they could cause.

Our therapist tried, unsuccessfully, for several days to contact the social worker because he never called her for a report. She was becoming as frustrated with the system as we were so she called and talked to a supervisor. Her report, she was told, was filed with the case. Therefore, we felt confident that all would be fine when we went to court. We could not have been further from the truth. The boys' representative told the judge they accused us of not only what we were told by the social worker but several other lies. They said that I did not allow them to wear socks with their rubber boots, we did not feed them, and we locked them in sheds, just to name a few. I looked at my husband in disgust. "That is not true" I told the judge when he asked if I had any thing to say. It did not matter, the judge said the boys would stay in protective custody until the investigation was complete. He also told us we could visit the boys after we finished the hearing. "Oh that is just what we want to do" my husband told me. I told him I only wanted to talk to Charlie and ask him what was going on because he had had such a good summer that I did not understand what had changed his attitude. My husband agreed and told the social worker. She said that was fine because he wanted to see us but Chris did not. We stood outside the room while she went in to get Chris. When he walked out of the room, he turned his nose in the air, faced the wall, and walked down the hallway. "That's it," I said. "I do not care if we see him or get him back." However, my husband was not yet convinced.

As soon as I walked into the room, Charlie gave me a hug. I asked him what had happened to him. He said he did not know but was sorry for lying. I asked if he wanted to live at home or go to foster care. He said he wanted to come home but did not think he could now that he lied about me. I told him that only he could fix the problem he caused. He also told me that it was his brother's idea to runaway because he did not like doing his chores. "I did not want to go but I thought I needed to take care of him" he told me. I told Charlie that was the adults job, not his. "I am sorry mom, I want to come home." I told him that it was up to the judge and social workers. "All you can do now is tell the truth, but, after so many lies no one may believe you" I told him. He said he would try to do the right thing. We told him we had to leave. We also told him he could call us and it was up to him whether he associated with his brother. I told him "that is a decision you have to make on your own."

On the way home I told my husband that we needed to find a long-term placement for Chris because I could not have him at home and keep my sanity. I also thought Charlie would do better without his brother at home. I suddenly remembered their first case manager's words "we were going to split the boys and adopt them out because we think they have a better chance at making it by themselves." "Why didn't I listen" I asked myself. Five days later, the social worker called and told us to pick up our sons because there was no reason for them to keep them any longer. We called my best friend and she met us at the shelter. She agreed to help us with Chris because he was being obstinate. We stopped on the way home to get a hamburger to celebrate my husband's birthday. It was his this time, not mine. While driving to the restaurant, Chris told my friend he was on his way to my parents' house. When she asked why he would not tell her. Also, he told her that he "was going to get mom put in jail somehow." When she told me this I was more determined than ever to get him out of my house. "He is not going to stop until he hurts me, my parents, my sister, or my husband" I had to admit.

Although we had lived through our sons' many hospital and treatment center placements, they were all short-term, three months or less, admissions. Therefore, with adolescence upon Chris, my husband and I were prepared to face the problems that accompanied *teenageness* and were expecting additional treatment center stays. Yet, the extent of his problems convinced us he was a danger and could not live at home, at least for a while. My husband contacted several group homes, foster care agencies, and a boys ranch. Fortunately, the Baptist Boys Ranch located across town from us accepted him. Although I was still very angry with him, I was glad he was close enough that I could visit if, and when, we were both ready. Charlie seemed to flourish at home by himself. He started school and played football. He did very well.

A couple of months after school started, we received an offer to fully relinquish our remaining parental rights of the oldest brother. It had been more than five years since he left our home. We felt no emotional tie to him nor did he feel any for us. We asked our boys how they felt and were surprised to hear them voice the same feelings. In reality, they seemed to be relieved to have the situation finalized. Although their brother asked to have contact with them, neither one of them wanted to have contact with him. Their desire was further solidified when they received a letter from him in which he signed his birthname. Both of our boys were disgusted and said they were glad it was over. However, my husband and I convinced them to write a good bye letter to their brother. Although I knew they would have to face their emotions regarding their brother again in the future, I was glad we made them write the letter. We told them they could write whatever they were feeling as long as they did it respectfully. They complied, but did so hesitantly.

Chapter 20

It's Over

It was another year. Charlie had done so well the past four months that we told him he had earned a big birthday party. His birthday was the same weekend as the Super Bowl so we told him he could invite three friends over. My husband told him to get their names and phone numbers and he would arrange it with their parents. It was all set. The party was planned, the cake was ordered, and we were waiting for the weekend to celebrate the big event. Suddenly, my world ended. I experienced a hurt so deep I will never get over it. I did not have a favorite son, but, out of all of them, I developed a deeper closeness to Charlie. Even with all of the heartaches we had endured because of his behaviors, I never doubted that he would stay in our family. That is, until the week preceding his 14th birthday.

Chris was home for a weekend pass. During his visit he showed me his report card from school. This reminded me that I had not received Charlie's report card so I asked him about it. Charlie told me that they had not been handed out yet. I accepted his answer. However, I decided to call his school the next day to confirm without telling him that I was going to do so. The subject was dropped the rest of the day.

On Monday morning I called Charlie's school. The school secretary told me that their report cards had been sent home the previous week and that I should have already signed it and sent it back. I told her what Charlie had told me. I also told her that I would ask him again that afternoon and let them know his answer. When Charlie got home from school I asked him about his report card again. He told me, for the second time, that the teachers had not handed them out. I immediately rebutted him and said that I had talked to the school secretary and knew they had been handed out. For the next half-hour I must have heard nearly ten different stories regarding his report. For instance, when he heard that I had called the school his first excuse was that his teacher gave him the wrong report card and took it back. He said that his current grades were not posted on it. I told him that did not make sense and asked him again. He told me so many conflicting stories that I finally said "I don't want to hear anymore lies. You better bring home your report card tomorrow or I will call your teacher myself." He promised he would bring it home the next day.

When Charlie arrived home the next afternoon he was avoiding me. I asked him for his report card and he said he left it at school. I told him I would call the school and go pick it up. However, when I called the school there was no answer. Because I could not do anything at that time, I repeated my insistence that he bring home his report card the next day. Of course, he once more promised to bring it home. This went on for two more days. Finally, at my wits end with all of the secretiveness and lies, I gave him the ultimatum. I told Charlie that if I did not have his report card in my hand the next afternoon, Thursday, then his birthday party on Sunday would be cancelled. This took him by surprise and he told me that he had left it in his desk and he would remember it the next day before he left school. I gave him the benefit of the doubt.

To ensure that I would receive the report card, I called Charlie's teacher the next morning. She told me that she would send a copy of his "lost" report card home with him that day along with a note for me to sign acknowledging the fact that I received it. She said she would tell Charlie to bring the note back to her so she would know that I received it. I told her that if he did not bring either the report card or her note home then I would inform her and we would proceed with the consequence, no birthday party. She agreed because, in addition to the report card incident, he had been causing a lot of trouble at school over the past couple of weeks. He had been fighting with others, stealing, and lying about his work. He was being disruptive in class and had been sent to the principle's office and counselor several times. I thanked her for letting me know and told her I would keep her abreast of what happened when he got home.

I was waiting at the front door with my hand out when Charlie got home from school. He knew exactly what I wanted. He immediately began to tell me that he left his report card at school. I stopped him before he could finish and called his teacher. She told me that she had given him the copy of his report card and the note on his way out the door not even thirty minutes prior to my call. When I asked him about that he said "I must have dropped it on my way home." I said "okay, fine, let's go for a ride." I put him in the truck and we drove to the school. We retraced the same route he took home. Of course we did not find a report card or note anywhere.

Because it was his regular therapy day I drove him to his therapists office. He continued to lie to me on the drive to her office. With each lie I became more frustrated and angry. I finally had enough and told him that he had been given several chances but due to his lies and the trouble he was getting into at school his birthday party was cancelled. I walked him into his therapist's office and told her the situation. I also told her that my husband would pick Charlie up because I was too angry with him. She told me she would call me the next morning to discuss the situation. For the rest of the evening I stayed away from Charlie. Not only was I deeply hurt that he had lied to me, but I was also upset that he had fallen into his old behavioral pattern again. I was also exasperated that he had blown his birthday party because everything had been purchased and arranged. I had wanted him to have his big party so badly and when he behaved in a way to lose it I was very disappointed for him.

Charlie's therapist called me the next morning. She began to tell me about numerous problems, including the report card. She said that she had known for a week about the report card. Charlie had told her he had torn it up and thrown it away because he made one bad grade. She had discussed this with him and told him it was a better idea to tell us about it so we could help him. She also told him that one bad grade compared to the rest of the A's and B's was good. He had told her that if we knew about the bad grade he would lose his party. She tried unsuccessfully to convince him that we would be more upset with his deceitfulness and lying than about the grade. She told him that if he lost his party it would be for the lies, not the bad grade. However, she could not convince him to tell us and decided to let him endure the consequences of his behavior. She told him he had made the choice and he would have to live with the consequences. I agreed that she had done the correct thing because if she had told us about it, he would have lost confidence in their trusting relationship.

Once the truth came out about the report card, we told Charlie he had to call his friends parents and inform them the party was cancelled. All of the parents agreed that he had done the wrong thing. Next, we began to deal with the other behaviors, the stealing, lying, and disruptions at school. We knew from past experience that Charlie needed more intense therapy than outpatient therapy session. However, due to his runaway behavior, the youth shelters were unwilling to admit him. Also, he did not quality for hospital treatment because he was not exhibiting suicidal behavior. Therefore, my husband contacted the state senator's office for assistance in securing a therapeutic placement for Charlie. During the week that the senator's staff was busy searching for a placement, the boys' adoption case manager called with some very disturbing news.

The adoption case manager she had received a call from out of the blue from someone claiming to be the birthfather's wife. She was calling for him to find out if it was possible to get the boys back because "he really loved them and missed them". I could not believe my ears. After all the turmoil this man had caused in at least five people's lives, the boys and ours, not to mention others of which we were unaware. She informed the woman that the boys were adopted and there was no way for him to get them back. After she told me this, I was determined that he was not going to get near them. It also occurred to me that, once again, there was a reason that both boys were not at home at the time of this phone call. Although I do not understand all that has happened since becoming the boys' parents, I do know there is a reason for each and every event. I reminded myself that I must continue to follow my gut instinct and not bow to those who have not lived our family's life.

My husband called to inform the senator's staff about a stolen wallet Charlie had hidden in the lawn mower. While relating this information to the senator's staff member, he mentioned the phone call from the adoption worker. The staff member's comment summed up perfectly the life we had shared with our boys. The staff member told my husband "Your story is something only seen in the movies!"

A few weeks after Charlie was admitted to the treatment center, Chris began to ask to come home. We discussed it with his therapist and decided it may work since he would be the only one at home. The boys had always exhibited a love-hate relationship. They continually fed off of each other's behaviors. Also, Chris had also been the one who needed constant attention. Therefore, we were optimistic that Chris would be fine if he was home without Charlie. Against the advice of the boys ranch, the therapist, my husband, and I decided to bring Chris home. The first couple of weeks seemed to go very well. Because he had been working with farm animals at the boys ranch, we decided to buy him a horse of his own so he would have something to care for. We found a young filly that had been neglected and abused. Chris immediately formed a bond to her. We were becoming comfortable and confident that Chris was going to be okay and make things work at home. Then, it all started again.

I was cleaning the bathroom while Chris was at school. When I pulled the carpet off the floor to wash I was taken by surprise. Underneath the sink and hidden under the carpet was a knife. I was not sure if it had Charlie or Chris that put it there. Both had plenty of opportunity. I was immediately struck by a fear for my own safety. I decided to hide the knife until my husband came home. At that moment I realized that by staying in our house I was in danger. When my husband got home from work I showed him the knife and told him that I could not live with either boy. It simply was too dangerous. I had received threats from Chris the year before but I did not take them seriously until then. Therefore, I planned to move out of our home. I knew I was doing what needed to be done to protect myself. Unfortunately, I did not think about his next victim—my husband.

A few weeks later, husband came home early from work and saw Chris sitting on the couch. Thinking nothing of this, he went to the bedroom to change out of his work clothes. While changing he noticed the gun cabinet had been pried open. He investigated it and found a small screwdriver hidden behind the dresser in an old purse that I had not used in years. Next, my husband examined the ammunition drawer and found that it had also been pried open. The guns and ammunition were still there, fortunately. Before he turned to leave the room and question Chris, my husband looked at the top of our dresser. It had been marred and had deep chunks of wood gashed out of it. This infuriated my husband even more.

He confronted Chris about the gun cabinet and dresser. Chris instantly told him that as he was walking up the hill from the barn he saw a blue truck with green stripes driving away from the house. My husband could tell he was lying and asked him again. Each time he was asked, Chris changed his story. We had learned the behaviors each boy exhibited when lying and, therefore, my husband knew this was just one more story fabricated to cover his attempts at stealing guns. My husband called the police and they sent an investigator to the house to file a report. The officer agreed with my husband that Chris was the culprit and he should be watched very closely. After the officer left, my husband gathered all of the guns and ammunition and took them to a friend's house for storage as a precaution. As punishment for the incident, my husband took Chris' house keys away and told him he would have to earn them back. After school, instead of coming inside the house, Chris would have to feed all of the animals and do his homework on the gazebo during the hour until my husband arrived home from work. When he got home from work then he would open the door and allow Chris to go in. My husband told Chris to take an extra snack in his backpack each day so he would have something to eat after school. He also told him to get his water bottle and leave it on the gazebo so he could fill it with water after school.

During the next few days things went smoothly. However, towards the end of the week we began to notice damage done to the house. One of the first things I noticed when I came home the following weekend was caulking pulled out from around the windows. At first I thought maybe it had dried from the sun and needed to have some added. Next, I found that there were several screws, used to hold the logs on the side of the house, were missing. This confused me because I had helped put the siding on when we built the house and did not remember missing any holes. It still did not occur to me that the damage I was finding was intentionally done. Later that weekend I was cleaning the garage windows and found large holes gouged into the doors directly beside the windows. It looked like a large stick or hammer had been used in an attempt to pry out the windows. After finding this I wondered if Chris had been telling the truth about the "green truck with blue stripes" so I told my husband what I had found. He decided not to say anything to Chris until we had investigated it further.

I went back to my apartment on Sunday night and planned, as always, to be back home the next weekend. My weekend was cut short when I received a devastating telephone call. My grandmother had passed away and I needed to get home. The call came midweek so only a couple of days had passed since I had left the weekend before. I called my husband and told him a couple of friends were driving me home because I was too upset to drive. We decided not to say anything to Chris until that evening when we all were together. That evening we sat in the living room and told Chris what had happened. He appeared sad at first but then just went about his business of getting ready for school the next day.

I was busy the next day helping pick up family members from the airport. I was nervous also because I still had no contact with my parents or sister. They knew nothing that had occurred with the boys over the past few years except what they had heard from others in passing. I was not sure how to explain Charlie's absence but decided I was not going to cover for his behavior any longer. Therefore, when I was asked, I decided I was going to tell the truth about his placement—he could not stop stealing and he decided he did not want to live in a family any longer. As for Chris, I was going to explain all of the trouble we had been dealing with including the many hospital and treatment center stays. I was not going to tell them the attempted threats on their life. I did not think it would do any good to get into the details of the gun thefts and run away episodes that were intended to find my mother and sister to do "kill" them. After dropping off family members I went to the mall to get a new suit for the funeral. I had not seen any family members except for the Aunt and Uncle that I picked up at the airport.

I did not want to get home before my husband and be alone with Chris so I browsed the mall for an hour looking for a suit. I do not enjoy shopping for clothes and could not find anything that I liked. I left. I calculated that I would get home about the same time as my husband so I should be okay since there were no guns in the house and Chris should be on the gazebo doing his homework or reading a book. As I drove up the drive I noticed our 5-year-old neighbor boy standing by the side of the road. His shirt was hanging half way out of his pants and his boots were on the wrong feet with his pant legs pushed up over their tops. I thought to myself, he must have been in a hurry after school to get outside and play. He was a playful little boy and it was not unusual to see him outside playing in dirt or water. However, I had never seen him so haphazardly dressed before. I assumed it was his attempt to take care of and dress himself without his mom's help. As I turned to pull into our driveway I noticed Chris running from the barn. He stopped and sashayed to me when I got out of the truck. With so much else on my mind I did not question what he was doing in the barn. Later that evening, this incident came flooding back into my consciousness.

My husband pulled up a few minutes later. I told him that I needed to go to the funeral home after dinner. He said he would go with me. We called our neighbor and asked if she could watch Chris for a couple of hours. Because of his behaviors, she was the only person we knew who was still willing to watch him. We were taken by surprise when she told us that if we had called an hour earlier she would have had no problem with it. However, she was in the middle of talking to her son about an incident that happened between him and Chris that afternoon. She told us she would call us back and explain. We had no idea what had happened but I related to my husband what I saw when I drove home. We assumed there had been a fight and Chris had hit or hurt her son. Since he was eight years older, we were afraid that he had caused some bruises or cuts on the younger boy. Never in our wildest dreams did we expect what we would soon learn that he had done.

My husband asked Chris what had happened he said they were "play wrestling" in the barn. That explained why I saw him running from the barn that afternoon but not the rumpled looking little boy I saw. Each time my husband questioned Chris he, as always, changed his story somewhat. My husband told Chris he had to go to bed after dinner and better be in his bed when we got home. We left to visit the funeral home. Unfortunately we were late and it was already closed. We drove to my grandmother's house and saw that my parents were there. Uncertain what to do my husband went to the door. We were invited to come inside. We were upset not only about my grandmother, but also about the latest "unknown" incident with Chris. After some coaxing we went inside.

When I saw my parents I lost control of my composure. The past seven years of turmoil, hurt, frustration, anger, helplessness, and depression, combined with the current loss of my dear grandmother, was more than I could take. All of these emotions and uncertainty flooded upon me and I could not keep it inside any longer. Although it would be several months before the past was resolved, this proved to be the beginning of the healing process for my family. I remembered thinking that "grandma would be happy" to see this. It was a start at mending old emotional fences. The only thing I was still confused about was what to do about Chris' latest episode. Should I try to explain it now or wait? As it turned out the following morning provided the answer I needed. Sadly, when Chris' attempt to harm my husband with the guns was foiled, he pursued another victim; he did the unthinkable with the young neighbor child. The very worst part of our adoptive experience had begun!

Chapter 21

The Final Straw

The phone rang early the next morning. It was our neighbor. She proceeded to tell my husband what had occurred the previous afternoon between her son and Chris. I watched my husband's face become stone cold as he listened to her. My thoughts were that Chris had started a fight and caused a broken bone or large bruise to her son. I could not, however, believe my ears when he told me what she had related to him.

She told my husband that Chris had sexually molested her son in the barn the previous afternoon. At first I could not believe it. I found myself thinking of all types of explanations for the incident. I thought that she had misunderstood her son's story. I knew that the boys had done some very deviant things in the past but this I could not comprehend. Without alerting Chris that we knew something had happened, my husband went to the neighbors to talk to them in person. He sat quietly as the young boy told my husband the torrid details of the incident. When he was done my husband apologized and said he would check back after he discussed this with the therapists and police. He came home and told me what was said. I knew by the explicit details that the boy gave that it had to be true. I told myself that, in hindsight, it all made sense why I saw him so haphazardly dressed the day before and Chris running from the barn with a "blue truck with green stripes" story. I was totally disgusted. To me this was the final straw. I had endured the threats to myself, my husband, my family, the birthparents, and animals. However, now innocent children were in danger of being harmed. I simply could not allow it to continue. The risk was too great. Also, there were three other young children in our neighborhood and I could not take the chance that they could be his next victim. My husband agreed. We immediately called a youth shelter and had Chris admitted until after the funeral. This would give us time to make other arrangements.

A week later my husband was contacted by a police detective. He was instructed to bring Chris for an interview to determine if charges would be filed. While being questioned, Chris continued to change his story. Afterwards, the detective told my husband that she did not believe his denial and she was forwarding a recommendation to the juvenile district attorney for charges of lewd molestation with a minor child. My husband agreed and told her that we had no other recourse; we had done everything possible to help him. She told my husband to keep Chris in the shelter until his court date because he was a danger to the neighborhood children and us. My husband informed the shelter staff of this when he returned him that afternoon. They agreed to keep him until then. However, if he caused disruptions with the other youth, they said he would have to leave.

Two weeks passed with no word from the juvenile court. The shelter had begun calling and reporting to us that Chris was causing disruptions with the other residents. He was making racial slurs and provoke fights. He had been attacked by a group of the residents and had a large bruise from being punched. My husband told the staff that we had not received a court date yet, but that he would call and see if it had been set. When he called the court he was told that it was still in the district attorneys office waiting to be filed. He explained the situation and they said they would put a rush on it. He called to inform the shelter staff. They agreed to keep Chris a couple more days.

The next day the shelter worker called again and said that Chris needed new shoes because his were falling apart. We informed her that they were only a month old and it was our guess that he tore them up because he saw a pair that someone else had and he wanted them. We told her that he did this frequently with all of his belongings—clothes, bikes, etc. She said the shelter had a pair of "plain jane" shoes that he would have to wear instead. We agreed that was fine.

That weekend we had to go out of town. When we returned there were numerous calls on the answering machine from the shelter. They had to take him to the hospital because he was having trouble breathing. We called them and were told that he was put on an asthma inhaler. When we were informed of this, we assured the staff that he had never had this problem before. He was very good at getting attention with these types of behaviors and we deduced that he wanted an inhaler so he could look "cool" puffing on it. He was notorious for doing things like that. They said they had no choice but to take him since they could not reach us by phone. However, since returning to the shelter he showed no signs of breathing problems so they felt we were probably correct.

While still waiting for a court date, the shelter once again called and told my husband that they had to discharge Chris because he was attempting suicide. He told the staff that if his dad did not come to get him that night he was going to drink poison or run away. We told them that he always threatened to do things like this when he did not get his way or wanted attention. They expected that he was threatening it because the other youth were ganging up on him due to his behaviors. However, by law, they had to have him removed and taken for a mental evaluation. My husband reluctantly agreed to pick him up and drive him to the hospital. When my husband told me what was happening I told him that the hospital would more than likely admit him. I had been with him all of the other times he was admitted and had learned that he knew exactly what to say to meet the criteria for admission. He had learned it by working the system to his advantage. Unfortunately, these kids are quick to pick up the language and knew exactly how to use it to get what they want. As it turned out, I was correct. My husband told me that Chris used all of the buzzwords that intake counselors listen for. He even used the correct "mental health" terms. The intake counselor believed that he knew what he was saying, but, as with the shelter, she had no choice but to follow the law and admit him under a suicide watch.

The hospital agreed to keep him until his court date. They had tried and failed to enroll Chris in a juvenile sex offender course because he would not admit that he had molested the boy. Although he continued to change his story about what occurred that day in the barn but he would not admit what he had done. Therefore, my husband was told that after the court hearing they could not readmit him. The social worker informed us that the court would more than likely accept custody of Chris and place him in a juvenile shelter because he continued to be a sexual predator risk to other children. Having faith in the justice system, my husband proceeded to take Chris to his court arraignment.

Despite all the evidence of his guilt, the judge ordered that my husband take Chris home for the two weeks until his trial. My husband pleaded with the judge to keep him in their custody due to the danger he posed to others. She informed my husband that if he could convince the juvenile system to keep him she would order it. He spent the next two hours talking to every person in a position to help. No one wanted to take custody of Chris. My husband was told numerous times that it was our problem. Fearing for the safety of the neighborhood children, my husband refused to take Chris home. He told the authorities there was nobody willing to watch him. The hospital would not readmit Chris, the shelter refused to have him back and the boys ranch where Chris spent the previous year refused to take him because of the sexual charge. Furthermore, no family or friends would keep him, he did not qualify for a treatment center because this was a criminal not psychological problem, and even the foster care system was not willing to take a chance of a short term stay when other children would be placed at risk. Still, no one at the juvenile justice system was willing to help.

It was nearing five o'clock and the office was closing for the day. When my husband continued to ask for assistance he was finally told that if he did not take Chris then he would be placed in emergency custody with the child welfare agency. My husband felt that this was better than taking a chance that another child would be harmed or molested. Once all of the paperwork was completed, the juvenile officer took Chris. My husband inquired when he needed to be back in court for Chris' trial. The officer told him that Chris was now in the custody of the state and we were no longer involved. The officer told my husband to go home. He did.

In the meantime, we contacted an attorney who agreed to appear with us on the day of the hearing. We did not meet him until walking into the door. He asked us what we wanted to do. We informed him that we wanted to relinquish parental rights. He asked us if Chris was adopted. We told him that he was and the attorney said "that is all I need to know". We walked into court. Once in front of the judge our attorney took over. He informed the judge that we agreed to relinquish parental rights. The next thing I knew we were completing paperwork and signing it. When the judge asked us if we understood, we both believed that we were agreeing to relinquishment. We learned two months later that was not all that was being entered into the court records.

We had decided that I should continue to live out of the home until all of this was resolved because Chris had made threatening phone calls to me and written letters threatening to "get me". During the next two weeks, my husband continued to keep me informed. In the meantime, we contacted a family law attorney in an attempt to relinquish our parental rights. Unfortunately, we did not have the money to hire him. If we had known what lie ahead of us we would have borrowed the money from somewhere because, two weeks later, in the middle of the night, my husband was arrested at home for child abandonment. He was taken to jail!!

I received a phone call the next morning from my mother. My husband could not reach me so he called her. I was in absolute shock when she told me what had happened. After all that we had done to help the boys we were now being treated like criminals when the real criminals who abused the boys were free as could be. I, never in my life felt so much distrust in the justice system. To me this was the **Final Straw**—I was not going to make excuses for, try to help, or be victimized by those boys anymore. From here on out, all that mattered to me was my marriage and my immediate family and close friends. I had taken more than any human being can take—I had nothing left to give!

My parents drove to get me and take me to their house. They posted the bond for my husband and my dad accompanied him to all of the arraignments. He was given a trial date for three weeks later. Over the period of the next two years, my husband and I were in and out of the courtroom for his charge. We had been directed by the senator's office to an attorney who agreed to take our case. This attorney turned out to be our saving grace. He got to work immediately on my husband's case. The first thing he wanted was a letter from anyone who had knowledge of our situation. In the end, we had over 37 letters of support ranging from friends to political officials to mental health authorities. Our attorney fought the district attorney. My husband refused to admit guilt for trying to protect innocent children. I supported him 100% and so did our family and friends. Our story appeared in two separate newspapers and garnered even more support for our case. After two years of continuances in the case, the district attorney finally agreed to back down. She accepted a no guilt plea from my husband. After a one year time period, our attorney filed adjudication paperwork and my husband's record was eradicated. It was the first time in nine years that we could sleep peacefully at night and get up the next morning and enjoy our lives.

Chapter 22

Reflections

We have traveled a long road since the first day we saw the boys. Many things have occurred, good and bad, sad and happy, frightening and peaceful. My husband and I have questioned our decision to adopt the boys more than once both during and after every trying episode. We both would be the first to admit that our answer has changed over the years, depending on the situation at hand. However, we are very adamant with our answer—it is a resounding **NO!!** The guilty feeling we used to experience on those occasions we wished we had never seen the boys have long since faded. We now realize that what others refer to as guilt, is only a matter of perception. In all actuality, if we find ourselves not questioning our decision every so often we feel "guilty" for not doing so. Not doing so would imply that we are superhuman or that the consequences of our sons' behaviors did not effect us individually or as a couple. Once we realized that it is perfectly legitimate, and healthy, to express our true feelings, we noticed a stronger inner peace. I have come to firmly believe that this is absolutely necessary for all parents, not only adoptive parents. "Do not judge me until you have walked a mile in my shoes" is very apropos and fitting for all of the hardships that we, as adoptive parents, have had to overcome.

Although they were few and far between, I will always cherish the good times. For instance, I will never forget each Christmas when we, as a family, did a good deed for others less fortunate. These deeds included playing our instruments and singing Christmas carols at the local nursing home or passing out candy canes to residents in assisted living centers. The most fulfilling Christmas deed occurred the year that the boys each selected a less fortunate family and worked to provide them with Christmas cheer. Charlie found a family without money for gifts or dinner. He worked odd jobs to make money then went shopping to buy a gift for everyone in the family and dinner for Christmas day. Chris called the Ronald McDonald house and got the name of a little boy who was being treated for medical reasons at the local hospital. The boy was from Mexico and was not able to be home for Christmas. Chris worked to earn the money to buy the little boy some American gifts. We as a family delivered the items to both families.

Also, I will always remember the boys climbing up the trees each year to gather mistletoe. They then brought it home, bagged it up, and sold it to make their Christmas money. We made a fun time of this annual event by drinking hot chocolate as they bagged their treasured mistletoe. We drove them to neighborhoods to sell it then treated them to a hamburger and ice cream cone after they had sold their allotment.

Other memorable times include the many sporting events that we attended. Both boys played football, baseball, soccer, and basketball. We also were involved in the school-wrestling program. We thoroughly enjoyed these times when we were just like parents watching their kids have fun. Other events included the 4-H llama that Charlie showed at the state fair, the jams, jellies, and pickles that the boys helped me make and then entered into the state fair, and the boy scout activities that Chris participated in with my husband. Charlie also planted and pampered his garden two summers in a row after he learned from me how to care for the vegetables. His work paid for itself when he had people offering to buy his fresh vegetables. One of the most fun activities we did, as a family, were the camping and fishing trips. We would spend hours at the lake with our lines in the water waiting for that "big catch" that never came.

Emotionally, I will always cherish the bond that Charlie and I had formed. If only he could have held on to this rather than revert back to his delinquent problems then he may have had a chance in our family. I will also remember the skunk family that Charlie brought home one day. He found them in the woods and wanted to keep them as pets. The look on his face when they sprayed him was priceless. Finally, my proudest moment was when Charlie gathered his own toys and those donated from his school and delivered them to the children of the Oklahoma City bombing. To see him interviewed by CNN and other news stations around the country filled my heart with hope. If only these good times could have been the majority part of our life instead of the minority part of our family life then we may have been able to make it. Unfortunately, this was not to be.

Going into an adoption with preconceived notions of how your family life will be or how your children will respond to you as their parent will more than likely not be how it actually turns out. Odds are, you will be disappointed by the actual events which unfold before your eyes. This disillusion is a very difficult reality to accept, but it does not indicate the original dream of an adopted child was abnormal or undesirable. *Failed intentions and lost dreams are a part of the daily lives of adoptive parents.*

Excerpts from my husband

As the man that has been labeled the *second* Dad in the boys' lives, I will attempt to summarize my experience as a well-meaning adoptive father.

First off, the boys were mistreated and abused extensively by their birth-parents. All three boys have, at one time or another, admitted to me that they wish I were their only father. Father to me means only one thing, the man that helped in the process of child rearing. Coming from a family where my Dad is not my birthfather, I fully understand why the boys, at times, say and do things that do not make sense to any one else but myself. I am grateful for my Dad's presence when I needed him and I can only hope that the boys will someday understand the extent my wife and I went to in an attempt to help them. We have done everything humanly possible for the boys. I know they do not understand now why we did the things we did for them but maybe they will as they grow older. My Dad instilled in me the strength I needed to raise the boys but there were times when I was sure I would collapse. I am still in the process of forgiving the youngest for what he did to my wife and I.

In the past I blamed myself for his condition, but I have come to real-ize it was not my doing. I personally feel that those responsible for the mistreatment will pay for their actions. If the boys realize why we did the things that we did they will be better people themselves. Due to the evil things that were inflicted upon them, they are, unfortunately, unable to live in a family setting. My hope is that they find someone that can care as we did and love them as deeply as we did. They will always be in our hearts and memories and no one, no matter how evil, can take that away from us. Sadly, they will spend the rest of their lives trying to mend the evil thrust upon them by their birthparents. There have been times that I felt, as a Dad, I could do no more, but deep within me a voice tells me to keep going. My dreams as well as the families' dreams will come true with time and love. Families come and go but the love my wife and I *first* expe-rienced for the boys will always be in our hearts.

Appendix

Attachment Disorder— Diagnosis and Treatment

Attachment Disorder is a psychological diagnosis for children who exhibit problems with attachment during infancy or early childhood (DSM-IV, 1994). Children who did not attach to a caregiver do not form basic trust for those around her/him. When a child is capable of trusting others, the trust facilities the development of empathy for others. It is empathy that precedes the development of a conscience. However, a lack of trust generates feelings of aloneness, pervasive feelings of anger, and an excessive need to be in control of the environment. An Attachment Disorder child relates control to survival and will do anything to keep the attachment figure(s) at a distance. The child, therefore, reasons that "they must take care of themselves" and will display behaviors of self-parenting. Because the child perceives their past caretakers as unresponsive to their needs, they feel it is too risky to cede their position, and the trust involved with it, over to any caretaker. The child displays behaviors designed to specifically keep the caretakers, especially the mother figure, at a controllable distance. The caretakers become confused over the child's distancing behaviors and may react in by (a) trying harder to parent the child or (b) distancing themselves from the child. Unfortunately, the caretaker's coping methods are often misunderstood by society and the caretakers are deemed as the problem. When these children present for counseling, they are seen as very charming and likeable individuals. Ironically, this type of behavior is an enormous insight into the controlling aspect of the Attachment Disorder child.

Causes of Attachment Disorder

Infants are born with an innate drive to attach to a caregiver (Bowlby, 1973). The degree of attachment to a specific caregiver decreases over time, but does not disappear. The attachment is merely directed to other significant individuals throughout the lifespan. However, for the individual to experience positive attachments at later stages of development, the attachment drive must be properly satisfied during infancy. The infant is vulnerable and incapable of taking care of itself. Therefore, evolution has equipped the infant with a mechanism to alert the parent or other primary caregiver of her/his basic needs. A reciprocal process of needing, by the infant, and needs meeting, by the caregiver, begins strengthening the infant's attachment to the caregiver. Furthermore, by meeting the infant's needs, the responsive caregiver enhances the probability of the infant developing feelings of security and safety. These feelings of security and safety then translate into feelings of trust. However, if the caregiver is not response to the infant's needs, the infant perceives itself as unworthy and will begin to develop insecure feelings and become untrusting of those around her/him. Failure to develop an attachment during the first year of life can result in negative and potentially dangerous psychological consequences that can be carried into childhood, adolescence, and eventually adulthood (Ainsworth, 1989; Barth & Berry, 1988, 1991, Berry & Barth, 1989, 1990).

Several hypotheses exist to explain the development of Attachment Disorder. Although empirical studies in the field are lacking, the consensus among those who have researched this disorder agree than an interference occurred during the critical attachment period (e.g. Bowlby, 1969) in the infant's or young child's life. This incidents include, but are not limited to (Sadler, 1997):

1. Prolonged separation from a caregiver due to
    a. Hospitalization of infant or caregiver
    b. Depression in caregiver resulting in distancing from the infant
    c. Death in family causing caregiver's prolonged absence
2. Frequent change of caregivers
3. Dysfunctional marital of relationship status of caregiver and significant other
4. Stressful pregnancy
5. Illness of infant and inability of caregiver to provide comfort
6. Abuse and/or neglect of the infant
    a. Physical abuse
    b. Sexual abuse
    c. Emotional abuse
    d. Neglect
    e. Any combination of the above

Co-Morbidity

Attachment Disorder is most often accompanied by symptoms of Attention Deficit Hyperactivity Disorder (ADHD) and Attention Deficit

Disorder (ADD) and it is common to be diagnosed with a degree of either disorder (Cline, 1995). Therefore, a complete medical examination is necessary to address this possibility. If the child is diagnosed with ADHD or ADD, medical intervention may be considered a viable treatment. The most common drug intervention for either of these disorders is Ritalin.

In addition to the ADHD and ADD, children with Attachment Disorder are commonly diagnosed with Depression, Post-Traumatic Stress Disorder, Anxiety, Oppositional Defiant Disorder, Conduct Disorder, learning disabilities, family problems, and suicidal ideation (Parker & Forrest, 1993).

Misdiagnoses

If the child is younger than 5 years old, a diagnosis of Reactive Attachment Disorder (DSM-IV 313.89) is appropriate. However, the DSM-IV fails to classify older children as Attachment Disorder. Instead, children older than the age of 5 years are more commonly diagnosed with Oppositional Defiant Disorder (ODD) or Conduct Disorder (CD).

Prevalence

Unfortunately, empirical studies are lacking on Attachment Disorder. Thus, the prevalence rates are estimated at 10% of the clinical population of children with behavioral problems (Parker & Forrest, 1993; Richters & Volkmar, 1994). As more children present to mental health professionals and treatment facilities with severe behavior problems, the diagnosis of Attachment Disorder should be considered in addition to ODD, CD, ADHD, and ADD (Cline, 1995).

Diagnosing Attachment Disorder

No standardized assessment instrument has been identified for diagnosing Attachment Disorder. However, the most widely used diagnostic instrument for the older infant and young child is the Strange Situation assessment (Ainsworth & Wittig, 1969). This assessment situation was designed to assess the infant's attachment to the mother or primary caregiver by observing the infant's behavior while in the presence of the caregiver and when the caregiver leaves then returns to the room. For instance, a securely attached child will exhibit proximity seeking behaviors in the caregiver's absence and exploratory behaviors in her/his presence. Specifically, when the caregiver is present, the child feels secure enough to explore the surroundings and will become frightened when the caregiver, or secure base, is absent from the child. On the other hand, a child with attachment problems reacts in the opposite manner. The child may cling to the caregiver in her/his presence but behave indifferently when she/he is not within proximity. Upon her/his return, the child may exhibit anger and resentment towards the caregiver.

In addition to the Strange Situation, the diagnostic criteria of Reactive Attachment Disorder of Infancy or Early Childhood in the DSM-IV (1994) may be used to assess the child. Lastly, a symptom checklist developed by a prominent treatment facility for Attachment Disorders at the Attachment Center in Evergreen, Colorado may be helpful for assessment purposes. The work done there with Attachment Disorder child has been instrumental, albeit controversial, in the devised symptom list.

Although the caretakers most often identify attachment problems, teachers, therapists, and medical professionals may also identify those with symptoms. Behavior most often exhibited by Attachment Disorder children include (Sadler, 1996):

1. Superficially engaging and charming
2. Indiscriminately affectionate with strangers
3. Lack of eye contact on parental terms
4. Not affectionate on parental terms
5. Destructive to self, others, and material objects
6. Lying about the obvious
7. Lack of cause and effect thinking
8. Lack of conscience

9. Abnormal eating problems

10. Poor peer relationships

11. Preoccupation with fire, blood, and gore

12. Persistent nonsense questions and chatter

13. Abnormal speech patterns—baby talk, mumbling, low tone and volume

14. Stealing

15. Blaming others

16. Inappropriately demanding and clingy

17. Animal killing

18. Running away

If a child fits the behavioral criteria of Attachment Disorder, a complete history of the child is extremely important. Occurrences of any of the following should be addressed and explored:

1. Medical problems experienced by birthmother during pregnancy

2. Medical conditions of the infant at or after birth

3. Separation of infant or child and caretaker(s)—divorce, illness, depression, death

4. Frequent change in daycare, babysitters, homes

5. Disturbed of dysfunctional family interactions

6. Illness of the infant or child resulting in long periods of hospitalizations and separation

7. Frequent change in medical providers

8. Inconsistent comforting of the infant and child

9. Physical, sexual, emotional abuse and neglect

Neglect includes any activity that disrupts meeting the physical meeting of the child's needs. Emotional abuse includes lack of touch, eye contact, rocking, and holding. The timing of the abuse is also critical. If the abuse or neglect occurred in the preverbal stage of the infant, this may result in the child directing anger in an all pervasive manner, they are angry at the world because it is an unsafe place. If, however, the abuse or neglect occurred in the verbal stage, the child may direct the anger towards the person(s) responsible. In addition, all children tend to direct anger at the mother figure no matter when the abuse or neglect occurred.

Treatment of Attachment Disorder

Treating the Attachment Disorder individual includes not only the child, but the caretakers as well. Quite often the caretakers are foster parents, adoptive parents, or other substitute caretakers (Sadler, 1996). However, it is essential that anyone who is the primary caretaker for the child be involved in the treatment process. Both the child and the parent are taught specific responsibilities for interaction. One without the other may not be successful in treating the symptoms of Attachment Disorder.

Conventional parenting styles are designed in accordance with Erickson's (1963) psychosocial model of human development. However, the Attachment Disorder child has not progressed past the trust-mistrust level of development, and, therefore, does not allow the parent to provide the opportunity to establish parental trust. Because the basic physical needs were not met, or were interrupted, during an earlier period, the child does not benefit from other aspects of parenting. Due to the lack of basic needs at an earlier stage of development, the child did not learn trust for the parents and will not respond to the parental expressions of love. In addition, after repeated abuse and neglect, normal discipline techniques do not affect these children. No spanking will be as bad as the abuse and no deprivation will be as bad as the neglect. Therefore, these children ignore the conventional discipline techniques.

Conventional psychotherapy also fails with the Attachment Disorder child because:

1. Only the child is seen
2. Parents are not provided information or advice on how to parent the child

3. Therapist may no be knowledgeable about the abuse, neglect, or adoptive issues

4. Therapist does not help the family change the child's environment

5. Families are not provided with support by social systems

6. Emphasis is placed on adoptive status rather than traumatic effects of abuse/neglect

7. Play therapies are ineffectual

8. Therapists lack appropriate behavioral interventions for children who do not respond to conventional love and discipline

9. Therapists blame the parents for the child's behavioral problems

10. Therapists are unfamiliar with schools and their policy and procedures

11. Therapists fail to recognize the marital distress that the troubled adoption and child's attachment issues are causing

Therapeutic interventions which have proven to be effective in working with Attachment Disorder children include (Sadler, 1996):

Children's responsibilities and jobs

1. Child must learn to be respectful of parents by
   a. Engaging in eye contact
   b. Being alert of their tone of voice with parents
   c. Being alert to their body posture and to stand/sit straight when talking to parents

2. Child must be responsible by
   a. Establishing time frames for consequences of their behaviors
   b. Accepting the consequences of their behaviors

3. Child must be pleasant to be with
   a. They do not need to do anything with parents, just be together

b. They need to think of activities to do with parents that do not involve money

Parent's responsibilities and jobs

1. Provide basic needs for child and do not withhold as a punishment
2. Establish rules for behavior and follow through with consequences
3. Provide closed-ended choices rather than open-ended—i.e. "PJ's now or after story"
4. Define the adult's role and the child's role—i.e. I need to cook the dinner, you need to eat it
5. Provide monologue regarding rationale for behavior—i.e. If I had done that it would have upset your friend. How do you think your friend would feel if you did it?
6. Establish firm time frames for routine and insist on knowing child's whereabouts
7. Always look for situations to address the child's feelings
8. Insist that the child ask permission for all needs, major or minor
9. Teach child appropriate ways of expressing anger
10 Do not accept any kind of stealing, lying, or dangerous behaviors
11. Always confront and assign consequences for unacceptable behavior
12. Provide consistency and predictability for all behaviors and interactions
13. Use humor and provide fun activities
14. Do no pressure the child to engage in physical contact unless they initiate

References

Abikoff, H., Courtney, M., Pelham, W. E., & Koplewics, H. S. (1993). Teachers' ratings of disruptive behaviors: The influence of halo effects. *Journal of Abnormal Child Psychology, 21*, 519-533.

Ainsworth, M. D. S. (1980). Attachment and child abuse. In G. Gerbner, C. J., Ross, & E. Zigler (Eds.) *Child abuse: An agenda for action* (pp. 35-47). New York: Oxford University Press.

Ainsworth, M. D. S. (1989). Attachments beyond infancy. *American Psychologist, 44*, 709-716.

Alexander, P. C. (1992). Application of attachment theory to the study of sexual abuse. *Journal of Consulting and Clinical Psychology, 60*, 185-195.

American Psychiatric Association. (1994). *Diagnostic and Statistical Manual of Mental Disorders* (4th ed.). Washington, DC: Author.

Austad, C. C., & Simmons, T. L. (1978). Symptoms of adopted children presenting to a large mental health clinic. *Child Psychiatry and Human Development, 9*, 20-27.

Bandura, A. (1977). *Social Learning Theory.* Englewood Cliffs, NJ: Prentice-Hall.

Barth, R. P. (1988). *On their own: The experiences of youth after foster care.* Berkeley, CA: University of California, Berkeley, School of Social Welfare.

Barth, R. P. & Berry, M. (1988). *Adoption & Disruption.* New York: Aldine De Gruyter.

Barth, R. P. & Berry, M. (1991). Preventing Adoption Disruption, pp. 205-222. In *Families as Nurturing Systems.* Haworth Press, Inc.

Berry, M. & Barth, R. P. (1989). Behavior problems of children adopted when older. *Children and Youth Services Review, 11*, 221-238.

Berry, M. & Barth, R. P. (1990). A study of disrupted adoptive placements of adolescents. *Child Welfare League, 69,* 209-225.

Biringen, Z. (1994) Attachment Theory and Research. *American Journal of Orthopsychiatry, 64,* 405-420.

Boer, F., Versluis-den Bieman, H. J. M., & Verhulst, F. C. (1994). International adoption of children with siblings: Behavioral outcomes. *American Journal of Orthopsychiatry, 64,* 252-262.

Bohman, M. (1981) The interaction of heredity and childhood environment: Some adoption studies. *Journal of Child Psychology and Psychiatry, 22,* 195-200.

Boneh, C. (1979). *Disruptions in adoptive placements: A research study.* Boston: Department of Public Welfare, Office of Research Evaluation.

Borgman, R. (1981). Antecedents and consequences of parental rights termination for abused and neglected children. *Child Welfare, 60,* 391-404.

Bowlby, J. (1969). *Attachment and loss: Attachment.* New York: Basic Books.

Bowlby, J. (1982). *Attachment and loss: Separation.* New York: Basic Books.

Bowlby, J. (1988a). *A secure base. Clinical applications of attachment theory.* London UK: Routledge.

Boyne, J., Denby, L., Kettenring, J. R., & Wheeler, N. (1984). *The shadow of success: a statistical analysis of outcomes of adoptions of hard-to-place children.* New Jersey: Spaulding for Children.

Brodzinsky, D. M. (1987). Adjustment to adoption: a psychosocial perspective. *Clinical Psychological Review, 7,* 25-47.

Cicchetti, D., & Carlson, V. (Eds.) (1989). *Child Maltreatment: Theory and research on the causes and consequences of child abuse and neglect.* New York: Cambridge University Press.

Crittenden, P. M. (1992). Children's strategies for coping with adverse home environments: An interpretation using attachment theory. *Child Abuse and Neglect, 16,* 329-343.

Deutsch, C. K., Swanson, J. M., Bruell, J. H., et al. (1982). Overrepresentation of adoptees in children with attention deficit disorder. *Behavioral Genetics, 12,* 231-238.

Dickson, L. R., Heffron, W. M., & Parker, C. (1990). Children from disrupted and adoptive homes on an inpatient unit. *American Journal of Orthopsychiatry, 60,* 594-602.

Dubow, E. F., & Tisak, J. (1989). The relation between stressful life events and adjustment in elementary school children: the role of social support and social problem solving skills. *Child Development, 60.* 1412-1423.

Eagle, R. S. (1994). The separation experience of children in long-term care: Theory, Research, and Implications for practice. *American Journal of Orthopsychiatry, 64,* 421-434.

Erickson, E. (1963). *Childhood and society.* New York: W. W. Norton.

Fagot, B. I. & Kavanagh, K. (1990). The prediction of antisocial behavior from avoidant attachment classifications. *Child Development, 61,* 864-873.

Fatout, M. F. (1990). Aggression: A characteristic of physically abused latency-age children. *Child and Adolescent Social Work, 7,* 365-376.

Festinger, T. (1986). *Necessary risk: A study of adoptions and disrupted adoptive placements.* Washing, D.C.: Child Welfare League of America, INC.

Fine, M. A., Overholser, J. C., & Berkoff, K. (1992). Diagnostic validity of the passive-aggressive personality disorder: suggestions for reform. *American Journal of Psychotherapy, 66,* 470-484.

Fingerhut, L. A. & Kleinman, J. C. (1990). International and interstate comparisons of homicide among young males. *Journal of the American Medical Association, 263,* 3292-3295.

Fraiberg, S. (1977). *Every child's birthright: In defense of mothering.* New York: Basic Books.

Frick, P. J., Lahey, B. B., Loeber, R., Stouthamer-Loeber, M., Green, S., Hart, E. L., & Christ, A. G. (1991). Oppositional defiant disorder and Conduct disorder in boys: Patterns of behavioral covariation. *Journal of Clinical Child Psychology, 20,* 202-208.

Frick, P. J., Lahey, B. B., Loeber, R., Tannenbaum, L., Ban Horn, Y., Christ, M. A. G., Hart, E. L. & Hanson, K. (1993). Oppositional defiant disorder and conduct disorder: A meta-analytic review of factor analyses and cross-validation in a clinic sample. *Clinical Psychology Review, 13,* 319-340.

Gabel, S., & Shindledecker, R. (1991). Aggressive behavior in youth: Characteristics, outcome, and psychiatric Diagnoses. *Journal of American Academy of Child and Adolescent Psychiatry, 30,* 982-988.

Gadow, K. D., Nolan, E. E., Sverd, J., Sprafkin, J. & Paolicelli, L. (1990). Methylphenidate in aggressive-hyperactive boys: I. Effects on peer aggression in public school settings. *Journal of the American Academy of Child and Adolescent Psychiatry, 29,* 710-718.

Ghuman, H. S., Jayaprakash, S., Saidel, D. H., & Whitmarsh, G. (1989). Variables predictive of the need for placement in a long-term structured setting for adolescents. *The Psychiatric Hospital, 20,* 31-34.

Groze, V. (1986). Special Needs Adoption. *Children and Youth Services Review, 8,* 363-373.

Hadley, J., Holloway, E., & Mallinckrodt, B. (1993). Common aspects of object relations and self-representations in offspring from disparate dysfunctional families. *Journal of Counseling Psychology, 40, 348-356.*

Hartman, A. (1984). Working with Adoptive Families Beyond Placement. New York: Child Welfare League of America.

Hinshaw, S. O. (1994a). *Attention deficits and hyperactivity in children.* Thousand Oaks, CA: Sage.

Hinshaw, S. P. (1994b). Conduct disorder in childhood: Conceptualization, diagnosis, comorbidity, and risk status for antisocial functioning in adulthood. In D. Fowles, P. Sutker & S. Goodman (Eds.). *Psychopathy and antisocial personality: A developmental perspective* (pp.3-44). New York: Springer.

Horowitz, F. D. (1992). John B. Watson's legacy: Learning and environment. *Developmental Psychology, 28,* 360-367.

Jacobsen, T., Edelstein, W., & Hofmann, V. (1994). A longitudinal study of the relations between representations of attachment in childhood and cognitive functioning in childhood and adolescence. *Developmental Psychology, 30,* 112-124.

Jerome, L. (1986). Over-representation of adopted children attending a children's mental health center. *Canadian Journal of Psychiatry, 32,* 526-531.

Jerome, L., Cohen, J. S., & Westhues, A. (1987). A review of the literature on the prevention of harmful sequelae of adoption. *Journal of Preventive Psychiatry, 3,* 261-277.

Jewitt, C. (1978). *Adopting the Older Child.* Harvard, MA: Harvard Common Press.

Kagan, R. M. & Reid, W. J. (1986). Critical factors in the adoption of emotionally disturbed youths. *Child Welfare, 65,* 63-73.

Kaye, K. & Warren, S. (1988). Discourse about adoption in adoptive families. *Journal of Family Psychology, 1,* 406-433.

Kazdin, A. E. (1992). Overt and covert antisocial behavior: child and family characteristics among psychiatric inpatient children. *Journal of Child and Family Studies, 1,* 3-20.

Kim, W. J., Zrull, J. P., Davenport, C. W. & Weaver, M. (1992). Characteristics of adopted juvenile delinquents. *Journal of American Academy of Child and Adolescent Psychiatry, 31,* 525-532.

Kirk, H. D. (1964). *Shared fate.* New York: Free Press.

Kotsopoulos, S., Cote, A., Joseph, L., Pentland, J. (1988). Psychiatric disorders in adopted children: A Controlled Study. *American Journal of Orthopsychiatry, 58,* 608-612.

Lipman, E. L., Offord, D. R., Racine, Y. A., Boyle, M. H. (1992). Psychiatric disorders in adopted children: A profile from the Ontario child health study. *Canadian Journal of Psychiatry, 37,* 627-632.

Livingston, R. Lawson, L., & Jones, J. G. (1993). Predictors of self-reported psychopathology in children abused repeatedly by a parent. *Journal of American Academy of Child and Adolescent Psychiatry, 32,* 948-953.

Loeber, R. & Le Blanc, M. (1990). Toward a developmental criminology. In N. Morris & M. Tonry (Eds.), *Crime and Justice* (pp. 375-473). Chicago: University of Chicago Press.

Loeber, R. & Schmaling, K. B. (1985). Empirical evidence for overt and covert patterns of antisocial conduct problems: A meta-analysis. *Journal of Abnormal Child Psychology, 13,* 337-352.

Loeber, R. Green, S. M., Lahey, B. B., Christ, A. G., Frick, P. J. (1992). Developmental sequences in the age of onset of disruptive child behaviors. *Journal of Child and Family Studies, 1,* 21-41.

Mahler, M. S., Pine, F. & Bergman, A. (1975). *The psychological birth of the human infant: Symbiosis and individuation.* New York: Basic Books.

Malinow, K. L. (1981). Passive-aggressive personality. In J. R. Lion (Ed.), Personality disorders: Diagnosis and management (2nd ed.). Malabur, FL: Robert E. Krieger Publishing Company.

Martin, H. P. (1980). The consequences of being abused and neglected: How the child fares. In C. Kempe and R. Helfer (Eds.), *The Battered Child* (3rd ed). University of Chicago Press.

Melina, L. R. (1986). *Raising adopted children: A manual for adoptive families.* New York: Harper and Row.

Menlove, F. L. (1985). Aggressive symptoms in emotionally disturbed adopted children. *Child Development, 36,* 519-532.

Moore, D. R., Chamberlain, P. & Mukai, L. H. (1979). Children at risk for delinquency: A follow-up comparison of aggressive children and children who steal. *Journal of Abnormal Child Psychology, 7,* 345-355.

Morey, L. C. (1988). A psychometric analysis of the DSM-III-R personality disorder criteria. *Journal of Personality Disorders, 2,* 109-124.

Nelson, K. A. (1985). *On the frontier of adoption.* New York: Child Welfare League of America.

Odenthal, S. G. (1995). *Parenting a child with attachment difficulties.* Unpublished manuscript.

Offord, D. R., Aponte, J. F., & Cross, L. A. (1969). Presenting symptomatology of adopted children. *Archives of General Psychiatry, 20,* 110-116.

Parker, K. C., & Forrest, D. (1993). Attachment disorder: an emerging concern for school counselors. *Elementary school guidance & counseling, 27,* 209-215.

Partridge, S., Hornby, H., & McDonald, T. (1986). *Legacies of loss/Visions of gains: An inside look at adoption disruption.* Portland, Maine: University of Southern Maine, Center for Research and Advanced Study.

Patterson, G. R. (1982). *A social learning approach, Coercive family process.* Eugene, Oregon: Castalia.

Pearce, J. W., & Pezzot-Pearce, T. D. (1994). Attachment theory and its implications for psychotherapy with maltreated children. *Child Abuse & Neglect, 18,* 425-438.

Pike, V. (1995). Understanding Attachment Disorders, *Family Matters: Oregon's Special Needs Adoption Newsletter,* Portland, OR.

Richters, M. M. & Volkmar, F. R. (1994). Reactive attachment disorder in infancy and early childhood. *Journal of the American Academy of Child and Adolescent Psychiatry, 33,* 328-332.

Rogeness, G. A., Hoppe, S. K., Macedo, C. A., Fischer, C. & Harris, W. R. (1988). Psychopathology in hospitalized, adopted children. *Journal of American Academy of Child and Adolescent Psychiatry, 27,* 628-631.

Rosen, M. (1977). *A look at a small group of disrupted adoptions.* Chicago: Chicago Child Care Society.

Rosenthal, J. A., Schmidt, D., & Conner, J. (1988). Predictors of special needs adoption disruption: An exploratory study. *Children and Youth Services Review, 10,* 101-117.

Russo, D. C., Cataldo, M. F., & Cushing, P. J. (1981). Compliance training and behavioral covariation in the treatment of multiple behavior problems. *Journal of Applied Behavior Analysis, 14,* 209-222.

Rutter, M. (1985). Family and school influences on behavioral development. *Journal of Child Psychology and Psychiatry, 26,* 349-368.

Saal, F. E., Downey, R. G., & Lahey, M. A. (1980). Rating the ratings: assessing the psychometric quality of rating data. *Psychological Bulletin, 88,* 413-428.

Sack, W. H., & Dale, D. (1982). Abuse and deprivation in failing adoptions. *Child Abuse and Neglect, 6,* 443-451.

Sadler, M. (1996). *Attachment Disorder.* Paper presented at the Oklahoma Adoption Coalition, Northwest Marriott Convention Center, Oklahoma City, OK.

Salo, F. (1990). "Well, I couldn't say no, could I?": Difficulties in the path of late adoption. *Journal of Child Psychotherapy, 16,* 75-91.

Senior, N. & Himadi, E. (1985). Emotionally Disturbed, Adopted, Inpatient Adolescents. *Child Psychiatry and Human Development, 15,* 189-197.

Skinner, B. F. (1953). *Science and human behavior.* New York: Appleton-Century-Crofts.

Small, I. F., Small, J. G., Alig, V. B., & Moore, D. F. (1970). Passive-aggressive personality disorder: A search for a syndrome. *American Journal of Psychiatry, 126,* 973-981.

Sonne, J. (1980). A family system perspective on custody and adoption. *International Journal of Family Theory, 2,* 176-192.

Sorosky, A. D., Baron, A., & Pannor, R. (1975). Identity conflicts in adoptees. *American Journal of Orthopsychiatry, 45,* 18-27.

Stone, S. M. (1997). *Overt and Covert Behaviors of Abused Children as Indicators of Placement: Adoption or Structured Treatment Facility.* Masters Thesis, University of Central Oklahoma, Edmond, OK.

Stroufe, L. A. (1988). *The role of infant-caregiver attachment in development.* In J. Belsky & T. Nezworski (Eds.), Clinical implications of attachment, pp. 18-38. Hillsdale, NJ: Erlbaum.

Tizard, B. & Hodges, J. (1978). The effect of early institutional rearing on the development of 8-year-old children. *Journal of Child Psychology and Psychiatry, 16,* 61-73.

Turner, P. J. (1991). Relations between attachment, gender, and behavior with peers in preschool. *Child Development, 62,* 1475-1488.

Urban Systems Research and Engineering. (1985). *Evaluation of state activities with regard to adoption disruption.* Washington, DC, Urban Research and Engineering.

Valdez, G. M. & McNamara, J. R. (1994). Matching to prevent adoption disruption. *Child and Adolescent Social Work Journal, 11,* 391-403.

Verhulst, F. C., Althaus, M. & Versluis-den Bieman, H. J. M. (1990a). Problem behavior in international adoptees: I. An epidemiological study. *Journal of the American Academy of Child and Adolescent Psychiatry, 29,* 94-103.

Verhulst, F. C., Althaus, M. & Versluis-den Bieman, H. J. M. (1990b). Problem behavior in international adoptees: II. Age at placement. *Journal of the American Academy of Child and Adolescent Psychiatry, 29,* 104-111.

Verhulst, F. C., Althaus, M. & Versluis-den Bieman, H. J. M. (1992). Damaging backgrounds: Later adjustment of international adoptees. *Journal of the American Academy of Child and Adolescent Psychiatry, 31,* 518-524.

Warren, S. B. (1992). Lower Threshold for referral for psychiatric treatment for adopted adolescents. *Journal of the American Academy of Child and Adolescent Psychiatry, 31,* 512-517.

Watkins, C., & Cline, F. W. (1995). *Attachment: Crisis in older adoption.* Unpublished manuscript, Evergreen Attachment Center, Evergreen, CO.

Westhues, A. & Cohen, J. S. (1990). Preventing disruption of special-needs adoptions. *Child Welfare, 69,* 141-155.

Whitman, R., Trosman, H., & Koenig, R. (1954). Clinical assessment of passive-aggressive personality. *Archives of Neurology and Psychiatry, 72,* 540-549.

Widom, C. S. (1991). Avoidance of Criminality in Abused and Neglected Children. *Psychiatry, 54,* 163-174.

Young, J., Corcran-Rumppe, K., & Groze, V. (1992). Integrating special-needs adoption with residential treatment. *Child Welfare, 71,* 527-535.

About the Author

Dr. Stone is an Assistant Professor of Psychology. She was an adoptive mother for Attachment Disorder boys. Her professional work examines human-pet bonding, the use of animals for therapeutic interventions, and animal learning/cognition. She is the founder and owner of Pet-Me Pets®, a therapy pet program.

0-595-19294-7

362.734 STO
Stone, Sherril M.
More than love :

Printed in the United States
146725LV00003B/42/A